LIBRARY CATALOGUING

LIBRARY CATALOGUING

Manohar Nanda

ANMOL PUBLICATIONS PVT. LTD.
NEW DELHI - 110 002 (INDIA)

ANMOL PUBLICATIONS PVT. LTD.
H.O.: 4374/4B, Ansari Road, Daryaganj
New Delhi - 110 002
Ph.: 23261597, 23278000
B.O.: No. 1015, Ist Main Road, BSK III Stage
III Phase, III Block
Bangalore - 560 085 (India)
Visit us at: www.anmolpublications.com

Library Cataloguing

First Published, 2006

PRINTED IN INDIA

Published by J.L. Kumar for Anmol Publications Pvt. Ltd., New Delhi - 110 002 and Printed at Mehra Offset Press, Delhi.

Contents

Preface

"Library Cataloguing" as a paper is being taught at B.L.I.Sc. and M.L.I.Sc. in 'Library Science' at various universities and institutions. This book is designed as an introductory text to the above paper, encompassing vital information on all pertinent aspects. Thus the material presented here would be of interest as well as of great use to the students, teachers and professionals of Library Science. This book will provide complete knowledge of the history of cataloguing, information sources, document description, techniques of cataloguing, codes of cataloguing, subject cataloguing etc. to the students.

The major topics dealt in this book are—Introduction to Information Sources; History of Cataloguing; Document Description; Forms of Document Cataloguing; Cataloguing Technologies; Evolution of Catalogue Codes; Subject Cataloguing; Study of AACR and CCC; Resource Sharing.

It is hoped that all those will benefit from the contents of this book for whom it is meant. The author will feel amply rewarded, if motive is achieved.

Editor

1

Introduction to Information Sources

A catalogue is a list of and index to a collection of books and/or other materials. It enables the user to discover:

What material is present in the collection and where this material may be found.

The 'collection' may relate to one or a number of libraries or information service points. In the fitter case, the catalogue is termed a union catalogue.

The catalogue has much in common with the bibliography, which is also a list of books and/or other material. The same principles are applied to their compilation and they are used interchangeably. For example, the NECRT General catalogue of printed books or the National Book Trust catalogues also act as important bibliographies. The pure bibliography is not an index to a specific collection but simply a list of books and/ or other materials within some restricted field, since it would clearly be impossible to list all materials from all countries and all periods on all subjects.

This entry could also be used, without amendment, in a bibliography although there might not be any need to include the classification number and, on the other hand, further detail such as the price of the item might be required. Nevertheless the close relationship between the entry as used in a catalogue and the entry as used in a bibliography is obvious.

The art of cataloguing relates to both catalogues and bibliographies. It is the art of describing and listing material in such a way as to make it as easy as possible to discover the nature and extent of what is available and, if appropriate, where this material may be located or obtained.

The library catalogue is a list of books and other material in the holdings of library or a group of libraries. The list contains entries of books; arranged according to same definite plan. *(C.G. Vishwanathan)*. It is a list of books; as distinguished from the Bibliography, it is confined to a contents of a particular library or collection. Arranged in a reconized order the entries which it contains, are formulated in accordance with specific rules, providing bibliographic information and often further elucidation and appraisals. (*Encyclopedia of Librarianship*).

The terminology group at a International Conference on Cataloguing Principles (ICCP) held at paris in 1961 defined a catalogue as a "Comprehensive list of a collection—or collections of books, documents or similar material". (ICCP. Report). The ICCP has defined a library catalogue "a comprehensive list, with the idea that by no means all catalogues aim at comprehensineness. Originally, the word catalogue means a list or an enumeration having a systmatic and methodical arrangement of items in alphabetical or other logical order and color. A library catalogue is a systematic listing of the books, and materials in a library with descriptive information about each one: author, title, edition, publisher, date, physical appearance, subject matter, special features and location. (Jean Key Grates). Thus the library catalague is an index to the contents of a liberary, which help the reader in discovering and locating material in a library.

The definitions of various authors are said as under:

A catalogue is "an explanatory, logically arranged inventory and key to the books and then contents and it is confined to the books in a particular library". (James Duff Brown).

According to (CA. Cutter). A library catalogue is a list of books which is arranged on some definite plan. As distinguished from a bibliography it is a list of books in some library or collections.

According to (Margaret S. Taylor). A catalogue is also a list of books like 'bibliography but its scope is limited to a particular collections.

According to (Margaret Mann) A catalogue is a record of the material in library.

According to (L. Jalley) A catalogue is a communication.

According to (Isadore Gilbert Mudge) A catalogue is to provide a tool which will give the reader accurate information on four different points: Accurate information, bibliographical details, by a given author, and on a given subject.

According to (S.R. Ranganathan) A library catalogue is a list of documents in a library or in a collections forming a portion of it.

According to (S. Akers) A catalogue is a record of the material in a library.

According to (J.S. Sharma) Catalogue is essentially a laboratory art. Accuracy is its cordinal principle.

According to (H.A. Sharp) Catalogue is the recording of information regarding Manuscripts, Books, pamphlets, Musical composition, illus, prints, maps, slides.

According to (T.S. Rajgopalan) Cataloguing is a technique.

Catalogue is a list or catalogue of items of library.

In view of the above definitions, it is clear that library catalogue is a:

(i) list and record—of;

(ii) Documents including books, manuscripts Maps, Charts etc.—which is;

(iii) a art of Communication, guidance and information which is;

(iv) arranged systematically—in a;

(v) alphabitical order—and help in;

(vi) locating, aiding, identifying, indicating of locality, position, date, price, size etc.—and represent;

But this definition is elaborated in I.C.C.P. Conference (Paris, 1961) and placed the library catalogue at par with bibliography by defining it as a "comprehensive list," According to their concept catalogues are themselves a form bibliography.

Dr. Ranganathan has defined the library catalogue involving three aspects:

(i) The list,—of;

(ii) Documents,—in a;

(iii) Library (single library or group of libraries.)

It may be a printed list or the manuscripts, the card or the loose leaves. The list may be in a form of book, or in the paste down form. It is called library catalogue.

Documents includes the books, periodicals, Microfilms, photo graphs, gramophone records, tap records, etc.

Brown defines the library catalogue as one of the important key and inventory of books. Key in the sense that it indicates the location or the identification of the book and inventory in the sense that it contains the bibliographical information. But Broven has confined the catalogue limited to books while catalogue is also prepared for other reading material. Moreover, a catalogue may also be prepared for a group of libraries.

The term 'Catalogue' has been formed from Greek phrase "Katalogos." 'Kata' means "According to", and "Logos" means "order" or "reason". 'Logos' also denotes to logical concept which is based on the reasoning. Thus the catalogue may be regarded as a:

(i) work in which contents are arranged in a reasonable way;

(ii) work which is done on a set plan; and

(iii) work whose contents are arranged in a systematic way.

Catalogue is an important tool of a modern and well equiped library. A library always need a systematised and well planned catalogue in order to provide up-to-date information to the users. If there is no catalogue in a library or a incomplete catalogue, it will pe like a house which has been built without keeping in view the need, nature of the accomodation. While the talk of efficient service, we interprete a well planned catalogue, qualified staff and the adequate reading material.

Library Service

↓

Reading Resources

↓

Library Staff

↓

Library Catalogue

Therefore, catalogue is a guide for the directing element to a reader. It is as important to library resources such as the key to a lock. A library may. possess good collection. But if it lacks in good catalogue, the collection will not be properly used. Hence the extent of the use of library resources depends greatly upon the quality of library catalogue.

Catalogue denotes the standard of the library service. Good catalogue enhance the reputation of the library on one side but mars the reputation of the library on the otber side. Catalogue is also a first grade librarian in material.

Librarian—I grade librarian in person

Catalogue—I grade librarian in material.

Librarian has to consult or take help of the cataloguer at every stage of reference service, book selection etc.

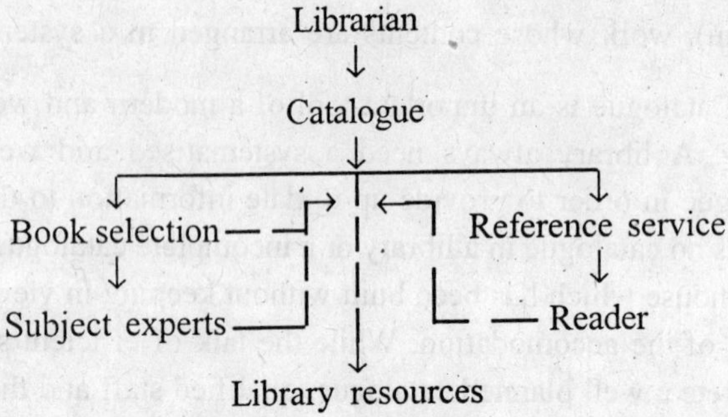

Edward Edwards say that here is no matter connected with the administration of a public library which can be, in point of importance, with the character and the conditions of its catalogues." However, liberal book collection, able chief, well trained staff, large collection, it will fall lamentably and could not achieve the true standard of a library, if the library catalogue is not:

(1) well planned,

(2) well up-to-date;

(3) thoroughly systematic.

OBJECTIVES OF LIBRARY CATALOGUE

Catalogue serves tbe reader and as such the community. While we prepare a catalogue we consider the community or the institution which is to be served.

(a) Nature of the committee or institution-whether it is growing or Shrinking;

(b) Size of the library; and

(c) Material acquired.

To make best use of the material and maximum service to the reader community, the help of the catalogue is always sought. Reader attend the library with the object of consulting more material in shortest time without spending more money. In others words, library should provide, quick service, free or cheap service, and large number of reading material. This is possible if we maintain a good catalogue in library, as it:

(i) saves the time of the reader by directing him the location of the book;

(ii) knowledge to the extent of the stock *i.e.*, total collection.

(iii) saves money of the reader as he has nothing to purchase of its own, if the required books are available in the library;

The main purpose of the catalogue can be digout if it solves the following problems. (C. A. Cutter) that:

1. It should enable a person to find a book of which either *(a)* the author, or *(b)* the title, or *(c)* the subject is known;

2. It should assist in the choice of a book *(a)* as to its edition (bibliographical) and *(b)* as to its character (literary or topical).

3. It should show what the library has *(a)* by a given author, *(b)* on a given subjeet, or *(c)* in a given kind of literature;

The above statement of cutter clearly groups the main objectives of a catalogue as under:

1. Locate and Identify a Book of Which Either:

(a) ***Author.*** Author is clearly identified by the entries made under the name of the author popularly known, or written on the title page. Needham has suggested that in case of controversial authors, the name out of the title page should be considered.

(b) ***Title.*** Title can be identified by preparing entries under title. Title entries are generally made for striking and significant titles, *i.e.*, for novels and other works in the "form" classes like plays and major power, and works likes periodicals which has no recognized author.

(c) ***By a Author.*** Reader's approach is not only the author, title or the subject of a book, but he also needs all works of one author at one place. Catalogue fulfill this requirement—by showing reference entries based on various approaches of a reader. These necessary references serve the purpose and supplement the author.

(d) ***Subject.*** Subject can be identified by preparing subject entries made under a classification number in classified catalogue and under the subject headings or descriptive term, in dictionary catalogue.

(f) ***In a Given Kind of Literature.*** There are various forms of literature: dictionary, encyclopaedia, year books etc. A list is prepared for the collection of one form, such lists fulfill the objective of providing information of the whole collection of a particular term of literature. The term of presentation may also be a sub-heading.

2. Objective of Assisting in the Choice of a Book as to Edition and Nature.

It is covered by the descriptive cataloguing. Catalogues are prepared in two ways: as a bibliographical tool and as a finding list. Cutter provided edition and in print alongwith notes but their application is made, when found necessary.

Reader require sufficient information in a catalogue to find the right book and the right edition. No doubt that the library catalogue act as a finding list. But a decision has to be taken as how much information is sufficient to find the right book and the right edition. Whitley has the same opinion and gave more emphasis on providing the sufficient bibliographieal details which is suitable to the reader.

The objectives stated by Cutter were formulated in 1901 but they stands to the right test in modern concept of library Catalogue to a great extent. There have been general criticism on these objectives from time to time. It has been said that the three objectives are the repetition of one over the other. But even than the concept of the cutter was approved by all corners.

According to Dr. Ranganthan (library Manual) the main purpose of the catalogue is to provide to readers answers to questions such as the following:

1. Is there a book in the library by such and such an author? What are all the book in the library by him?

2. Is there a book in the library with such and such a title—that is, name?

3. Is there a book in the library in such and such a publisher's series? What are all the books in the library in that publisher's series.

4. Is there a book in the library with such (and such a collaborator—that is, editor, translator, reviser, compiler, commentator, etc? What are all the books in the library with him as colloborator ?

5. Is there a book in the library on such and such a subject? What are an the books in the library on that subject and on its sub-divisions and on subjects of which it is a sub-division?

From the above statement of Dr. Ranganathan the purpose of a catalague is to identify to:

(a) Is there a book on—a author,
a title,
a callaborator,
a subject.

(b) What are they on—a auther,
a title,
a collaborator,
a subject.

Generally there are two approaches of a reader: auther approach and the subject approach. The first approach is fulfilled by the alphabetical part or the dictionary catalague while the second approach can be fulfilled by the classified part or the classified catalague. But the second approach can be fulfilled only if the reader know the exact subject he wanted. Ranganathan has expressed his view on the objectives stated by Cutter that the classified part is designed to suit the functions marked by Cutter as (C), (E), (F), (G) and (H); while the alphabetical part corresponds to the functions (A), (B), (D) and to same extent (H) also.

Lubętzky has stated two objectives:

1. To enable the user of the catalague to determine readily whether or next the library has the book he wants. The catalague is constantly searched by the readers, library staff. If catalague is better, the information may be found quickly.
2. To reveal what works the library has by a given author under one form of Buthor's name and the edition or translation of a given author.

FUNCTIONS OF CATALOGUE

On the basis of the objectives of library catalague, its functions may be grouped in two catagories:

1. Functions in reader's service.
2. Functions in library operations.

The first function includes reference service, guidance to the reader about particular book; of a particular auther; and on a particular subject. The second function includes the assistance in book selection, guidance to library staff etc. Shera and Egan states two basic functions of catalague:

1. It provides speedy and accurate determination whether or not an item known by auther or title is in the callection or in the library, and if so, where it may be formed.
2. What materials the library contains upon a given subject, where they may be found and how they are related to one another.

According to Jeankey Grates, the chief function of the catalague is to make the total resources of the library fully and easily accessible to the user:

1. It points out the lacation of every book in the library by giving the location symbol, or call number.
2. It lists in one place, in alphabetical order, all books by a particular subject, regardless of their locations in the library.
3. It provides several way of finding materials, listing them by auther, title, subject, by author, translator, or illustrator, if there is one, and often by series, if book belongs to a series.

Dr. Ranganthan describes the library catalogue a essentially a tool and it should be designed as to:

1. Disclose to every reader his and her document;
2. Secure for every document its reader;
3. Save the the time of the reader; and for this purpose;
4. Save the time of staff.

He is of the opinion that the name of the auther is more important than the subject. Hence, the catalague should bear necessary rules for the rendering of the name of the auther. Less importance should be given in determination of the subject, but more importance should be given to location of the book' which direct to the specific place of book. It is possible by adopting a classified catalague which involves location symbola.

However, catalogue should provide the following functions:

1. It works as list (finding list or inventory) of the stock of the collection held by the library;
2. It groups the books of one characteristics, author, subject, and colloborator;
3. It gives information about the location of reading material;
4. It guides the reader to select his book of choice.
5. It works as a reference tool;

6. It let the reader know about the availability of book in a particular library;
7. It enables the reader to select the list out of the mass.
8. It gives the total account of the collection of a library i of an auther, title, and the subject.
9. If affiliates the subjects of one nature.
10. It satisfy the reader by giving all bibliographic information about the book. The library catalague is the most highly organised section of the whole net work of bibliographic references.
11. It is a instrument of communication; it communicates information about the book it records.
12. It display the library record before the reader. It brings reader's needs in relation with the resources of library.
13. It helps in book-selection;
14. It saves the time of the readen;
15. It directs the reader to identify his book from all sort of changed names of a author and title—pseudonym, show title.
16. It maintains discipline among the reading material.
17. To enterpret the library to the reader.
18. The Catalogue is the Codification of practice.
19. The Catalogue is a Social scientist not a philosopher.

DIFFERENCE BETWEEN CATALOGUE AND THE BIBLIOGRAPHY

There has been a little difference between the catalague and the bibliography. A catalague is confined to

(a) the holdings of one library, or

(b) in case of Union Catalague and Cooperative Catalague, a group of libraries.

While a bibliography is confined to

(a) a list of items within a particular subject field,

According to V.W. Clapp, there are no fundamental difference between bibliography and library catalague. A littie difference is:

1. A catalogue is concerned with the contents of a single library or group of libraries and describe only the copies of books to be found therein while a bibliography is not so confined, either as to the location of the material it records or to the description of the particular copy of each work which the library chances to possess.
2. A bibliography is concerned with the whole vast product of man's minds on paper, wherever he can lay his hands on it, for his aim is not to guide the seeker to the contents of one collection, but to help him to find his wayout in the great sea of literature which increases so alarmingly year by year.

In other words, a Bibliography is an organized list of reading material on one auther or subject. It is not limited to a particular collection. A catalague enlists, describes, records, and indexes the bibliographic resources of a particular collection.

A catalague may sometimes act as bibliography when it it prepare for a particular or special callection. Bibliography may also be used as adjunct to the card catalague.

We may enumerate the difference as under:

Catalogue	***Bibliography***
1	*2*
1. It covers the reading material of a particular library.	It is not confined to any one callection of books.

1	2
2. Its scope is limited to the a collection of a library or group of libraries in a locality or a country.	It's cope is unlimited. It may be limited to a library, group of libraries but also covers the whole universe on a particular collection of a country or the locality.
3. It groups the resources but bibliographical feature.	It enables the reader to identify particular positions in a published record from one point of view.
4. There is location symbol.	Location symbol need not be given.
5. It can be called as branch of descriptive bibliography.	It may not be the branch of catalague.
6. Details up to some degree' It is right and proper in its place.	There is no fixed degree of details.
7. It is usually found on card.	Usually in book-form.
8. It is based on standard code.	It is ncessary to follow any standard code. Much variation in practice.
9. There is sequence which is applied in uniformity.	There is sequence, but it may differ.

Inspite of various differences between the catalague and the bibliography, they have similar characteristics *i.e.*

1. Both are treated as list of books.

2. Both are arranged in definite order.

Sometimes a bibliography may include more details than the library catalague as it includes the price, type of binding and the channel of availability.

CATALOGUE IS SCIENCE OR ARTS

Science: means systematic and formulated knowledge of universe around us. It is a mode in which all phenomena are reasoned about, rendered precise and exect.

The definition of science clearly shows the basic factors of the Sciences, *i.e.*

(i) Reason—denotes Logic.

(ii) Precise—denotes Accuracy.

(iii) Exect—denotes fact finding.

Science involves techniques like methods of salesman in market weightingout his goods in common scales and the operations of a chamist in performing a difficult and intricate analysis by means of his balance and finaly graduated weights.

Science has its ever natural laws and causes. (causes+effect). (If there is flames, there was fire.)

Art : Art signifies a skill or ability. Art denotes.

Skill—Techniques.

Ability—Intelligency.

Both art and science are similar in persuit of truth, the process and methods by artist as well as Scientist.

Difference Between

Arts	*Science*
1	*2*
1. Synthetic approach.	Analysing material or events by separating them in to parts while artist select the materials, assembles, Composes and builds.
2. Individual reaction on experience basis.	General laws.

1	2
3. Art once completed stands as a final statement for all times. It may be destroyed but not disapprove.	The Theory once formulated stand best till new theory invalued.

Now we may evaluate the Catalogue whether it is a Science or art.

It is a Science : as

1. It has some normative principles. *i.e.*

    (a) Norms—Pattern, rules, authoritative standard.

    (b) Aims—drafting code, interpretation, provision for guidance.

2. Normative principles are based on some formulas.

3. Principles were extracted out of the facts.

4. Methods were established on the basis of the facts.

5. Canons.

6. Draw out fundamental principles after analysing general codes.

It is a Art: as

1 . It is a technique,

2. It has basic rules,

3. It can be eloberated,

4. It requires display of intelligence and sound judgement, and

5. It is govern by a code which involves some technicalities.

Like the science of Chemistry, cataloguing is essentially a laboratory art. It cannot be learned by memorizing a code but to be applied from the very beginning. A cataloguer has to use the active intelligance to decide on the particular rule applicable to the case in hand. (Henry A. Sharp) Every art is not mearly a practice but a discipline also. Accuracy & Consistancy is its first need.

Neither Art Nor Science:

Mr. H. W. Acomb has the opinion that cataloguing does not involve any of the qualities of art and Science as:

1. Cataloguing gives self expression which is not suitable to education.
2. It little depends on the ascertained and unalterable facts.
3. It is simple in technique.
4. It is simple in practice.

ESSENTIALS OF A GOOD CATALOGUE

Before approaching the practical problems of cataloguing it may be well to devote a little time and space to some introductory discussion of the qualifications required in satisfactory cataloguing, and of the importance of the catalogue itself in any library.

The three attributes most worthy of attention are:

Accuracy. Whether there is a case of style of cataloguing, compressed or abbreviated the entry, accuracy must be strictly adhared to. This may sound like the solomn enunciation of a platitude, aud yet it is no uncommon happening for a beginner work to be spoiled by small error in spelling, in the transcription of names with variant forms, or ever in the style of entry. In accuracy may cause serious misunderstanding and, loss of time and dislocation. Another aspect may be expressed in the dictum that a catalogue entry should represent exactly what appears on the title page of the book it stand for, subject to addition or omission only if indicated precisely in the way conventionally allowed.

General Knowledge. Knowledge purify catalogue. It is an asset in cataloguing by its very nature as dealing with the external details of books rather than with the value of their contents, demands it in a very special way. The changes in headings confront the cataloguer of old and rare books, and familiarity with psendonyms and library curiosities of that kind. All these problems can be dealt with satisfactorily if a cataloguer has enjoyed maximum General Knowledge.

Flair for Dealing with Book. The librarian should possess a quality of work and equally a gift which is possessed by nature, or else is very hard of acquisition. The possession of it will make difference between the routine worker and the first-class craftman. The catalogue of a library may be compared with the time-table if a railway service. Similarly then apply this simile to a large library without a catalogue, which depends on the memory of its staf for the location of books, and the initations of its public in going to equire what books might really be found on its shelves, some idea of the supreme inpertance of a catalogue may be gained.

Consistency. The paramount quality of a catalogue should be strictly consistency with the rules on which it is based. It matters less that the bast code should be adopted, in beginning to compile a catalogue, than that the most careful consistency should characterize the application of the rules when once they are Chosen Any departure from adopted practice, unless or rare occasions when, for the sake of convenience, such a variation is deliberately made and indicated, will inevitably cause trouble, and its cumulative effect will be infinitely greater in proportion to the apparent importance of the orginal lapse than can be foreseen.

Needs of the Readers. A good catalogue, whatever be its form, should be designed to meet the mulitiple needs of its users. A reader wants to know, what book a library has, or on a particular author, what edition, and on what subject, a library has. A user also want to evaluate the different materials in a library on a particular subject or a group of subjects for the purpose of study or research. The subject approach from the users point of view may be either by specific subject headings; or by exploration of the entire field covered. by the subject (class, division, sub-division and sections).

Well-Constructed. A good catalogue must be well-constructed to suit the needs of the people for whome it is intended. It should be suited to the clientele. Entry-arrangement should be simple, unifrom and easily understood. Descriptive details shouid meet the demands of the users.

Kept up-to-date. Catalogue should be kept up-to-date and thoroughly at the command of readers. It should be a occessible to all.

Meet the Problems. A well constructed catalogue should be as designed as to meet the various problems of entry represented by various complex materials or records of human thought and experience. Like entries should be arranged together. The same procedure should be followed in case of previous publications of a work.

Definite Principles. The catalogue, if constructed should be based on definite principles and followed uniformally throughout. Catalogue should, where necessary, rigid and unalterable rules for all times so that rules, may be revised the accomodate the incoming flow of complex material and to meet new requirements, but the revision should be rational, consistant and uniform.

Basic Parts. A library catalogue records the library stock. Each record consists basically of three important parts.

(a) Heading,

(b) Description, and

(c) Location.

Each document is recorded at general different parts in the catalogue to cater for a variety of approaches—author, editor, translator, title, subject. The first entry of these approaches is called Main Entry. In case of unit card entry, all entries, other than main entry, give the same amount of information about a document. The main entry is effective because.

(a) it is decided in term by which a document is sub-arranged at a class number;

(b) it is treated as the important and one likely to be looked for;

(c) it is used for selective reading lists and bibliographies.

Cataloguing Process

Contemporary society has experienced an extraordinary explosion in knowledge; this has resulted in a corresponding increase in the publication of books and other materials which act as information carriers. In general terms, without the aid of technology it is now impractical, if not impossible, to ascertain what material exists and where it may be obtained.

Two Operations

The cataloguing process basically consists of two operations: first, the creation of the appropriate entry relating to a particular item and, second the subsequent manipulation of this and other entries to form the actual catalogue.

The computer cannot replace the first of these, that intellectual element which only a human being can, at present, supply. The creation of a catalogue entry involves the answering of questions such as: What is the title of the item? Which person or body is responsible for its content? Who published it? When by a machine, which could not, for instance, distinguish between an author, *e.g.* Charles Dickens, and a title, *e.g.* David Copperfield.

However, the computer is capable of performing the various clerical functions involved in the manipulation of entries. For example, the computer can quickly sort catalogue entries into any desired order, or search for, entries which conform to a particular search profile. And the search facility that can be provided is a much more powerful one than would be possible in a manual index.

Because the computer can rearrange entries into any desired order, it may be used as a means of producing a catalogue or bibliography in 'hard' copy, *i.e.* 'printed' on to paper or film. However, it is becoming far more common to use 'on-line' access, *i.e.*, the catalogue entries are stored within the machine to use 'on-line' access, *i.e.* that catalogue entries are stored within the machine and searched for and displayed as necessitated by the requirements of a user.

Flexible Search Facility

Further, it should be noted that today's computerized catalogues and bibliographies can offer a far more flexible search facility than Cutter could ever have envisaged. For example, the user may need to know only part of an author, or part of a title, in order to find a particular entry.

Cataloguing must not be considered a self-contained unit; the relationship with bibliographies has already been stressed for example. There are also obvious links between cataloguing and classification; the same mental process must take place when deciding on the subject of an item, whether this is described in alphabetical terms or by a classification number. In addition, the catalogue can form the basis of an integrated system with ordering, acquisition and circulation control modules. Indeed, when the computerization of the cataloguing process is being planned, it should not be considered an isolation but as part of a larger entity.

Not everyone regards the catalogue as an essential tool. D.J. Urquhart showed, for instance, how effectively the National Lending Library for Science and Technology (now the British Library Document Supply Centre) in its early days could be administered without catalogue. It is seen by some people as a sacred cow and, in the 1960s, Grose and Line referred to it as a white elephant.

Certainly there are many more keys to unlock the doors of knowledge in the form of bibliographies, indexes and databases, and library users can find out very quickly via a computer terminal what is available, in global terms, in any subject field. But what they so often want to know is whether a particular item is available in their particular library, whether it be public, academic or special. Most readers want subject arrangement in the library, so that they can browse and this means that a catalogue is desirable to show not only what is available but also where it is shelved. The descriptive part of the catalogue entry will help the user to decide whether an item not immediately available is likely to be relevant.

There are other reasons for maintaining a library catalogue. It can provide analytical entries for parts of an item and it can record all items in a library's stock, acting as a valuable supplement to published bibliographic tools. At present, bibliographical control of English and American books and periodical article is excellent but this is by no means true of, for instance, report literature, semipublished material and the many forms of non-book media.

Standardization and the road to AACR 2. The requirement of cooperative and centralized systems make the acceptance of standards of vital importance. Such standardization might relate to the classification scheme used to arrange the stock of a library, to the alphabetical subject indexing methodology, or to the contery and arrangement of the catalogue entry. It is the latter with which this chapter is primarily concerned.

The manner in which a catalogue entry is organized with regard to the amdunt of detail to be included will depend upon the requirements of the particular cataloguing agency.

Despite differences in the amount of detail required, it is clearly advantageous for various cataloguing agencies to agree to work to the one standard, *i.e.*, a set of rules, to be used by all. The standard would prescribe how the content of the entry was to be organized and how the headings, or access points, under which an item was to be entered should be selected and presented. Whilst entries could be simple, because all elements advocated be compatible with those containing more detail because both had been produced using the same standard.

In USA

In the United States, standardization of author-title cataloguing has been a way of life in libraries, especially since 1901 when the Library of Congress took over the printed catalogue card service begun by the Library Bureau in 1893.

In Britain

In Britain, progress towards standardization was much slower perhaps due to the natural independence of British librarians, or perhaps because Britain's National Library did not attempt to take a central role in British librarianship until the 1970s, or possibly simply because no library was willing to accept the Anglo-American code of 1908 without considerable amendment. Even when the British national bibliography began to be published in 1950, using a much amended version of the 1908 code as the basis of its cataloguing, many libraries preferred to continue their own cataloguing practices.

When BNB started to issue printed catalogue cards in 1956 its cataloguing achieved greater acceptance, but there were still libraries which resisted, partly because they had reservation about the BNB's use of the Dewey decimal classification. What such libraries fail to appreciate that standardization does not mean accepting without question all of the data provided by a central cataloguing agency; rather it means using common practices as far as possible and lowing the agency to do work which cannot be done better locally.

Even though Americans accepted AA 1908 and later the ALA revisions of 1941 and 1949, many of them were not happy with these rules. Their dissatisfaction was voiced by Andrew Osborn on 1941 and, most notably, by Seymour Lubetzky in 1953. Lubetzky's Cataloguing rules and principles of that year came out strongly against the codification of catalogue rules via the elaborate and complex enumeration of innumerable 'cases' and pointed the way towards the possible formulation of a less complex set of rules based encyclopedia, for example, would not be regarded as a particular 'case' or type of publication, but would be treated in a similar manner to all other works, *i.e.* according to the particular 'conditions' of authorship of responsibility pertaining to it.

Lubetzky's ideas were widely welcomed and helped pave the way for the International Conference on Cataloguing Principles held in Paris in 1961. A draft statement of principles based upon Lubetzky's Code of Cataloguing rules: author and title entry; an unfinished draft

(ALA 1960) was submitted to this conference for discussion along with working papers on the various problems of rules prepared by delegates. A final version of the 'Statement of principles' was adopted and participants agreed to work in their separate countries revised rules which would be in agreement with these accepted principles.

The Anglo-American cataloguing rules of 1967 (AACR 1) was one of several codes reflecting the "Paris Principles'; though, unfortunately, it had to be published in two texts (British and North American) because there was not complete unanimity between the two countries' committees, particularly in the areas of description sand corporate headings.

AACR 1 was immediately accepted as a standard by the BNB and by several British libraries, but certainly not by all of them. In the United States its complete acceptance was hampered by the fact that the Library of Congress, one of the bodies responsible for the rules, adopted a superimposition or 'no conflict' policy-headings from AACR 1 were accepted only if they did not conflict with headings already in the catalogue.

AUTOMATED CATALOGUING

The development of automated cataloguing methods, particularly the MARC (Machine Readable Cataloguing) Project made the acceptance of an international standard more urgent, but already AACR 1 was being overtaken by events. Apart from the considerable influence of the computer, there were three factors which were of particular significance.

First, there were the rules being produced by a number of different countries throughout the world. Although these were also based upon the Paris Principles, there were some differences of opinion. European libraries, for instance, had never been happy with editors and compilers of collections being given the status of authors, preferring to enter collections under title, and so this rule was revised by the British and American in the interests of international cooperation.

Corporate responsibility was another problematic area where unanimity was difficult to achieve.

Second, there were the rules developed specifically for non-book materials, an area which was undergoing rapid expansion and for which AACR 1 was not considered satisfactory. In Britain there was Non-book materials cataloguing rules, produced by the Library Association's Media Cataloguing Rules Committee, published by the National Council for Educational Technology in 1973, and known as LANCET (the initials of its two sponsoring organizations); in Canada there was Non-book materials: the organization of integrated collections by Jean Riddle Welhs, Shirley Lewis, and Janet Macdonald, published by the Canadian Library Association in 1973; and in the United States there was Standards for cataloguing nonprint materials—an interpretation and practical application by Alma Tillin and William J. Quinly, the fourth edition of which was published by the Association for Edicatopma; Communications and Technology (Washington) in 1976.

Third, there was the continuous work being undertaken by the International Federation of Library Associations (now the International Federation of Library Associations and Institutions), a Working Group on the co-ordination of Cataloguing Principles was set up by IFLA as early as 1954 and in 1957 the IFLA General Council adopted a proposal to hold a world-wide conference on basic cataloguing principles. The International Conference on Cataloguing Principles of 1961 was thus IFLA inspired, the necessary financial assistance being forthcoming from the Council on Library Resources in America. The ICCP achieved international agreement on the principles to be adopted for choice of headings but for the international exchange of bibliographic information, whether in written or machine-readable form, it is obviously also necessary to have a generally accepted standard which lists the elements to be included in the descriptive part of an entry the order in which the elements are to be cited the punctuation which is'to be used to separate the elements.

A IFLA International Meeting of Cataloguing Experts in Copenhagen in 1969 set up a Working Party to study the possibilities for an International Standard Bibliographic Description for monographs. Such a standard ISBD (M), was subsequently drawn up and was officially adopted by the IFLA Committee on Cataloguing at its meeting in Liverpool in 1971. The publication of this standard necessitated the amendment of the relevant sections AACR I, in order to achieve conformity. These amendments included the introduction of a new area to accommodate the recently introduced International Standard Book Number (ISBN) as a unique identifier. Later, the International Standard, Serial Number (ISSN) also had to be catered for ISBD (M) was to be followed by similar standards for other media such as ISBD (S) for serials and ISBD (NBM) for non-book materials. Almost inevitably, because a different committee was responsible for each standard, certain discrepancies became apparent and, to counteract this, a 'general' framework for description was produced, ISBD (G).

The above brief historical account clearly illustrates that there was a strong case for revision of AACR 1. There was a need, to incorporate the ISBD (G) framework and to take account of other international developments. There was, also the very important need for one unified Anglo-American text, which would incorporate all amendments issued since 1967. In addition, there was the need to consider other proposals for changes and the effects of library automation. The latter was particularly difficult because these effects are on-going and have yet to be completely assessed and understood.

The Council on Library Resources agreed to fund the revision, with certain conditions, the major one being that royalties from sale should be placed in a common fund for future activities associated with AACR. A Joint Steering Committee for AACR meeting in 1974 confirmed the participation of five bodies as 'authors' (ALA, LC, LA, BL, and the Canadian Committee on Cataloguing). It was agreed to set up national committees to consider issues and proposals for revision. The new rules, the results of collaboration between the national libraries and professional associations of three countries, were published in 1978. The main objectives were to a great extent achieved and not the least part of this remarkable achievement was the fact that any institution, organization or individual with a point of view was given ample opportunity to express it during the process of revision.

Not Welcomed by All. The publication of AACR 2 was not welcomed by all librarians but, as Peter Lewis, later Director-General of the British Library Bibliographic Services Division, and former Chairman of the Joint Steering Committee for AACR, stated: 'for every powerful voice speaking against AACR 2, there is an equally powerful one calling for full implementation without delay'.

The major criticisms leveled against AACR 2 are that with the fast developing state of automation it is irrelevant, and its implementation increases library costs without increasing benefits.

Despite objections, four national libraries (the British Library, the Library of Congress, the National Library of Australia and the National Library of Canada) adopted AACR 2 from January 1981. Initially, the Library of Congress decided to retain certain pre-AACR headings for economic reasons but it reconsidered its position and decided to abandon this 'compatible headings' policy from 1982. Thus all of the national libraries were then agreed that the adoption of the rules, as they stood, would bring long-term cost and user benefits.

Whether an, individual library decides to use AACR 2 will depend upon factors such as the use made of centralized services and the staff support available to amend existing catalogues. Cataloguing agencies which have adopted AACR 2 are using what is, in effect, an international standard.

Work on the rules did not cease with the publication of AACR 2 in 1978, indeed, rather was the reverse the case in that a whole series of related activities was generated. These activities included. the implementation of training programmes, and the production of adoption aids, interpretative manuals, illustrative examples and translations. AACR 2 has spread its influence into a number of Non-English-speaking countries, and translations have been made into languages such as Arabic, Finnish, French, Japan see, Norwegian, Portuguese, and Spanish.

In 1981 the first edition of Gorman's 'The concise AACR 2', a rewritten and simplified version of the rules, was published. This was intended to provide a readily comprehensible summary of AACR 2 practice for librarians and cataloguers in a number of different situations, such as librarianship students, persons working in small libraries, especially 'one-person' libraries, and cataloguers working in a non-English-language environment.

AACR 2 has also encouraged research. For example, cataloguing rules for choice of access points involve conditional decisions; *i.e.* if a certain condition applies then take a particular decision. A computerized expert system functions in a similar way using a knowledge base expressed as a set of rules. Because of this similarity, several researchers have investigated the feasibility of creating an expert system for cataloguing.

The international Joint Steering Committee for Recession of AACR continued to meet regularly, as did the various national committees, and in 1981 it was agreed to add an Australian representative to JSC. The revision process also continued and three sets of revisions were prepared and published in 1982, 1984 and 1986. Many of these revisions have formed part of a general 'tidying-up' and correction process, whilst others have been of a more significant nature.

A major decision was taken by the Joint Steering Committee in 1985, when it was resolved to recommend that a consolidated was to incorporate all rule revisions passed, and topographical errors found, to that date. If possible, it was also intended to include revised rules for computer files, taking note of work that had already been done in this area such as that by 'Templeton and by Dodd, and for recently introduced media such as compact discs. This consolidation, including a new chapter for computer files and revised rules for recent media was published as Anglo-American cataloguing rules Second edition 1988 revision.

A survey of AACR 2 users taken in 1985 revealed that 98% favoured a loose-leaf format, and the new revision is available in three versions: soft back, hardback and loose-leaf. A new version of the concise AACR 2 has also been published. The period in which AACR 2 has developed has been a time when applications of the computer in cataloguing have also been developing at a tremendous rate. Therefore there are bound to be questions posed by library automation which have not been answered by the rules, even though some new concepts have sprung from, or been precipitated by, advances in automation. Forman, the editor of MCR 2, considers that the fact that AACR 2 has not been able to take I; library automation fully into account is not really the fault of those responsible for AACR but rather is due to the fact that the effect of library automation on catalogues has yet to be completely assessed and understood.

For these reasons, Forman predicts that there will never be an AACR 3 but a new type of code which will deal with the creation of machine-readable records for use in national and international networks. However, in the meantime, revisions to AACR 2 will continue to be made; cataloguing cannot stand still, and the fact that the new revision is available in looseleaf format reinforce this point.

Review Committee

An ISBD Review Committee was formed by IFLA in 1981 to implement a five-year review of the ISBDs for monographs, serials, cartographic materials and non-book materials, ISBD (M), ISBD (S), ISBD (CM) and ISBD (NBM), with the intention of publishing revisions in 1987. The Joint Steering Committee for AACR became concerned that ISBD(G), for which, as previously noted, the Joint Steering Committee was jointly responsible, might be effected by this review. Draft texts were circulated for comment in 1983-84; JSC AACR was one of the recipients of these drafts and was therefore given the opportunity to contribute to the review. Special attention has also been given to computer files; a Working Group net for the first time in 1986 and the final version of ISBD (CF) was published in 1990. The influence of AACR can be plainly seen in the latter publication with the ISBD adopting the AACR solution for differentiating between the type of file and physical carrier. A revised draft of the ISBD for rare, antiquarian books, ISBD(A), was circulated for study by appropriate persons in 1988.

The Main-entry Principle. Although rules for standardizing a bibliographic description (as the ISBDs and AACR2) and for selecting and formulating access points (as ARCS 2) may be necessary, one other aspect of AACR 2 is completely redundant in the machine-readable context, namely the concept of main entry. AACR 2 considers 'the concept of main entry to be useful in assigning uniform title and in promoting the standardization of bibliographic citation'. Some cataloguers defend AACR 2 on the ground that, although a number of on-line catalogues have appeared, the majority of present catalogues are still card catalogues. Other cataloguers would take issue with this defense. In Japan, for instance, cataloguers used codes based upon the main entry principle under the influence of AACR 2 and the Paris Principles until 1977, when a new code of Nippon cataloguing rules (NCR) was compiled. These rules abandon main entry not only because of progress in automation but also because of progress in automation but also because, in non-automated systems, it is seen to be less useful than the unit entry, which is now easy to produce and which ensures that each entry in the catalogue has an equal value.

The Japanese rules also differ from AACR 2 in another respect is that an attempt is made to define an item or unit more clearly. It is claimed that this leads to reader consistency where the cataloguing of multivolume sets and multipart items are concerned.

The Guidelines. AACR 2 reverses the pattern of all previous codes of cataloguing rules by placing the rules for description before the rules for choice of headings, because it is believed that this is the pattern followed in most libraries and bibliographic agencies. It also accepts the desirably of integrating bibliographic records of books and other kinds of materials.

Description. ACR 2 Part One-Description-is based upon the framework of ISBD(G). It begins with a general chapter containing rules which apply to all library materials. Each of the succeeding chapters in Part One, except for chapter 13, is concerned with more detailed rules for specific media, *e.g.* : chapter 2 Printed monographs; chapter 5 Music; chapter 6 Sound recordings; chapter 9 Computer files; chapter 12 serials. More than one chapter, apart from the general chapter, may need to be consulted; a serial, for instance, may also be sound recording. When this sort of situation occurs, AACR 2 states that the description of an item should be based in the first instance on the chapter dealing with the class of materials to which the item belongs. For example, a printed monograph in microform should be described as a microform.

The cataloguer brought up on earlier codes, which were concerned almost exclusively with printed material, must now, therefore, become familiar with some new terminology: publication, distribution, etc., area instead of 'imprint', 'Physical description area' instead of 'collation'; and terms such as 'statement of responsibility other 'title information' and 'statement of extent'. These new terms are largely a reflection of the integrated nature of the rules: 'statement of responsibility' includes the author of a book and the creator of a work of art; statement of responsibility includes the author of a book and the creator of a work of art; 'statement of extent' includes the pagination of a printed monograph or the playing time of a sound recording.

It is not necessary for all of the areas to be present in every case. An item may not, for instance, be influded in a series, or have a standard number. Similarly a note may not always be required. One area, the 'material specific details' are, in fact, used only for maps, music computer files and serials.

The number given on the right is the relevant rule number for that particular area. These numbers are used logically and mnemonically so that rule 1.1 will deal with the recording of the title in general terms, rule 2.1 will deal more specifically with the recording of the title of a printed monograph, rule 6.1 with the recording of the title of a sound recording, and soon.

Each area may be further divided into constituer elements, for example the publication, distribution, etc.; area could include such elements. the place of publication, distribution, publisher and date. These èlements are separated by a prescribed punctuation.

MANAGEMENT OF CATALOGUING

The quality of good management lies in the application of the principles in such a way as to provide the most effective catalogue fora library and its users. Correct decisions must be made on such matters as the fullness of cataloguing required; whether to use a conventional classified or alphabetical subject catalogue required; whether to use a conventional classified or alphabetical subject catalogue or some other system; the method to be used for establishing subject headings or subject index entries; what filing system to use; policy with regard to analysis and annotation; the physical form of catalogue; and the extent to which CIP (Cataloguing-in-publication) information, centralized services and or the computer are used.

With regard to centralized services, writers such as Foster maintain that to process books efficiently, every library, large and small, must have a good portion of its cataloguing performed by an outside source. If a centralized service is utilized, some decisions may, of course, be taken out of the individual cataloguing agency's hands.

Cataloguing needs may vary, not only in different kinds of library but also within the same library system. In some special libraries the major demands may be for current subject information and more use may be made of a subject-based retrieval system than of an author catalogue constructed according to AACR 2. In others, such as the library of a professional organization sending many items on postal loan, there may be a strong case for detailed cataloguing may vary according to the kind of material, some audio-visual materials may lack 'brows ability' and so be given more detailed cataloguing than books, and books which are on the open shelves may be catalogued less fully than those which are not.

Whatever the kind of library, there are certain management techniques which can be applied to the cataloguing process. There is a bewildering number of techniques, 'more than 250 of them being described in Finch's excellent of guide', but it must be remembered that they are only a means to an end-aids to decision-making or problem-solving. Just as cataloguers should not become so immersed in their cataloguing rules or methods that they overlook the overriding purpose of the catalogue-to help users of the library to find what they want-so managers should avoid becoming so immersed in a particular technique that they forget its purpose-to improve or optimize performance, to measure value or to rectify faults.

Foster, in his Managing the cataloguing department, cites 'management by objectives' (MBO) as 'typical of the most innovative management concepts found in libraries today'. MBO is so much a part of everyday normal management behaviour that the term is rarely used but it is still very relevant to cataloguing as 'an approach to assessing performance by reference to the achievement of results'. MBO involves formulating objectives (*e.g.* to ensure that library materials reach the public for whom they have been acquired with a minimum of delay); setting targets to allow these objectives to be met (*e.g.* cataloguing x number of items per day); and removing any obstacles to the achievement of these targets.

The cataloguing objectives can be defined as 'to ensure the maximum usefulness of the catalogue:

(a) surveying the use of the COM catalogues;

(b) reviewing the information required (*i.e.* considering the application of MARC and the latest edition of the Dewey Decimal Classification to new stock and old stock); and

(c) considering new applications for the catalogue database (organizing input and retrieving data to provide stock revision information, booklists on a subject and new accessions lists).

The specimen objective on cataloguing in the American Library Association's, 1980 planning manual for public libraries was concerned specifically with automation: 'to automate the acquisitions cataloguing, and circulation's functions within the five year period' with a view to lowering the elapsed time from receipt of materials to shelf to 20 days.

At New South Wales Institute of Technology the objectives of the cataloguing department were defined as to carry out the cataloguing and classification of all monographs, A/V and serials needed by the staff and students of the Institute, and the method of achieving these objectives reflected the underlying philosophy of the library: that the use of technological advances and resources sharing among libraries is the only effective and rational way of operating in these days of economic stringency.

Accepted Standards. In order to set targets it is necessary to have some generally accepted standards. In cataloguing, there are adequate standards of technique or practice but there are no generally accepted standards of timing or performance-inevitably, perhaps, in view of the different kinds of materials to be catalogued, the variation in difficulty of this material, and the differing amounts of information on catalogue entries.

A study at Cornell Lay Library, using the OCLC database, showed that the average cataloguing time was 8-9 minutes per record and, in a survey of members of OCLC network, 91 % of the libraries surveyed reported that the time required to catalogue items had been reduced by on-line cataloguing. A small study at Bath University Library showed that the cataloguing of 160 items took only 293 minutes, or an average of just under two minutes per item, but it must be borne in mind that this involved very brief catalogue entries. The average time taken to classify 148 items was just under five minutes per item, and classification normally forms part of the cataloguing process.

It should be possible for each library to determine its own standards. The Centre for Library and Information Management (CLAM., at Loughboroughy University, United Kingdom has shown how this can be done using the 'diary' techniques, with each member of staff keeping an accurate record of the time spent on every activity. A study by CLAIM's predecessor, the Library Management

Research Unit, of four libraries serving schools, colleges and institutes of a university, showed that one library spent an average of 8 minutes cataloguing each item, two spent an average of 10 minutes per item and one spent an average of 16 minutes per item. The four libraries were commensurate in size and staff involvement.

At La Trobe University, Melbourne, Australia, cataloguers kept detailed monthly statistics of the time spent on each operation. They did not object to the establishment of minimum output figures; rather, they requested such figures because they provided a target and a basis for assessing their performance. It should be borne in mind, however, that all human beings are different; they are not machines, and some people will inevitably perform tasks more quickly and efficiently than others.

Libraries Compared. A library may well find it helpful to compare its own activities and costs with those of their libraries in the same group, and published comparative statistics are useful from this point of view.

In the UK, for example, the Centre for Interfirm Comparison (CIFC), after its formation in 1959, carried out many comparisons of performance data in industry, showing that such comparisons can be a valuable management tool to help in the establishment of standards and in the evaluation of activities and procedures.

Flow of Work. A smooth workflow will help to streamline the cataloguing process, the various operations being performed in a reasonable chronological sequence and the layout of the cataloguing department being such that no member of staff has to exert himself more than necessary when carrying out his particular tasks. This is an example of ergonomics the relationship between the worker, his environment, and the equipment he uses. Ergonomics is a technique which is sometimes overlooked in librarianship.

Network Analysis

Network analysis can be of value in planning and controlling cataloguing operations, particularly those concerned with recataloguing or retrospective conversion. There are several network planning techniques, the best known being PERT (Programme Evaluation and Review Technique) and CPM (Critical Path Method). The time required for the activities and the sequence in which they should be performed are analyzed and represented in the form of a digram known as a 'network'; the activities forming the 'critical path' are then identified to enable the project to be completed in the shortest possible time.

Another management technique applicable to cataloguing is cost-benefit analysis which, as its name implies, involves weighing the cost of an activity against the benefit, accruing from that activity. It may be costly to make a lot of analytical entries, but is the cost justified by the time saved on searching for information and improved service to readers? Conversely, is the cost of full cataloguing justified if few readers use the cataloguing justified if few readers use the catalogue or if the majority simply want to locate an item and are not interested in publication details or physical description?

Item to be considered in costing include the cost of labour and materials, subscriptions to outside services, maintenance and depreciation costs, and overheads such as heating, and lighting. Factors affecting costs include:

CATALOGUING POLICY

Cataloguing policy, such as fullness of cataloguing, the rules to be used and the extent of analysis and annotation. The methods employed; for example, computerizing the catalogue. The proper use of staff; for example, it may be cheaper to use clerical staff for routine cataloguing and checking. The extent to which cataloguing is coordinated with other operations.

The benefit part of the cost-benefit equation should not be ignored. Where (d) is concerned, for example, a major advantage of computerization is that it allows on record to be used for many purposes, including ordering, cataloguing, circulation control, interlibrary loans, preparation of reading lists and production of management information. In a survey of OCLC members, 80% of the libraries surveyed reported that their primary objectives had been met. For some libraries the primary objective was reduced costs, whilst for others it was faster cataloguing or improved interlibrary loans. Thus both cost and efficiency benefits had accrued form membership.

A study by the Bath University Programme of Catalogue Research undertaken in 1979 to establish the size and distribution of the market for automated cataloguing services, produced a considerable amount of data relating to the cost of cataloguing. Unfortunately, the report did not relate these figures to the kind of cataloguing or the value of the catalogue to the user, in other words the cost-benefit element was missing.

To change to AACR 2 (or to any other code of cataloguing rules) is major management decision. How many headings in the catalogue will need to be changed? How costly will the change be and, more important, how cost effective? Will it result in a better catalogue or allow more effective use of networks?

A study at La Trobe University Library, Melbourne, indicated that the time spend on cataloguing might rise by 2.3% as a result of introducing AACR 2. Training would be an additional cost, though a one-off cost which need to be absorbed during a brief period of time. All in all, concluded George Sector, 'the adoption AACR 2. is likely to cause financial disaster to libraries with up to date practices'.

Five possible methods of implementing a change to AACR 2 are:

1. Starting a new catalogue for all items acquired after a specified date
2. Starting a new catalogue for all items published after a specified date
3. Changing the old headings as required
4. Superimposition

5. Interfiling the new entries with the old ones and linking as necessary with see also references, *e.g.*:

SMITH (W.H.) & SONS see also W.E. SMITH & SONS W.H. SMITH & SONS see also SMITH (W.H.) & SONS

Very large libraries are likely to opt for closure of the catalogue, but Rosenthal has pointed out that this step has implications for almost every library operation. He has also emphasized the importance of very careful planning of any change and that the public relations aspects should not be ignored. Any system must be properly explained to non-cataloguing staff and to the public. If a library opts to automate and to make use of MARC records in some way, *e.g.* by subscribing to the BLAISE Records Service or by joining a bibliographic utility such as OCLC, the decision to change to AACT 2 becomes implicit.

It is claimed that the 1988 revision of AACR 2 is a code supportive of the needs of library automation. Libraries of all sizes use automated systems and 'there is a greater reliance on, and indeed, a greater expectation of the availability of derived cataloguing copy'. With such 'realities serving as a backdrop, and, with the urgings of ABACUS (Association of Bibliographic Agencies of Britain, Australia, Canada and the United States) to facilitate machine transfer of bibliographic information by further standardizing, in particular, the choice and form of authors, titles, and series. JSCAACR has developed a revision more conducive to automated environments on the evolutionary scale of cataloguing codes, the 1988 revision of the Anglo American cataloguing rules carries us one step closer to the goal of universal bibliographic control'.

For those libraries maintaining non-MARC record-based systems there is more of an option to adopt AACR 2 or not. 'These non-MARC libraries must consider how not changing may effect exchange of information, or may impact on future plans for database or system conversion'.

The claims made for AACR 2 cited above are sweeping claims which some librarians might consider debatable but nevertheless the fact remains that the AACR 2 1988 revision exists; it does form the basis of the MARC record, and therefore the majority of libraries in English-speaking countries and even elsewhere must be prepared to take decisions about its use.

PRE-NATAL CATALOGUING

For many years Ranganathan urged the inclusion of a catalogue entry in each book on publication-'pre-natal cataloguing', as he called it. During 1985-89 the Library of Congress's 'Cataloguing-in source' experiment attempted to establish the feasibility of this, in collaboration with publishers and with the assistance of a grant provided by the Council of Library Resources. At the in-Souse programme could not be justified from the viewpoint of financing technical considerations, or utility. In 1971, 'cataloguing-in-source' was reborn in the United States as 'cataloguing-in-publication', initially for three-year experimental period, but it later became a permanent feature of Library of Congress record supply. For example, catalogue cards are printed from CIP records whenever full MARC cataloguing is not available. CIP' entries differ from full MARC cataloguing in that records are shorter and references to pagination and size are omitted.

Brazil implemented a cataloguing-in-publication programme in the same year as the United States (1971). CIP schemes now operate in many countries and they have become an integral part of bibliographic services.

In the United Kingdom, British Library Bibliographic Services began to provide brief catalogue entries on the verso of the title page of some British books in 1976. CIP entries began to appear in the British national bibliography and on MARC tapes in 1977. In January 1985, the first of a new-style CIP entry, conforming generally to AACR 2 Level 2 for description and containing full subject data, appeared in the BNB. Prior to 1985, the CIP entry was not intended to be definitive but the new programme was designed to realize the full potential of CIP as a major input source for the creation of permanent UKMARC records of both high quality and high currency. Thus the CIP record formed the actual basis of the, definitive "national bibliographic" record'. It was a radical move away from the long-accepted principle of using the actual item as the primary source of cataloguing data. An essential requirement for an effective CIP programme is the fullest possible participation of publishers. By 1990 well over 10000 British publishers were participating in the scheme. 'It is a mutually advantageous service getting early information to libraries and offering increased marketing potential to participating publishers'.

In 1988 the British Library entered into an agreement with Book Data Ltd. which was intended to lead to improvements in both the quality of data and the coverage of the CIP programme. Book Data's declared objective is to serve publishers, booksellers and institutional buyers-including libraries, with particular emphasis on the acquisitions function-by creating a database of very full descriptive records about titles currently available or about to be published. By 1990 the list of participating publishers include some 900 imprints accounting for more than 25,000 titles a year.

The British Library has stated that from April 1991 it will cease to create CIP records from advance information supplied by publishers. In order to continue providing this service, however, the Library intends, as an interim arrangement, to continue to buy in CIP 1 records from Book Data Ltd. These records will meet the minimum data requirement of AACR 2 Level 1 with some enhancement. They will include Book Data subject headings and will be classified according to Dewey Decimal Classification abridged edition. CIP records will continue to appear in BNB approximately six weeks before the expected date of publication.

As soon as the book has been published and received by the British Library Copyright Receipt Office a full authoritative record will be created which will then reappear in the main sequence of the BNB.

Whitaker is to supply CIP data to the British Library as from 1992.

Where Book Data is concerned, OCLC is also to mount a Book data file as part of its EPIC Reference Service.

Cataloguing at Low Cost

If necessary economies are not achieved by a more scientific approach to cataloguing, the library may resort to some form of 'limited cataloguing', an expedient useful also for reducing, cataloguing arrears and speeding up the cataloguing process and for reducing the bulk of the catalogue by eliminating unnecessary entries. The term 'limited cataloguing' is a generic one covering simplified cataloguing and selective cataloguing.

The most usual form of simplified cataloguing is the reduction of the descriptive element of the catalogue, such as the omission of all or part of the publication area or physical description area. Other possibilities include the simplification of author headings and the elimination of certain added entries. These limitations apply to the whole of the library's stock, whereas selective cataloguing involves the use of a variant form of cataloguing usually a simplified form, for certain items, and/or the omission of a catalogue entry for some items.

Most libraries can practice some form of selective cataloguing with little inconvenience to their readers. There seems little point in cataloguing standards specifications, especially if a library takes all of them, since they are easily retrievable via published indexes; alternatively they can be given a subject entry but not an author entry. Similarly, libraries which receive all government publications may rely on the official indexes rather than cataloguing each item, though the quality of cataloguing and subject indexing in the official lists may not be satisfactory for the library. Where UK official publications are concerned, a catalogue is also available on CD-ROM (UKOP). This provides over 180,000 bibliographic records for official publications published since 1980. Such materials' as town guides, trade catalogues and annual reports need not usually be catalogued as they may be regarded as 'self-indexing'. Some public libraries do not catalogue fiction, though many would consider this to be an undesirable economy.

The Library of Congress adopted a limited cataloguing policy between 1951 and 1963 when, in order to deal with arrears which had accumulated over the years, accessions were divided into four groups of documents considered primarily of interest as groups, and items given entry only. Care should be taken that the costs saved by adopting a limited cataloguing policy are not offset by greater inconvenience to library users because of reference and readers' advisory staff having to consult a large number of different sources for information. It is interesting that LC. ended its limited cataloguing policy in August 1963 following comments from card subscribers and others. We are back to cost-benefit analysis.

In 1987, the British Library, as part of a plan for future development, identified certain categories of material to receive 'ARC 2 level I' treatment, *i.e.* 'minimal level' cataloguing. These categories included modern English fiction (15%). Children's literature (10%), science and technology (25%), material with 32 pages or less (9%) and religion (4%). With overlaps, these categories cover 50% of BIB MACRO annual output and it was estimated that overall savings in record creation of 10% would be made.

An Essential Task

Catalogue maintenance is an important part of a cataloguer's responsibility. It is essential that new and revised entries are filed regularly and correctly; superseded entries are withdrawn; worn cards or sheaf slips are replaced; filing errors and other inconsistencies are rectified; obsolete subject headings are replaced; and new sub-headings are created when there are a large number of entries under one subject heading. Nowadays, simple instructions to the computer can often deal with these points.

MANAGING THE PERSONNEL

Communication is an essential feature of good staff management; staff must be kept informed of what is happening and why. Wherever possible some form of participative management is desirable, staff being involved in the decision-making process. One useful technique to employ is management by excepection, whereby matters are dealt with according to precise instructions or well defined objectives and only exceptional issues are referred to senior management.

The setting of objectives is an integral part of MBO techniques and there continues to be interest in MBO in British libraries, although the number of published references to its application has been on the decline. In the United States, however, academic libraries appear to have abandoned MBO in favour of Management Review and Analysis Programme (MRAP), an approach which relies very heavily on staff participation. MRAP was initially designed for use in large research libraries in the US in response to a perceived need to respond positively to the new economic, personal and external pressures of the 1970s. The focus is placed firmly on management functions: planning, budgeting, management information, policies, organization, staff development, supervision and leadership, personnel and communication for example.

MRAP is not concerned with appraising or even developing a plan but with improving the procedures for planning. In more general terms, MRAP can be seen as a method of introducing participatory management into a library, for analysing the library's functions and for providing a new framework for decision-making. MRAP has been used in a considerable number of American libraries with, it must be said, very mixed results and, does not seem to have caught on outside the United States.

Staff participation becomes absolutely essential when a library is implementing an automated system. In Norway, for example, the relevant trade union became interested in finding out what effect computerization had on personnel. After interviewing staff who had recently experienced automation in their libraries, one of the major findings was that adequate training is a very important requisite and this training should include staff participation at all stages as the system develops.

Lovecy tells us that 'the most damaging element for staff morale is run our and speculation'. From the initial consideration of possible automation, it is important to involve members of staff in discussions. ' This makes sense from all points of view, since no librarian really wants to make a decision on whether or not to computerize without someone to discuss it with ... the more staff that can be drawn in to the discussion at this early stage the better.' Good staff management is helped by the use of a procedure manual, which should ensure consistency without endless repetition of verbal instructions.

COMPUTERISED CATALOGUING

The quality of good management lies in the application of the principles in such a way as to provide the most effective catalogue for a library and its users. Correct decisions must be made on such matters as the fullness of cataloguing required; whether to use a conventional classified or alphabetical subject catalogue required; whether to use a conventional classified or alphabetical subject catalogue or some other system; the method to be used for establishing subject headings or subject index entries; what filing system to use; policy with regard to analysis and annotation; the physical form of catalogue; and the extent to which CIP (Cataloguing-in-publication) information, centralized services and the computer are used.

Increasing use of the computer; and of networks such as BLCMP and OCLC, is bound to have an effect on the management of cataloguing. The benefits of a computerized cataloguing system are indisputable but a decision to automate or not to automate the catalogue will depend upon a great many factors, including:

Size and type of library

Staffing levels

Financial support

Computer availability

Computerizing the Catalogue. It might be difficult, for example, in a small one-person library with very restricted financial provision and no access to any sort of computer. It is appreciated that some small libraries, unfortunately, cannot afford even an adequate book, stock, let alone consider automation. On the other hand, a large academic library with considerable resources and, in all probability, access to a large mainframe computer might find it difficult to resist automation. It is not unknown, however, in the case of the small library, for things to change overnight and if, for instance, a chance were suddenly offered to purchase a microcomputer system, as might happen in a school or college library, then the possibility of automation would have to be reviewed.

This is not, of course, to imply that the larger library will always find it easy to automate. A number of sizable libraries, such as Liverpool City Libraries, continue to have to manage with manual catalogues. Before adopting an automated system it is necessary to carry out a process of systems analysis, which means that the existing method of operation must be examined in order to ascertain whether computerization might lead to an improvement. Initially, objectives must be defined and a feasibility study undertaken.

The feasibility study will examine the various ways that the defined objectives might be achieved and it will look at the costs that might be incurred in relation to the benefit accrued (cost-benefit analysis). It will also investigate cost effectiveness in terms of manpower.

There are several options which a library planning to automate its catalogue might choose from:

> to develop a completely independent in-house system; to purchase a turnkey package; to join a bibliographic utility or cooperative network.

Whichever of the above is selected, it may be possible to make use of a centralized cataloguing service such as MARC in someway. Indeed, it may be obligatory to do so as in the case of the bibliographic utilities. Turnkey packages may not cater for the MARC format and for the importing of MARC records but many do and, in some instances, two approaches to the creation of the cataloguing database are offered-MARC and non-MARC. It should also be rioted that the bibliographic utilities usually offer some form of standalone turnkey system. This may also permit remote access to, and interaction with, the central database. There may well be, therefore, some overlap between options.

Go-in-One. The 'go-in-one', completely independent in-house system can vary from a single microcomputer configuration to a sophisticated set-up with large mainframe-computer support. If in-house development is chosen, care should be taken to ensure that on-goingbackup and maintenance are available and that enhancement will be possible as and when necessary. It is not unknown for an in-house system to grind to a halt as it grows and develops, owing to the lack of such facilities.

One library which preferred to use its own independent automated system was Derbyshire, UK, because it provided control over what to accept or reject, control over standards, and priority of access.

The prime example of an in-house development is probably that of the Upiversity of California's MELVYL catalogue system, which is recognized as one of the most sophisticated and advanced public online cataloguing systems in existence.

Follow-up studies have tended to confirm the above findings. For example, the University of Wyoming conducted a survey of online catalogue users in 1986. This was an adaptation of the Council on Library Resources study and the results were consistent with national findings, with very few exceptions.

Two Surveys. Liverpool Polytechnic has undertaken two surveys relating to PRECIS—a survey of reactions of indexers in all kinds of libraries, and a study of user reactions.

Of the 377 organizations respondings to the firstsur vey, 255 (67%) had given no thought to its adoption, and of the remaining 122, only 25 were actually using the system for indexing. The reasons quoted most often for rejecting PRECIS were its comlexity and labour intensiveness and it is interesting to note that the British Library is now simplifying the methodology. Some indexes regarded the document-specificity of PRECIS and the open-endedness of its vocabulary as advantages, and others say them as disadvantages.

The small number of organizations using PRECIS in their own systems is not, of course, an indication of the total number of users.

Anyone who makes use of the British National Bibliography or of UKMARC (1971-90) for subject access (including those he access British Library files online) can be considered a PRECIS user.

In the PRECIS user study, the main conclusion was that users generally reacted favourably, the document specificity was considered very useful. Users found the full subject statements more helpful than a string of terms, as in chain indexing, or broaded subject headings, as in the Library of Congress subject headings. Some non-librarian users found this aspect of PRECIS particularly Impressive. The ability of PRECIS to show relationships between terms was also appreciated.

Computerised Indexing

By removing the human intellectual element from indexing and allowing a machine, that is a computer, to select terms for index entries, a form of automatic indexing is obtained. Computerized 'keyword from title' indexes are automatic to a degree, but is there any way in which a computer can be programmed to identify appropriate terms from the text of an item? Initial attempts at automatic indexing were based upon determining, by statistical methods, the words which occur most frequently in a document. This method can be improved by comparing the number of times a particular word appears with the number of items it might be expected to appear. The advantage gained is immediately obvious; with the earlier technique a word occurring only a few times world be ignored but, using the latter method, the word might be proved to be very significant. Other experiments have concentrated upon the discovery that if words are 'paired' together in a document upon a number of occasions then this has an added significance.

In addition to the simple descriptors which are normally used in automatic indexing systems, it has also been shown that it may be possible to improve the quality of such systems by the addition of more complex descriptors, for example phrases, and other techniques evolve around the selection of sentences. Sentences can be weighed according to predetermined measure of significance. Sentences with the highest weights are likely to be those which best summarize the subject-content of an item. Examples of 'measures' are 'word frequency', as described above, and the position of a sentence-for example, the first sentence of a paragraph might be an important indication of the paragraph's subject-content.

An automatic indexing system can be linked with a machine-based thesaurus to provide controlled language indexing.

Research into techniques such as those described above has continued over many years and operational systems have been devised. Some of these systems have been shown to possess a number of defects and inadequacies; others have been put to practical use and are claimed to be successful. For example.

'Thonssen describes an automatic indexing system (PRIMUS-IDX) which interfaces with an automatic thesaurus management programme (INDEX) to enable large quantities of texts to be indexed quickly, consistently and cheaply. The recent application of expert system technology should also be noted. The overall objectives of research into automatic indexing can be said to be rather more than simply to represent the subject-content of a document by index terms; it is possible to produce an automatic extract ('autoextract') which compares reasonably well with an abstract prepared by a skilled abstractor.

The SMART project, which was developed in the United States by Saltine, and which is sometimes referred to as Saltine's Magical Automatic Retrieval of Text, is concerned with the effectiveness of computer-based retrieval systems relying entirely or almost entirely on machine processing of text. Out of the early experiments evolved new techniques for the construction of computer-generated thesauri. The system could be used online and a comparison with MEDLARS proved that the SMART procedures worked well. A detailed discussion is outside the scope of this work but it is, perhaps, worth recording that Salton came to the sweeping conclusion that there is little jurisdiction for maintaining controlled many indexes.

Computerised Classification

Allied to automatic indexing, although somewhat outside the scope of this present work, is automatic classification. At the Cambridge Language Research Unit, for instance, investigations panning a number of years from the early 1960s were involved with the machine analysis of documents for the discovery of 'keywords' for indexing purposes. Attempts were made to construct automatically a classification of key words based upon the way in which terms 'co-occur' in documents. Terms thus related are grouped together into 'clumps', terms 'outside'. Using clumps alone did not lead to very satisfactory results and later experiments utilized four different kinds of group, the original' clumps', together with 'strings', 'stars' and 'cliques', A 'string', for example is a set of terms in which each term is found to be most strongly associated with the one next to it.

This is 'clearly and indisputably a newer form of classification' which may have farreaching effects in the future. At present such work is still mainly at a theoretical level but there is a possibility that it could well improve the search capability in computerized databases to a marked degree.

Spark Jones considers that the immediate prospects for operational automatic classification are "not bright", because of the failure to fully establish appropriate methods and applications, and the high cost of experiments. Yet she believes that large files need more sophisticated tools, such as classification, and since automatic classification has not been conclusively shown to be unhelpful compared with human classification, its longer prospects should be interesting to all concerned with information systems.

It is certainly possible that some form of classification, whether 'automatic' or not, 'built-in' to computerized databases could improve the search capability to a marked degree. It might, for instance, be feasible that a search on one tern, could be translated automatically into a search for other related coordinate or subordinate terms indicated by the classification. This could greatly improve the efficiency of the system. If to take a simple example, an item dealing with the 'use of parachutes to stop ocean-going tankers' was searched for under 'parachutes' and 'slips', the automatic classification facility would reveal that 'tankers' was closely related to 'ships' and the relevant document would be retrieved.

The Embodiment

Part of the British Computer Society's approved definition states that an expert system is regarded as the embodiment within a computer of a knowledge-based component from an expert skill in such a form that the system can offer intelligent advice or take an intelligent decision about a processing decision. In other words, an expert system is a computer programme which can take the place of a human expert in some particular area of knowledge. As such, clearly there are possible applications within the cataloguing and indexing field.

For example, expert system techniques might be successfully applied to the task of selecting index terms. On such system is that operated by the Central Abstracting and Indexing Service of the American Petroleum Institute (API-CAUSE), which selects index terms from abstracts of articles appearing in the technical literature. A rule-based system has been created, using the API thesaurus as a base, which has been operational since 1985. The index terms selected by the computer are reviewed by a human index editor (as are the terms selected by CAIS's human indexers). After editing, the terms are used for printed indexes and for online computer searching.

Other examples include L-IDIA (L-Intelligent Document Information Analyser), which is the central part of an expert system designed to analyse automatically the content of documents in natural languages (relevant to well defined domains of knowledge) and an expert system described by Gauch and Smith for searching in full-text. Where the later is concerned, an intelligent search intermediary helps end-users to locate relevant passages.

An obvious possibility is automatic cataloguing based upon a set of rules as embodied in a code such as AACR 2, and there have been several pieces of research aimed at achieving this. One example of the research carried out by Hames at the University of Exeter, another is the work of Hjerppe at Linkoping University, and an investigation into automated title-page cataloguing has been carried out under the direction of Weibel at OCLC However, 'for an expert system to generate the required conditions for a specifically designed goal, the logic in the knowledge base must be consistent. There have been problems in every attempt to convert AACR 2 into the highly structured rules necessary to run an expert system'. Meador and Whiting conclude that this may well lead to further changes in the rules because the impact of technology will demand greater consistency. Apart from this, Weibel cites other unsolved problems as the incorporation of the cataloguer's general knowledge into the system, the complexity of the rules, and a lack of reliable data capture techniques.

Language to Language

One of the problems that has exercised the minds of librarians over the years has been that of switching from one indexing language to another. Apart from direct one-to-one translation, there is the possibility of the use of having an intermediate neutral languages designed to switch indexing decisions recorded in one indexing language into equivalent decisions in other languages. The intermediary should have the same coverage and specificity as the languages with which it is to be used and should be hospitable to index languages with different structure; that is, faceted or enumerative classification, thesauri or alphabetical word lists. Horsnell investigated the feasibility of a switching language in the field of information science. She reported that switching is possible and that overall recall and precision values far normal indexes and indexing obtained by switching are similar.

Other developments in this area include work conducted under the auspices of UNISSIST to provide an international switching language which could be applied to all publications to indicate the subject fields covered. The original intention was that this would be an intermediate language between two established languages, for example:

German natural language-switching language-French natural language, but the eventual product was the Broad system of ordering. This is a general classification scheme, with a fairly low level of specificity (as the title suggests). Although the scheme, which was the work of an FID (International Federation for Documentation) / BSO Panel, is intended for information exchange and switching, it is not a true switching language in the context of the criteria explained above. It can be concluded that we should investigate and attempt to evaluate indexing systems rather than take their performance for granted, but we should not be too surprised if the results of these investigations are sometimes inconclusive. Cleverdon wrote, when reporting on the second Cornfield investigations: 'As with Cranfield I, the outcome of this test is to raise more questions than it answers. It would be absurd for any organization to abandon conventional indexing and controlled index languages, whether thesauri or classification, on the basis of these test results.

INDEXING PROCESS

The requrement that the index a certain number of items per day will usually dictate that the indexer must accept less than a complete reading. A combination of reading and "skimming" is usually advocated. The parts to be carefully read will be those likely to tell the most about the contents in the shortest period of time: the title, abstract, summary and conclusions. Section headings and captions to illustrations or tables are also worth more attention. The rest of the text should be skimmed to ensure that the more condensed parts give an accurate picture of what the item is about. Nevertheless, the indexer should usually take into account the entire document (parts read, parts skimmed) and the terms assigned should reflect the whole.

The exception would be the case in which only part of the document (e.g., a lengthy multitopical item) is of interest to the user group to be served. Jones, quoting Anderson, points out that some parts of a document are especially rewarding to an indexer: "Opening paragraphs (in chapters or sections) and opening and closing sentences of paragraphs seem to be particularly rich in index able words." This agrees with the findings of Baxendale in her work on the development of procedures for the automatic indexing of documents. The international standard on subject indexing (ISO. 5963-1985 [E]) offers further guidance on the examination of the document:

> A complete reading is often impracticable, nor is it always necessary, but the indexer should ensure that no useful information has been overlooked. Important parts of the text need to be considered carefully, and particular attention should be paid to the following:
>
> — the title;
>
> — the abstract, if provided;
>
> — the list of contents;
>
> — the introduction, the opening phrases of chapters and paragraphs, and the conclusion;
>
> — illustrations, diagrams, tables and their captions;
>
> — words or groups of words which are underlined or printed in an unusual typeface.

All these element should be scanned and assessed by the indexer during his study of the document. Indexing from the title alone is not recommended, and an abstract, if available, should not be regarded as a satisfactory substitute for an examination of the text. Titles may be misleading; both titles and abstracts may be inadequate; in many cases neither is a reliable source of the kind of information needed by an indexer.

The largest group of indexers (about 85 percent of the total) 'stated that they routinely examine the entire document. However, these indexers stressed that certain sections of the document were examined more carefully than others. These sections included the abstract, introduction, summary, conclusion, methodology, findings, and charts and graphs. If one or more of these "condensed" sections were considered adequate by the indexer, he might lightly scan, or simply "page through" other parts of the document. The major reasons given for looking at the body of the document were to see if anything was overlooked, to facilitate greater depth in indexing, and to clarify any doubts or questions.

One assumption underlying all of this is that the item to be indexed can be read. As the international standard (ISO 5963-1985 [E1]) points out; different procedures will apply to other types of item:

> Non-print documents, such as audio-visual, visual and sound media, including realia, call for different procedures. It is not always possible in practice to examine a record in its entirety (for example by running a film). Indexing is then usually carried out from a title and/or synopsis, though the indexer should be allowed to view or hear a performance of the medium if the written description is inadequate or appears to be inaccurate.

The reason for examining the document, of course, is to decide what to include in the indexing (in the terms of Preschel, this is the identification of the "indexable matter"). To do this effectively the indexer must know a great deal about the interests of the community served by the index. Within a particular organization, indexers may be instructed to look for certain predefined elements in a document; if these occur they must be covered in the indexing.

Depending on the type of organization, such essential elements might include: materials of construction, temperatures involved, age group involved, educational level, and so on. In some cases the more essential elements may be preprinted onto an indexing form to remind the indexer that the appropriate terms must be used if they apply to a particular document. For example, the National Library of Medicine uses "checktags" of this kind to account for age groups, gender, types of animals used in experiments, and so on. This "conceptual analysis" stage of indexing should not be influenced by the characteristics of the vocabulary to Library be used in the translation stage. That is, the indexer must first decide what topics need to be represented; only later (momentarily perhaps) should he consider whether or not the vocabulary can represent these topics adequately. Put somewhat differently, an indexer should not ignore a topic because he knows or suspects that it cannot be expressed adequately.

It is possible that a careful examination of the vocabulary may prove him wrong in this. Moreover, an important function of the indexer is to improve the controlled vocabulary by bringing its inadequacies to the attention of those responsible for its maintenance. This is unlikely to occur if the indexer is encouraged to "think" in the controlled terms. In this respect we are in complete disagreement with ISO 5963, which states that: "Both analysis and transcription should be performed with the aid of indexing tools such as thesauri and classification schemes." The transcription, to be sure, cannot be performed without such tools, but the analysis should be completely independent of them. A related factor to bear in mind is that the terminology used by an author may not correspond exactly to the terms of the controlled vocabulary Even though author terms and controlled terms coincide, the way they are used may differ.

Factors affecting the performance of an information retrieval system that are directly attributable to indexing can be categorized as follows:

— Indexing policy

— Indexing accuracy

Policy decisions are established by the managers of the information service, and are thus outside the control of the individual indexer; the accuracy factors are under the individual indexer's control. The major policy decision is that relating to the exhaustivity of the indexing, which roughly corresponds to the number of terms assigned on the average. Exhaustive indexing implies the use of enough terms to cover the subject matter of a document rather completely. Selective indexing, on the other hand, implies the use of a much smaller number of terms to cover only the central subject matter of a document. The more terms used to index a document the more accessible it becomes and, presumably, the more it will be retrieved.

Policy decisions on exhaustivity should not take the form of absolute limits on the number of terms to be assigned. Rather, the policy might suggest a range of terms-e.g., "most items will be indexed with 8 to 15 terms." In a large information center, dealing with many different types of documents, the policy may vary with type of document. For example, the information center of a large company might establish a policy as follows:

Company's own technical reports	15-25 terms
Other technical reports	10-15 terms
Patents	15-20 terms
Journal articles	5-10 terms

Alternatively, the policy could be based on subject matter, the subjects of most interest to the company being indexed with most terms. Although a database indexed exhaustively will tend to allow for comprehensive searches (high recall), exhaustive indexing is likely to be more expensive than selective indexing. Moreover, exhaustive indexing will cause lower precision in searching. That is, more items will be retrieved that a requester judges not pertinent to his information need. This may occur for two reasons:

— "False associations" will increase with the number of terms assigned. For example, the item in Exhibit 3 might be retrieved in a search on telephone surveys in Egypt, but it has nothing whatever to do with this topic.

— The more terms used to index an item, the more it will be retrieved in response to search topics dealt with in only a very minor way. The item in Exhibit 3 is likely to be retrieved in a search for articles discussing political leaders of Arab states, but the person requesting such a search may decide that it contributes so little to this topic that it can hardly be considered useful.

The term depth is frequently used to refer to the number of terms assigned to a document. That is, depth is used in place of exhaustivity. Both terms are imprecise and can be misleading. To better understand the effect of increasing the number of terms used to index a document, one may consider it as having two dimensions. One can regard this as the breadth of coverage of the document. If the indexer attempts to cover all of these topics, the indexing can be considered exhaustive. The more topics covered the more exhaustive is the indexing.

Some of the topics identified could be indexed at more than one level of specificity. Suppose that the first topic is "architecture of cathedrals." This might be indexed under the term ecclesiastical architecture, which is not completely specific. To increase specificity the indexer might add a second term, cathedrals. The joint use of the two terms precisely represents the topic of discussion.

In other words, the addition of further index terms might increase the exhaustivity of a representation or might increase its specificity. Therefore, while it is true to say that "exhaustivity" roughly corresponds to the number of terms assigned, no exact one-to-one relationship exists between exhaustivity and number of terms.

The number of terms assigned to a document is really a cost-effectiveness consideration. Generally speaking, the more exhaustive the indexing the greater the cost and there is little sense in indexing more exhaustively than warranted by the needs of the users of the service.

Principle of Specificity

It is better to use several specific terms rather than a term that is more general. If an article describes the cultivation of lemons, limes, and grapefruit, it is better indexed under the three specific terms rather than the more general citrus fruit. The term citrus fruit should be used only for articles discussing citrus fruit in general and for those in which virtually all citrus fruit are discussed. This guideline could be extended to the situation in which several citrus fruit are discussed but not in enough detail (in the indexer's judgment) to warrant use of the specific terms.

In some cases, too, the audience served by the indexer may be interested only in certain fruit. In this situation it would be legitimate to index these only and not to include terms for the others. Some students of indexing make the mistake of indexing redundantly. Having indexed an article on oranges under the term oranges, they want also to assign citrus fruit and even fruit. This is quite unnecessary. Indeed, it is poor indexing practice. If the generic terms are assigned every time a specific term is used, it becomes difficult to distinguish general articles from specific ones. For example, the user who searches an index under the term fruit should expect to find items on fruit in general rather than items on individual fruit.

In the manual retrieval systems that were the predecessors of computer-based systems, it was in fact necessary to "post up" from specific to generic term *e.g.*, the use of the term oranges in indexing an item caused citrus fruit, fruit, and even, perhaps, crops, to be assigned also. This was done to allow for generic searches. Were it not done, it would be virtually impossible to perform a complete search on, say, all fruit. If a computer-based system is properly designed, however, posting-up in this way should not be necessary, at least when a controlled vocabulary is in use. For example, it should be possible to ask the computer to search on the term fruit and everything below it in the hierarchical structure.

Then, one would not expect the terms citrus fruit and oranges to be applied to the same item. The only situation in which this combination is justified would involve an article dealing with citrus fruit in general but including a lengthy discussion on oranges, or one on citrus fruit that uses oranges as an example (*e.g.*, the irrigation of citrus fruit with examples drawn from the irrigation of oranges).

The indexer must remember that specificity may be achieved through the use of combinations of terms. If no single term exists, an appropriate combination should be sought in the controlled vocabulary. Some hypothetical examples:

— Medieval French Literature

— Indexed under medieval literature and

— French literature

— Medical Libraries

— Indexed under science libraries and

— Medical sciences

— Canadian Literature

— Indexed under Literature and

— Canada

— Groundnut Oils

— Indexed under vegetable oils and

— Groundnuts

In theory, Medieval French Literature could be expressed by medieval literature and France, but the combination of medieval literature and french literature expresses the idea more accurately. Likewise, medical sciences is combined with science libraries rather than libraries to express the idea of medical libraries, since medical libraries are clearly scientific, and groundnuts is combined with vegetable oils rather than oils since groundnut oil is a vegetable oil.

The process of subject indexing seems to be unsusceptible to precise rules. Beyond the principle of specificity, no real rules for the assignment of terms have been developed, although many exist for what to do with index terms once they are assigned. A number of "theories" of indexing have been put forward, and several have been reviewed by Borko, but these tend not to be true theories and they offer little practical help for the indexer. Fugmann has presented several axioms of "indexing and information supply" but not all of these are directly related to indexing per se. The only real indexing principle put forward, referred to as "mandatory indexing," states that an indexer is to use the most appropriate terms available to describe the subject matter discussed in a document.

Since this will usually mean the most specific terms, this is essentially a restatement of the principle of specificity. Most of Fugmann's axioms are really factors affecting the performance of information retrieval systems rather than elements of indexing theory, although several have implications for indexing. For example, the axiom of definability relates to the ability to define an information need clearly and unambiguously. This can obviously be extended to the ability to define the subject matter of documents clearly and unambiguously. Fugmann's axiom of predictability states that the success of a search in a retrieval system depends largely on the predictability with which subject matter is described, which points to the importance of consistency in indexing. The axiom of fidelity states that another factor affecting performance is the ability to precisely and accurately describe subject matter (of information needs and, by extension, documents), which relates more to the vocabulary used to index than it does to indexing itself.

It is possible to identify only two fundamental rules of indexing, one related to the conceptual analysis stage and the other to the translation stage, as follows:

— Include all the topics known to be of interest to the users of the information service that are treated "substantively" in the document.

— Index each of these as specifically as the vocabulary of the system allows and the needs or interests of the users warrant.

Of course these rules are subject to interpretation. For example, what does "substantively" really mean? One possible guideline would be that topic x should be indexed if it is felt that the majority of users seeking information on x 'would find this item of interest. It is clear that "substantively" is not a property that can be expressed or measured in any precise way. Whether or not a particular topic is worth indexing will depend largely on three factors: *(1)* the amount of information given on the topic, *(2)* the degree of interest in the topic, and *(3)* how much information already exists on the topic: a single, brief mention of a compound may be worth indexing if the compound is known to be quite new; years later much more information would be needed to warrant inclusion. The statement "needs or interests of the users" in the second rule implies that the principle of specificity can and should be modified when it is known that users of a particular system or tool would be better served by indexing a particular topic at a more general level under certain circumstances. For example, in a medical database, articles on veterinary medicine applied to dogs might be indexed under the names of the dog breeds involved. Some indexers, particularly those who consider themselves to be subject "experts," may be tempted to see things in a document that the author never intended (*e.g.*, applications of a device beyond those claimed in the document). While it may be an important function of certain information specialists (*e.g.*, those in industry) to bring potential applications to the attention of users of an information service, this is not really, the function of the indexer perse. It is much better that he stick to the text and the author's claims. The ERIC Processing Manual gives some advice on this:

> Index the document in hand, not the document the writer would like to have written or intends to write the next time. Do not confuse speculation, or referrals to implications and possibilities, with real content.

"Results not claimed by the author," of course, should not be confused with negative results. It will usually be desirable to index the latter.

Post-coordinate Indexes

The subject matter discussed in a document, and represented by index terms assigned to it, is multidimensional in character. Consider, for example, an article discussing labour migration from Mozambique to the mines of South Africa indexed under the following terms:

— Mozambique

— South Africa

— Migrant workers

— Miners

— Economic Relations

Although the terms are given here in the form of a list, they actually represent a network of relationships: One should be able to retrieve this document in a search involving any single term or any combination of them: any two terms, any three, any four, or all five. An information retrieval system that allows a search to combine terms in any way is frequently referred to as post-coordinate (post combination or manipulative are other terms that have been used).

Post-coordinate systems emerged in the 1940s, when they were implemented through the use of various types of cards. A modern computer-based system, operated online, can be considered to be a direct descendant of these manual systems.

The files of an online system comprise two major elements:

— A complete set of document representations: bibliographic reference usually accompanied by index terms or abstract or both.

— A list of terms showing which documents have been indexed under them (sometimes referred to as an inverted file or a postings file). The documents are identified by accession numbers.

Indexing Aids

The indexer must have some way of recording the results of the indexing operation. Four possibilities exist:

— recording on the document itself,

— completing some kind of form printed on paper;

— recording on an audiotape; or

— completing a form displayed online.

In some organizations the indexer merely marks up the document at hand and a typist transcribes the indexer's markings. This mode would usually be appropriate only to situations in which a relatively simple approach to indexing is employed *e.g.*, the augmentation of titles coupled with the addition of a relatively small number of index terms or codes.

In some highly specialized indexing environments it might be possible to preprint the entire controlled vocabulary onto an indexing form, allowing all terms to become essentially checktags. The pioneer of this approach was probably Mooers.In analysing a document, the indexer essentially considers every descriptor in the schedule as potentially applicable. In effect, the indexer asks himself the questions posed by the indexing form itself. If, for example, the answer to "are there specific aerodynamic loads?" is "yes" (i.e., the document at hand discusses specific loads), the indexer must account for this by assigning the most appropriate aerodynamic load descriptor or descriptors. The descriptor list, presented in this way, simplifies the indexing process because it takes some of the intellectual burden from the indexer. The potential uses of a document of interest to the organization are represented by the list of "leading" questions which has been carefully compiled by senior scientific personnel.

In the past the U.S. Patent and Trademark Office has developed small retrieval systems restricted to a single class, or limited number of classes, in the patent art. Specialized vocabularies have been devised for these areas, and they are small enough to be printed on a few sheets. Exhibit 11 illustrates part of such a vocabulary for the patent subclass dealing with general purpose digital computers. As with the Mooers descriptor schedules, the entire vocabulary can be easily scanned, preventing the indexer from overlooking an important term, and eliminating the need for entering terms on an indexing sheet. In this case, multiple copies of the term list are available, and a patent is indexed merely by circling the appropriate terms or their codes on a copy of the list. All subsequent processing is clerical. The "microthesaurus" of the Air Pollution Technical Information Center, as described by Tancredi and Nichols, was also designed for use by circling of terms.

Success has also been achieved in some organizations by having the indexer dictate terms into a tape recorder for future transcription by typists. This approach does have some problems associated with it. Many typing errors may occur when a large technical vocabulary, unfamiliar to the typist, is used, necessitating very careful editing. Some indexers do not work well in this mode because they have trouble remembering which terms they have already assigned to an item.

The producers of databases are converting to online indexing procedures. In this mode of operation various formatted displays are presented on the screen and the indexer enters data into the fields thus displayed. This mode of operation offers significant advantages over its predecessors: the indexer can be prompted in various ways; some indexer mistakes can be recognized by error detection programmes and the indexer informed immediately, and the intermediate clerical step of converting the work of the indexer into machine-readable form is avoided. Moreover, it should also be possible for the indexer to switch from an input mode to a retrieval mode. Thus, precedence can be used to guide certain indexing decisions. That is, the indexer can switch into the database to find out how a particular term has been used in the past or how an earlier document, related to one at hand, was indexed.

The controlled vocabulary used by an information service will be a tool of paramount importance to the indexer. It should be organized and displayed in such a way that it gives the indexer positive assistance in the selection of the terms most appropriate to use in a particular situation. While closely related to the subject of indexing, the construction and properties of controlled vocabularies are topics outside the scope of this book. They have been dealt with in detail elsewhere.

A published thesaurus will usually incorporate a limited entry vocabulary in the form of see, use, or see under references. A large information center may also issue a separate entry vocabulary for in-house use by indexers, searchers, and lexicographers. Such a vocabulary may be available in several forms: card file, loose-leaf, machine-readable for printout or online display, or microfilm. Published reference works can be of great value to the indexer, most obviously in defining the meaning of unfamiliar terms. Specialized and general dictionaries and encyclopedias, and glossaries of all kinds, will be of particular importance.

BIBLIOGRAPHIES

Bibliographical control is a term variously defined but conveying the idea of a goal which has proved to be tantalizingly elusive. It is an idea which Dorothy Anderson sums up as: 'Ever since published material appeared in quantity—since the advent of printing in fact—librarians have been concerned with problems of controlling the bibliographic record of that material, and in the process, have developed an assortment of bibliographical tools with their purpose to supply answers to a variety of questions...' In the first two hundred years of the printing-era it was independent scholars rather than librarians who were the principal compilers of bibliographies; it is possible to see in Dorothy Anderson's words the basis of the concept—the compilation of bibliographies and their creative application to the problems of seeking information.

In 1964, the British Library Association published a new syllabus for their professional examinations, paper four of part-one was entitled 'Bibliographical control and service', Accompanying the syllabus was a very serviceable definition: 'Bibliographical control is the development and maintenance of a system of adequate recording of all forms of material published and unpublished, printed, audio-visual or otherwise, which add to the sum of human knowledge and information'.

The influential UNESCO/Library of Congress bibliographical survey provide a detailed definition which, although published about twenty years earlier, goes further than the Library.

Association's definition and links with a broader concept than simply listing records, bringing in the question of access to sources themselves: 'Bibliographical control is defined to mean the mastery over written and published records which is provided by and for the purposes of bibliography. Bibliographical control is synonymous with effective access through bibliographies. Thus a reference to the bibliographic control of medicine means effective access through bibliographies to sources of medical information'.

Bibliographic Listing

Bibliographic listing so that would be users of documents might be alerted to their existence is, then, most important. Gaining direct access to documents is obviously even more important and, whilst it is necessary to have the means of becoming aware of their existence, access is the ultimate goal. The study of the total system of listing and access is usually entitled 'bibliographic organisation' and whilst a definition of this term appears only a very little different from 'bibliographic organisation is derived from a seminal work by Jesse Shera and Margaret Egan: 'Bibliographic organisation may be defined as the pattern of effective arrangements which results from the systematic listing of the records of human communication. Such listings are themselves called bibliographies, and the art of making them is bibliography'.

Shera and Egan's definition of bibliographic organization provides a reminder that the compilation of bibliographies is not an end in itself but merely the means to an end. The end product of bibliographic control is 'the pattern of effective arrangements which result from ; systematic listing. Bibliographic organization is, thus, a much broader term than bibliographic control. It encompasses a study of the means by which access is obtained to record knowledge especially with regard to the reduction of barriers of the political, legal, intellectual or oganizational kinds. The barriers will include copyright problems, secrecy and security, trade, postal and tariff restrictions on the international dimension and differences in cataloguing and other internal arrangements at the national, local and even single library level. In truth, however, the two terms bibliographic control and bibliographic organization are often employed as synonyms and although an academic dissertation on the differences might be interestirg, it is hardly a very crucial topic to spend time on. The task faced Libraries are concerned with the collection of the records of human culture and achievement and organizing them effectively so that they may be easily retrieved and used. It is the most important single factor distinguishing man from other life forms that he is able to record and transmit his culture from generation to generation building upon it progressively. Libraries are the repositories of the records produced and they have been aptly described as standing in the see relationship to society as does the memory to the individual.

Formidable Task

The task set by society for the librarian becomes increasingly formidable in terms of the amount of recorded culture that needs to be collected and organized. Many daunting statistics and graphic images have been drawn to indicate the immensity of the problems for those who seek to organize recorded knowledge so that it may be quickly retrieved in case of need is educational expansion, goes forward throughout the world, following economic improvements, as education, industrial development and national pride develops so too does the quantity of published records. In 1953 UNESCO estimated that 269,000 books were produced throughout the world; by 1965 this figure had jumped to 426,000 and, according to their Statistical yearbook 1977, the number of books published in 1976 was 591,000, less than a fifth of the total production emanated from the Third World where nearly two thirds of the world's population live. Obviously as and when the economies of such countries stabilize and begin to develop, it is likely that massive additional increments of new publishing will result. There seems little reason to expect that the growth of published record seen in Europe and North America in the past fifty years will significantly abate. The 'paper storm' or the 'literature explosion' are evocative terms coined to draw attention to the dramatic nature of the growth of literature. It is easy to understand why there is the need to improve bibliographic control. In former times research and discovery was duplicated in different countries and even different parts of the same country through ignorance of the efforts of other workers in the same field due to the inadequacies of the available means of communications have improved immensely. Obviously with very large numbers of researchers at work it is likely that much research effort will duplicate or nearly duplicate other work which is in progress. What is alarming, however, is that such is the vastness of the published literature upon even the most limited fields that work which has been completed and fully reported in the literature is often duplicated in ignorance of earlier efforts or because the repetition of the research is probably cheaper than the cost of carrying out a detailed literature search. These days, duplication is often a function not of the under supply of literature but an undigested surfeit.

It is easy to become carried away by the sheer rise of the so-called 'information explosion' and to regard the growth of literature as a phenomenon as threatening to civilization as a virulent epidemic or the 'population explosion' in the Third World. Many writers have, indeed, written about it in this way. Herbert Coblans, in a forceful article, takes issue with the sensation seekers. He dismissed the image of overloaded libraries collapsing under the weight of a surfeit of paper as 'mythology'. Coblans conveys great conviction when he argues that the massive growth of the literature is no new thing. Given a particular stage in technical and intellectual development previous generations have had to cope with a growth of published record at least as awkward for them as the problem of the present generation. There is no reason to believe, Coblans' opinion, that this and succeeding generations will not be able to devise adequate means of coping with the growth of literature if it should continue.

Perhaps more significant than the optimism about technological innovation meeting any possibie crisis in literature growth is the conviction Coblans shows in his paper that, in fact, the 'explosion' is largely immaterial anyway due to the sheer irrelevance of much published literature. It has been pointed out by a number of writers on bibliographic control that the bulk of published literature is duplication, repetition or simply redundence. Coblans puts the proportion of 'useful' material at between a fifth and a tenth of the whole. Other writers are less generous in their estimates and will argue that only 5% of the published literature can be regarded as significant. Henry Voos points out how much the problem is caused by papers being published twice (or even more) in different periodicals and thus leading to an apparent growth in the literature rather than a real one. Voos makes the good point that with so much dual publication around we should not talk about 'an 'information explosion' so much as a 'paper explosion'. Harrison Bryan agrees with Coblans that the supposed problems have been much exaggerated though he points out that, although there is no doubt that technology will be able to keep up with the growth of publication and bibliographical control it, that is not the true problem. In recent years, then, there has been much less scare mongering about the imagined horrors of downing in a sea of paper. Librarians and bibliographers, whilst accepting as a fact of their lives the exponential growth in pieces of recorded knowledge, recognize that much of it is irrelevant to their needs. They do have the problem, however, of being able to sort out the nuggets of literary gold from amongst the torrents of published dross. The major problem is not in finding out what has been published, but in finding the most significant papers from a mass of mediocrity. Librarians have always been afraid of the danger of failing to collect important material or of disposing of it simply through ignorance of its value. The establishment of back up stores of little used material along the lines of the Centre for Research Libraries in the United States or of voracious collectors and disseminators of literature on the British Library Lending Division model reduces the risk of total failure of the bibliographic system to be able to supply required items. Individual libraries are, thus, somewhat freer not only to dispose of little used material but also to fail to collect material they are doubtful about. Not least of the means of controlling the flow of paper, or even reducing it, will be that because of these back up stores individual libraries are able to be much more selective. A substantial amount of publishing is done simply because librarians buy large quantities of material.

Talk of increased selectivity by librarians is a reminder that, when first coined, the term 'bibliographic control' was thought to be an attempt to censor the output of publishers and to make value judgements on the quality of literature in unacceptable ways. The argument revolved (and still does revolve) around the sense in which the word 'control' is used. It is a matter of historical fact that bibliographers over the centuries have constantly exercised the functions of selection and rejection in the compilation of their works. In evaluating the fitness of certain items for inclusion or exclusion from their bibliographies it could, indeed, be argued that 'control' could be thought of as a repressive, censoring, device. The mere term 'selective bibliography' indicates a degree of control which uses. that word in a disciplinary-sense. Selectivity in bibliographic activity is only one element in the total picture, however, and not really the most important. It is the task of national and universal bibliographers to record everything. In this sense 'control' is a more passive word implying an attempt to ensure that all is gathered in without any attempt at selection. This is not to say, though, that in some countries the 'all' that is available to gather into a current national bibliography is only that which the ruling government approve of. Twentieth century manifestations of press Licensing and Star Chamber which controlled printing in sixteenth century England still exist. The control function is, in these cases, not one exercised by the bibliographer but by a political power much superior.

Human Communication

The 'records of human communication', the definitions are indicating that it is more than simply books or even books and periodicals which are being referred to. Clearly the intention is that bibliographic control must extend further than simply to those two most obvious and ubiquitous forms of record. Just how wide the scope needs to be is indicated in that most seminal of the documents on bibliographic control—the record of the proceedings of the UNESCO conference held in Paris in 1950. In this record was embodied an enumeration of the various kinds of record of human communication needing to be controlled arranged in such a way as to indicate which bibliographies and indexes were needed before a country could claim to have achieved current national bibliographical control satisfactorily. The relevant statement in the report reads:

> All member states should be asked to give early consideration to the publication of current national bibliographies and lists as enumerated below wherever such do not already exist:
>
> 1. A general bibliography of all books and pamphlets published and on sale in each country, regardless of the language in which they are written, and preferably including published theses and academic publications and government publications of public interest. According to local conditions these three categories of publication might be published in separate bibliographies.
> 2. A bibliography of books and pamphlets published but not on sale.
> 3. An index of important articles in periodicals including newspapers.
> 4. A bibliography of maps and atlases.
> 5. A bibliography of musical works.
> 6. A bibliography of local government publications.
> 7. A directory of periodicals and newspapers currently published.
> 8. A list of audio-visual materials.
> 9. A bibliography of unpublished theses and academic publications.
> 10. A directory of publishers and booksellers.
> 11. Directory of learned societies, institutions, libraries and other related organisations.
>
> Consideration should also be given to the publication of select lists, annotated or 'otherwise, of books and articles in periodicals.

Absolute completion would require that some means be found to record current manuscript sources though this is a very difficult task more usually attempted retrospectively. The other principal omission from UNESCO's 1950 listing was report literature—a field of published record which has burgeoned in the last thirty years.

Systematic Listing

Bibliographies are always systematic in some way or another even if sometimes they are less than thoroughly comprehensible. In the terms of the definitions cited earlier the implicit requirement is for some agency or agencies to organize the system of producing the bibliographies needed. If we think of agencies being government sponsored bodies then it is only in recent years since the Second World War in fact that there has been any large scale involvement of official bodies. If, however, we think of agencies being defined more widely to include libraries, learned societies, or even groups of like minded individuals not formally organized, then almost since record began there have been people dedicated to their systematic listing. UNESCO's unique role, since 1950, in heightening the awareness of government agencies to the importance of assisting the development of bibliographic services cannot be over stressed. This role will be dealt with fully later. Sufficient to say here that the growth of bibliographic activity and of government involvement in it can be traced through the various UNESCO series devoted to bibliographic affairs notably Bibliographic services throughout the world (Paris, UNESCO 1950). The aim of 'systematic listing' is to ensure that nothing which is available as written or other form of recorded knowledge is left unlisted or uncontrolled.

In the history of bibliographic activity, there is a need for one complete universal source of reference, a catalogue of the entire stock of the world's recorded knowledge kept constantly up to date. It is a quest without a satisfactory conclusion a holy grail of librarianship which continues because librarians and bibliographers are as deeply fired with the idealistic favour which is alleged to have imbued the medieval knights. The story of the production of one single Source of universal reference begins with Conrad Gesner

(1516-1565). If Theodore Besterman, who wrote so engagingly about Gesner, is to be believed the story begins and ends there. Besterman claims that not only was Gesner the first universal bibliographer he was the last one of have any chance of success. Whilst this might be an arguable proposition it is true that there were no other serious attempts at universal bibliography for over 250 years. Gesner produced his Bibliotheca Universalis between 1545 and 1555 but, despite its title the work was never truly universal in scope. Contemporary scholarship has established that even within its limitations he was no more than 20%-25% complete. Gesner's bibliography attempted universality within closely prescribed limits and this is, in fact, the situation of every later attempt at bibliographic completeness. Bibliotheca Universalis lists more than 15000 titles and is, considering the problems of communication in the sixteenth century, an amazing work even given the fact that Switzerland was some thing of a crossroads for scholarship and printing at the time. Bay's essay was produced to commemorate the 400th anniversary of Gesner's birth and draws upon a mass of contemporary source material. The range and depth of Gesner's talents are disconcerting for lesser mortals to contemplate for his bibliographic endeavours were but one small aspect of his work.

'The noble art of describing a useful and beautiful book fully and adequately is recognized as one of the necessary elements in a librarian's education. It is a noble art because its perfection rests with an unattainable ideal. Considered as necessary work in the interest of humanity and general enlightenment, bibliography gains ground as the years pass. Times and conditions might be pointed out when bibliographers were tolerated. But to the person fortunate enough to possess the sacred fire of the art, his work is its own reward, and he blesses the men, living and dead, who kindled the spark within him. It is true even more of bibliographic compilation, or the recording of sources of study in the interest of students and librarians. Let it be said openly: it is its own reward.

To produce universal bibliographies unrestricted as to time, form and country have not been very successful, though they have often resulted in useful general bibliographies. K.O. Murra records briefly the destiny of several large scale attempts noting that even with substantial financial backing on an international basis the task of universal bibliography has proved beyond solution. It is true to say, however, that many of the bibliographies often cited as universal bibliographies. were never intended as anything other than selective works. For example J.C. Brunet's 'Manuel de libraire et de I' amateur de livres' is the compiler's selection of rare or otherwise notable books with the emphasis upon French and Latin titles. JGT Graesse's 'Tresor des livres rareset precieux' (Dresden, R.R. Kuntze, 1859-1869) is similar in scope to Brunet but stronger in German titles. W.S. Sonnenschein's Best books (London, Routledge, 1910-1935) lists a selection of books judged to be outstanding of their type. In the sense of these three works, library catalogues could be described as 'best book' lists but they are never thought of as universal bibliographies as Brunet and Grasse have sometimes been erroneously described. The most determined effort at universal bibliographic control undertaken in one .place by a single organisation has been that sponsored by the Institute International de Bibliographie founded in Brussels in 1895 by Paul Otlet and Henri la Fontaine. Their work, or at least Otlet's major part in it, has been chronicled by W. Boyd Rayward in a readable work.

Otlet and la Fontaine were both lawyers and their interest in bibliography began with the specific interests of lawyers in mind and gradually expanded first to the social sciences and then to the universe of knowledge. Although ultimately surrounded by a veritable maze of other activities the basic activity envisaged by Otlet was the creation of a manuscript record listing the totality of man's published records entered upon individual slips and systematically arranged. It was envisaged that the project would ultimately become self-supporting through the sale of transcripts of sections of the work to libraries and other organisations and individuals in a manner which would nowadays be thought of as 'print-outs' of a computer data base. Initially and in fact principally for so long as the project was seriously in being the Belgian Government underwrote the finance with some contributions erratically received from other sources. More than sixteen million records were transcribed from printed bibliographies, sales catalogues and library catalogues and arranged in a classified order.

Originally the Dewey Decimal Classification was employed as the arrangement device but soon proved inadequate and caused Otlet to experiment with the derivation of a more appropriate system to classify his massive work by. The Universal Decimal Classification was the result and it remains with us as the most lasting contribution to bibliographic control, aside from the lessons learned from the bibliographic work, because the attempted production of a universal bibliography foundered under its own weight and the difficulties caused by the First World War. It lingered on in much diminished vigour for some years after the War but did not prosper. The Institute itself lives on in much transmuted form as the International Federation for Documentation (F.I.D) in whose charge the maintenance and further development the Universal Decimal Classification is vested.

The First World War was, in part, to blame but it is probable that the scheme was never fully viable, for despite the 'international' superscription of the title the venture was never truly such Although there was, at one point, a measure of extra-Belgian support there was never a coherent management system internationally organized and single mindedly directed. Even without that kind of support something substantial might have been achieved on a lasting basis but the temperaments of the two founders-especially that of Otlet—were such that lasting success was unlikely. They were splendid starters of projects but like so many bibliographers poor sustainers of momentum. Fired by intellectual delight in the conception of ever more ambitious schemes they easily became bored by the drudgery of day-to-day management of the operation. A mass of bibliographic and other ventures were commenced before the basic work was securely grounded. The scheme took on all of the characteristics of a pyramid sales organization or galactic phenomenon which must continuously expand if it is not to collapse in upon itself.

Modern technology that probably could have given the goodwill and active co-operation of every country in the world for an activity based upon one of them, but there are certainly better ways available of approaching the same goals. The creation of the Universal Decimal Classification a more far reaching benefit has been handed down to later activity. This benefit was that of indicating how important co-ordinated international activity was and how much the success of international ventures depended upon the quality of national bibliographic services. Temperamentally Otlet was a loner wishing to be able to do everything himself in his own way and, of course, this was an impossibility given the ultimate size of the ambitious ventures sponsored. From the beginnings of the UNESCO activity after the Second World War the emphasis ever since in universal bibliographic control has been upon collective endeavours.

It is worth continuing the consideration of bibliographic control by examining the various major styles of bibliographic compilation to determine the contribution each makes to the creation of complete control. It will then be possible to return to the themes explored in this chapter to add further detail to later work especially as it has been sponsored by UNESCO and developed by the advent of the computer to bibliographic activity. Before making this departure, however, a few hints upon the methods of examining bibliographic compilations with a view to learning how to use them effectively are necessary. The careful examination of bibliographies can be an excellent means of understanding the structures of bibliographic control better and providing a better service to library users.

Bibliographical Study

Usage of materials in real life situations is the way to deepen and broaden knowledge.

There is no substitute for this method but it is possible to develop good habits for the formalization and structuring of information which is obtained by the careful examination of bibliographies.

Without a thorough understanding of how bibliographic works are made and of the aims of editors of particular bibliographies the librarian's use of them will always be clumsy and probably ineffectual.

There are a number of reasons why the careful study of the forewords, introductions and prefaces to bibliographic works are indispensable reading for anyone interested in acquiring a deep knowledge of enumerative bibliography. In them are detailed the hopes, aspirations and problems in producing the work together with a description of the manner of arrangement and the reasons for adopting it. When read in conjunction with authoritative reviews of the bibliography in the major reviewing sources—for instance The library—they provide a picture of the intention of the bibliographer and an assessment of the degree of success attained. This can hardly fail to inform the librarian, who would use the work, of its' strengths and weaknesses.

Accumulating experience and many years of close study and acquaintance with bibliographic works that a really substantial body of knowledge of the potential of bibliographic sources is acquired. In a curious way one failure to find particular information in expected sources can often tell the librarian more about the scope of a particular bibliography than half a dozen easy successes using the same source. It must be said that some librarians never seem to acquire any broadening or deepening of their knowledge of sources. This is because they fail to make an effort to formalize their study, to think about the reasons why a particular source did not help them as much as they expected, to read introductions to bibliographies and to develop a formal discipline for their searching.

The range and complexity of the structures of bibliographies available makes it difficult thoroughly to understand how to use them effectively without having a framework to build upon. Edwin Willoughby listed a sort of typology of bibliographies thus: Books published within Cumulative book index certain periods of time Book published in a city, country or other locality Book published in specific languages Books available to readers in a single library Books available to readers in an entire country. Books intended for certain classes of readers; Books recommended to be read; Books recommended not to be read Madan, Oxford books Schyns, 1500 modern Chinese novels and plays; The general catalogue of the British Museum; The union catalogue in the Library of congress.

The children's catalogue compiled by Giles, Cook & West Books for you issued by the National Council of Teachers of English. Index librorumprohibitorum of the Catholic Church Books sold at auction within certain periods of time.

The aim of the study of the structures of bibliographic apparatus is to be able to interpret the structure in relation to the questions asked of librarian and how they are asked. The aim is to achieve conditions in which a question, when asked, immediately begins to create in the mind of the well skilled librarian or bibliographer thoughts about the types of bibliography or specific bibliographies which will be of value in solving the enquiry. For example the question: 'Who wrote Joan and Peter?' A question put in this way immediately indicates that only bibliographies which enable a search by title will be useful. Rejection of any bibliography without the title indexing facilities is inevitable—The British Library catalogue is of no use except in the somewhat rare event of the work in question is put, gives no indication of the publication date, it will not be wise to search bibliographies with many separate sequences for example The English catalogue of books—as a first source of recourse. British books in print or Books in print suggest themselves as the first place to look because they provide a 'One sequence guide to a large number of titles. Of course, if such a convenient source proves ineffective then there is no alternative to more fatiguing searches through separately sequenced works. If the question was modified to ask when the first edition of the book was published then the search is a two part one. First the title has to be related to an author and then the enquiry has to be related to the best source which will comprehend the work and writing of H.G. Wells.

A question which requires a subject approach might be: 'Have you any recent books on stick insects?' The question requires that bibliographies with a subject approach need to be used and in case an alphabetical subject approach will not be precise enough insuch a very specialized case it will be necessary to acquire as precise a classification number as possible for Dewey Decimal and Universal Decimal Oassification—for these are the claissification schemes most frequently encountered in classified subject bibliographies. In. this particular case, however, the word 'recent' in the question adds an extra dimension and makes British national bibliography an obvious first choice because besides a classified main sequence the index offers precise alphabetical subject indexing facilities. Other qualifying additions to the basic question will seriously modify the question further and require very careful thought; 'they must be Book prices current suitable for an eleven year old' or 'only periodical articles which are will illustrated will do in the absence of suitable books'.

A question which is posed in the form: 'Can you suggest a really nice glossy picture book I could buy as a Christmas present for my father who is interested in travelling and motoring?' might tempt the librarian to point out where the nearest good bookshops may be found but bibliographically the dimension which suggests itself is the use of publishers catalogues or, perhaps more usefully, the twice yearly 'Export numbers' of the bookseller.

Actually the librarian who is the recipient of questions as straightforward as those above is probably in a very dull job. More likely to be asked is the more complex question such as, 'Can you give me any information on the influence of social class and social status on the quality of educational opportunity in various European countries?'. Again the need is for subject bibliographies and those which are limited to the social sciences seem the most likely sources. It is possible to guess that books will be few which address the problem squarely and periodical articles, these and reports may be needed. The question is international in scope and the enquirer will need to be questioned about their ability to read foreign languages. The internationally garnered UNESCO bibliography International bibliography of the social sciences will suggest itself to the librarian who takes the trouble to think out the question and check the library shelves at tile approximate classification number for social science bibliography, education bibliography etc.

The need arises to develop a mental checklist drill which will relate itself to the characteristics of bibliographies and those of the question which was asked. The raw materials of the checklist begin with producing the mental discipline to analyse questions and think about them clearly and go on to the gathering of a deep knowledge of the scope, contents and assumed reliability of a large number of bibliographies. Such knowledge grows with experience and constant use and, perhaps, most especially through failures to find information where it is expected. Over time, instincts, insights and self discipline can be developed. The experienced librarian has learned almost to the point of it being second nature to build up impressions such as: The London Library catalogue is strong in listings of nineteenth century fiction, British and European. For some reason Lowndes Bibliographers' manual of English literature is strong on the publications of scientific societies of the eighteenth and nineteenth century. Engineering index is a misleading title in that its subject scope is much wider than its title implies. Chemical abstracts is similarly misleading.

National Bibliography

The methods of creating complete bibliographic control of recorded knowledge almost invariably is led by a consideration of the means of developing effective current bibliographies, at the national level, of printed books. It might be argued that to give precedence to the printed book is to fall to appreciate the growing significance of non-printed sources or to ignore the historical fact that manuscript sources pre-data printed materials, Worldwide, however, the printed book is still the most ubiquitous source of record and it is right that the bibliography of printed books is considered first here, for despite the proponents of the media revolution the continued preeminence of the book into the forseeable future is an indisputable fact.

The development of a complete national bibliographic record requires the fulfilment of two conditions:

1. The establishment of a mechanism for the production of a current bibliography on a regular and continuing basis which adequately encompasses the whole publishing programme of the country.
2. The development of a retrospective programme of bibliographic listing to complete the bibliographic control

> of a nation's resources given the usual circumstances that at least some fragmentary retrospective provision pre-exists the establishment of a formal organisation charged with the responsibility to do so.

Most bibliographies are subject bibliographies. But there cannot be effective subject bibliographies unless there are wide-ranging and efficient general bibliographies are extremely important as they are, with a few exceptions, national bibliographies. They are serial bibliographies, mainly of books and pamphlets, relating to individual countries, covering all languages but keeping a particularly close watch on publications put on sale, and therefore available from bookshops. Serial bibliographies referred to as 'current bibliographies, but in that they can be used to find details of books published years ago, and no longer in print, they can also be regarded as 'retrospective'.

All the national bibliographies to be mentioned later are serial bibliographies which can be used for current and retrospective information, but their retrospective use is limited to the present century, or a small part of it. Details of books published more than a decade ago are often obtained from the published catalogues of the great national libraries.

The year 1950 was a landmark in the history of bibliographic control. In January the BNB was established. In November UNESCO held an international Conference on the Improvement of Bibliographical Services. In the General Report of this conference there were recommendations. Each of UNESCO's member states was urged to encourage the publication of a comprehensive series of current bibliographies of its country's publications, that is, bibliographies of all books and pamphlets published (including those not on sale), plus lists of maps, music, audio-visual materials and theses. As far as it went, the UNESCO recommendations were quite sensible. But they did not go far enough. Looking at the situation today, from the point of view of the main users of national bibliographies, namely, libraries and bookshops, three main types of serial bibliographies of current publications are wanted, namely:

1. Lists of new books and pamphlets, including revised editions and reprints which involve change of publisher, price or format (particularly the release of paperback editions of books first published in hard cover).
2. Lists of all books in print.
3. Lists of books due to be published during the next two or three months.

This broad classification of current bibliographies will be used later in this chapter when dealing with the national bibliographies of the UK and the USA. First, however, it is necessary to draw attention to three things which have affected national bibliographies in recent years. The first is the elimination, owing to their cost, of multi-annual printer cumulations. The second is the increasing use of high reduction microfiche in addition, to, or in place of, printed lists. The third is the addition of International Standard Book Numbers (ISBNs) to the entries for books and pamphlets. An ISBN identifies a book, and that particular edition of it, absolutely. It can be used for book ordering and a number of other purposes. It is made up of ten digits whose significance is indicated by the following example:

The Book with ISBN 0 406 55500 10 406 signifies: the UK/ USA group of publishers signifies: the name of the publishers-Butterworths 55500 signifies: the author, title, edition, and date of the book-J.H. Baker, Introduction to English legal history 1st edn, 1971. signifies: a check digit which will detect an error in transcription.

National Centre for Bibliography

Librarians developed the art of compiling bibliography centuries ago, but the idea of analysing bibliographic data till the last decade of the last century. Campbell in his 'Theory of the national and international bibliography advanced the idea of bibliographic analysis for the first time in 1896 and showed the scattering of information. In 1917 Cole and Eales applied statistical method for the analysis of literature on the history of comparative anatomy.

Analysis of bibliographies using statistical methods was gradually gaming ground and the activity required christening. Hulme proposed the term 'Statistical bibliography in 1923. Ranganathan proposed the term 'librametry' in a conference discussion in 1948 to denote measurement of various library activities and services using statistical and mathematical methods. The term bibliometrics, however, emanated from the pen of Pritchard in 1967 which he used in preference to 'statistical bibliography' following the suggestion of Kendall, the famous statistician.

Scene in India

Bibliometrics made a modest beginning in India when Dutta and Rajagopalan conducted a survey of citation practices followed by 200 Indian and foreign periodicals. It received a boost when DRTC convened a seminar on Documentation Periodicals in 1963. About a dozen papers on bibliometrics were read in the conference. The tempo which this conference built up continued to earn a distinct position for India in the world map of bibliometrics.

Visualising the potentialities of bibliometrics as an effective tool for analysis of various research outputs and generation of indicators that may prove highly useful, in planning, decision making and various other functions of science management. Dr. A. P. Mitra, Director General, CSIR entrusted Insdoc in 1987 the job of carrying out the bibliometric analysis of CSIR research output of 1986.

The job entrusted was completed in just three months. A completely new methodology was evolved basing impact factor and normalised impact factor of periodicals for the analysis of research output. Methodology had also to be evolved for determining the impact factor of periodicals not covered by SCI. This methodology has since been perfected and used for determining the impact factors of some Indian journals.

After the completion of the aforesaid job, the group was assigned the responsibility of selecting significant CSIR papers published during the last forty years. The papers were to form the Commemoration Volume to be published in the 40th year of Indian Independence. Preliminary selection of papers was done by the laboratories themselves. Citation study was to be done for more than

3000 papers for each year after its publication. SCI in mag-tape form was not available to the country; the cost of on-line search was too prohibitive: Hence a decision was taken to complete the job manually, a stupendous task. While completing the job, the inadequacy of bibliometric tools in Delhi became amply evident. The complete run of Science Citation Index was not available at anyone place in Delhi.

Genesis of National. The problems faced in determining the impact factors of Indian periodicals not covered by SCI; the extremely poor coverage of Indian periodicals in SCI (18 in 1986 out of 300-odd periodicals); the non-availability of the complete run of SCI at one place; lack of coordination of bibliometric activities within CSIR as well as in the country; inadequate facilities for the training of bibliometricians existing in the country, etc., led to the thinking of a national centre on the subject.

NISSAT was considered as the appropriate funding body for such a project. Hence, a proposal was forwarded to NISSAT for their consideration. Dr. A. Lahiri, Director, NISSAT too, keen interest in the project and through his untiring efforts, an initial grant of Rs. 6 lakhs was made available in April 1988 to start the Centre.

The Centre is going to function as a NISSAT project under the overall supervision of the Bibliometrics Section of Insdoc. The objectives of the Centre are:

1. To create S&T citation databases of Indian contributions appearing in Indian journals. The comprehensive collection of research journals in the National Science Library will be the base for the creation of such database. The format could be the same as developed for SCI.

2. To analyse the research outputs of selected research institutes, agencies, universities and other similar cognate bodies. The initial thrust will be on CSIR research output.

3. To develop tools, techniques and modalities for the analysis of research output based on SCI data and the Indian S&T citation database to be created.

The efforts enumerated above could result in the development of science indicators that could be useful in the planning, funding, policy making for R&D management, assessment of R&D output, etc. in any specified system and conglomeration of systems.

Facilities. The Centre will have all the cumulative volumes of Science Citation Index from 1945 till date. All these will be available for consultation by users. The Centre will also develop a reprint collection on bibliometric studies done in India and abroad.

Services. The services of the Centre will include the following:

1. Reply to queries pertaining to bibliometrics.
2. Supply of impact factor of all S & T journals including those not covered by the SCI.
3. Consultancy relating to bibliometric studies, improvement of the impact factor of journals, etc.
4. Analysis uf research outputs at individual scientists teams, institutions, etc.
5. Offer training courses on bibliometrics.

Progress. The order for the supply of the cumulative volumes of Science Citation Index for the periods 1955 to 1980 in paper-print medium, and 1988 in CD ROM has already been placed and the volumes are expected soon. The bibliometric analysis of about 180 papers of the Foundation for Medical Research, Bombay has already been completed. The formula for determining impact factor of journals not covered by SCI has been worked out; and applied to determine the impact factor of some of the non SCI journals.

British Approach

The methods of creating complete bibliographic control of recorded knowledge almost invariably is led by a consideration of the means of developing effective current bibliographies, at the national level, of printed books, It might be argued that to give precedence to the printed book is to fall to appreciate the growing significance of non-printed sources or to ignore the historical fact that manuscript sources pre-data printed materials, Worldwide, however, the printed book is still the most ubiquitous source of record and it 15 right that the bibliography of printed books is considered first here, for despite the proponents of the media revolution the continued preeminence of the book into the for seeable future is an indisputable fact.

The development of a complete national bibliographic record requires the fulfilment of two conditions:

1. The establishment of a mechanism for the production of a current bibliography on a regular and continuing basis which adequately encompasses the whole publishing programme of the country.
2. The development of a retrospective programme of bibliographic listing to complete the bibliographic control of a nation's resources given the usual circumstances that at least some fragmentary retrospective provision pre-exists the establishment of a formal organisation charged with the responsibility to do so.

A number of basic decisions should be taken before a creating national bibliography. Firstly, measures must be taken to ensure that information is available to the compilers of the bibliography which enables them to be fully comprehensive in their listing. Consideration is also needed to decide whether the bibliography will be national only in the sense of including items published within the country, for example, British national bibliography, or including all items relating to a nation's culture regardless of where published, for example, Bibliography of Scotland, which Ian Mowat describes the origins of. The form the bibliography must take is another basic decision-method of arrangement, frequency cumulative pattern and physical format.

The UNESCO series Bibliographic services throughout the world demonstrates clearly, the way in which the task of organizing the current record has been approached in different ways in various countries is due, no doubt, to local circumstances and historical precedents. That the precedents are Katherine O Murra reveals. Roger Greer charts the salient features of many current national bibliographic services in an interesting comparative way. His analyses of the frequency of publication pattern, modes of arrangement and cumulating of a number of services worldwide then is followed by an examination of the multiplicity of bibliographic activities which serve for an approximation to current complete bibliographic control in the United States. The United States case is interesting. It is not that there is no current bibliography indeed there is almost a surfeit-it is that no single co-ordinated activity can be recognized as the national Current bibliography. It is not uncommon in the economically and bibliographically advanced countries (the two almost invariably go together) for the degree of coordination and organization of bibliographic activity to be less clear than in newly developing countries.

The difficulties of establishing a current national bibliography are considerable, once established with adequate financial support it is an enterprise providing a variety of immediate benefits to a country's libraries and book trade organizations without too much difficulty. The provision of a record of material published previous to the establishment of a current national bibliography the retrospective record-is much more difficult for a number of reasons. Whilst the economic and technical benefits of operating a current bibliography are extremely persuasive and likely to appeal to librarians, booksellers etc., in a very direct way this is net always the case for a retrospective bibliography. The initial financing of a current national bibliography is probably much easier to underwrite than that of a retrospective bibliography. There is the promise of a quick return on an investment in a current bibliography, if not in financial terms then certainly in service terms.

The most effective means of evolving accurate and reliably produced retrospective records is to have developed a current national bibliography. The best possible retrospective record is the earlier volumes of a well established current bibliographic service. There are not many countries who can boast of an effective current bibliographic service with a history longer than thirty years a handful of countries have a fifty year continuous run of reliable current bibliography, few more than that. Beyond the span of the current bibliographic record the basic problem of producing retrospective bibliography lies in finding out what was published in previous years. The accuracy of current bibliography depends upon the availability, usually through a legal deposit-mechanism, of copies of text for the current bibliographer to work from in compiling the record.

The main props to any retrospective bibliography must be a well formed national library which has a long history of collecting the records or a nation's culture. Here the retrospective bibliographer will find the basis of the projected work and will be able to inspect copies of many of the items to be induded much as the current bibliographer might. Supplementation of the record derived from the use of a national library and its collections can then be achieved by the inspection of other notable retrospective collections, comparing their holdings with those of the national library, to find additional items. Booksellers and publishers catalogues and pre existing bibliographies and printed library catalogues will then be checked to try to ensure completeness.

The Retrospective Bibliography of the United Kingdom. It is convenient to commence a study of the complete national bibliographic record by a study first of the retrospective scene. Because enumerative bibliography was not always the well organized craft it has now become many retrospective bibliographies produced in former times must be regarded with suspicion. Often they were compiled not from an examination of the actual texts themselves but from the more or less uncritical incorporation of entries from other bibliographies, from booksellers lists and even from references to earlier work since lost which the bibliographer has discovered. Bibliographies developed in this way are rarely totally reliable and are sometimes downright misleading. A particular feature of much retrospective bibliography is that it was often compiled by individuals rather than the official sources which are most often responsible for current bibliographies. This fact alone indicates grounds for suspicion of the quality of many retrospective bibliographies and calls attention to the fact that one of the most accurate and reliable forms of retrospective bibliographic record is the printed catalogues of libraries.

In examining the landmarks of the retrospective bibliography of the United Kingdom it is convenient to group them into several chronological periods thus; 1475-1640, 1641-1700, 1701-1800, 1801 to date. The significance of the breakdown into such periods may be briefly explained as a mixture of logic and convenience. The first period begins with the date at which printing first came to England according to some authorities (1476 is the generally accepted date but the first English printer, William Caxton, was certainly printing in 1475 but probably in Bruges). The end of the period, 1640, is the begining of a period of difficulty and disruption in England due to the Civil War down to the end of Press Licensing representing a period in which several important bibliographies cover more or less exactly that period. It ends in 1700 at a time when the final lapsing of the Press Licensing Acts was encouraging the spread of printing throughout the country with a consequent massive growth in publishing and book trade activity. 1701-1800 is simply a period division and represents a century in which bibliographic control is exceedingly poor. The huge upsurge in publishing activity outran the rudimentary abilities of libraries and contemporary bibliographers to contain it. 1801 to date is used as a period division simply because there is a continuous, though variable quality, history of the production of a current bibliography of British books from that date.

A number of significant bibliographies exist which list British or English language publications over the whole, or major parts of the period of the history of printing. It should also be recalled that especially during the first two and a half centuries of printing, when there were severe restrictions upon printing in England, a great deal of printing in English was carried out in Continental Europe and, of course, later in North America and elsewhere. The most notable general bibliography of English/British and English language books printed elsewhere is the British Library's General catalogue of printed books. The Library of Congress' National union catalogue and other major British, Commonwealth and American printed library catalogues are other important sources of retrospective bibliographies.

General work of importance is Allibone's Dictionary of authors to use the familiar title rather than the more laboriously exact, Allibone, Samuel A Critical dictionary of English literature and British and American authors living and deceased, from earliest accounts to the latter half of the nineteenth century, containing over 46,000 articles (authors) with forty indexes of subjects (Philadelphia, Lippincott, 1858); a supplement compiled by John Foster Kirk added 37,000 more authors in 1891. All Allibone's work reveals how important it is for bibliographers to cross check their references and not take earlier work at its face value. Many errors in Watt's Bibliotheca Britannica are repeated by Allibone and Bibliotheca Britannica was littered with error! The fourth general retrospective bibliography worthy of mention in The new Cambrdige Bibliography of English literature. Although based upon an earlier edition (1940) it does not entirely replace it and both editions are normally kept in libraries taking their bibliography seriously. The whole work covers the period from 600 AD and is a complete and detailed work worthy of study in its own right as an example of effective bibliographic arrangement.

None of these general works can be regarded as anything other than useful sources of quick reference for fairly straightforward material. Certainly the first two cannot be relied upon unsupported by careful cross checking. For more scholarly and detailed purposes it is necessary to turn to more specialist bibliographies restricted as to period covered and more carefully compiled by authoritative hands.

During 1475-1640, a paper which provides a stimulating insight into the fascinations of the study of enumerative bibliography and the uses scholars put bibliographies to Howard W. Winger has this to say about the retrospective bibliographic control of English books: 'In range, comprehensives, varied points of access, and well considered articulation, the bibliographical tools for the study of English books printed from 1475 to 1700 have no equal'.

The cornerstone of the comprehensive coverage is the catalogue inspired by the Bibliographical Society which originally was intended to be but the precursor of a more ambitious work which never reached fruition: Pollard A Wand Redgrave, G R Short title catalogue of books printed in England, Scotland and Ireland and of English books printed abroad 1475-1640 London. The bibliographical Society, 1926, 4 volumes. This great work, of which no equal exists for any other country or language group, illustrated in its mode of compilation the way the retrospective bibliographer must work if the resultant compilation is to be used with confidence. Pollard and Redgrave and their assistants examined copies of the works they listed 133 British and 15 American libraries and provided selective locations for the rare items. In all they listed some 25,500 titles with entries giving author, short title, size, printers' name and date of printing where known. A reference was given to the Stationers Register entry and Pollard and Redgrave provided a running number to their entries which has subsequently become a standard reference to early printed books in English familiarly used by libraries and the book trade and referred to as the 'STC number'. STC, meaning Short Title Catalogue, is a familiar way of referring to such catalogues, the distinction between the different STCs now available being the employment of compiler's names thus, 'Pollard and Redgrave's STC or 'Wing's STC.

The significance and virility of the Pollard and Redgrave STC can be measured by the large body of ancillary works which have been spawned by the basic text. For the revised edition the Bibliographical Society plan to produce themselves an index of printers, publishers and booksellers and a chronological index to the basic work listing publications in order of printing. The first edition created a quite active 'market' in catalogues and hand lists produced by individual libraries listing their STC books and additional materials in their libraries which relate to the period.

Reading about bibliographic control of early British printed books abound as they do for all early printing. On the generality of the early history of printing and its associated bibliography emphasizing particularly the uses of the bibliographies is Winger's paper already mentioned which included a large and unusual reading list citing papers not frequently referred to in the literature. Dr. George Watson Cole instances the role of the Bibliographical Society as a vital one in the evolution of effective retrospective bibliographic control and his paper is also a reminder that the compilers' preface to the STC is an easy work and how it came to be executed. Much of the more valuable readings on the craft of retrospective bibliography and critical comment on the available tools of the trade lie half forgotten and largely unread in the forewords, introductions and prefaces of bibliograpnical works.

The nearest thing to a current bibliography of sixteenth and seventeenth century publications was the register kept by the Stationers Company in London in which printers were expected to enter the details of all new books they were intending to print. This register which came into being as a result of an ordinance issued at some time shortly before 1557 was never entirely accurate in the twin senses of printers not always completing work they had registered as an intention and of printers intending to produce work which would be defined as seditious by the highly sensitive rulers in those times, naturally refraining from registering such work. During 1640-1700, the second period of English bibliography is more widely diffused in the sense that the printing press had reached the North American colonies and other areas of English influence and also into Wales. The vigorous suppression of unauthorized presses whilst no less strongly attempted was more difficult to achieve in the circumstances of political upheaval implied by the Civil War and Commonwealth. Dissidents at home and the emigre communities established on the continent were producers of material difficult to control either in the contemporary legal sense or in later terms of bibliographic control. The period 1641-1700 as a whole is reviewed by D. G. Neill in a paper which also encompasses the eighteenth century and should be remembered in that context. The problem in tracing valuable papers for this period for those without ready access to a good bibliographical/ librarianship library is that many of the best items appear in relatively obscure sources.

A constant reminder that, these days, retrospective bibliography and technology are hand in hand is the realization that all of the items listed in both Pollard and Redgrave and Wing are available to purchase in microform editions. Recent developments in retrospective bibliographic work on the eighteenth century drive home this lesson of technological association even more firmly. During 1700-1800, the eighteenth century, by general consent, has been thought of as the period least adequately bibliographically controlled. It was a period of enormous increase in publishing activity but there were'no really effective libraries in publishing activity but there were no really effective libraries collecting and preserving on a planned basis nor were there private collectors active on a scale necessary to ensure effective means of retrospective bibliographic control on the model indicated by the treatment of the Thomason Tracts. The British Museum Library, the national library de facto, was founded in mid-century, and during the rest of the century was hardly properly organized to make adequate collections of currently published material. Legal deposit regulations, though in force from 1709, were never Effective throughout the century.

The bibliographies available are at best merely partial, moreover none of them is to be trusted as reliable and accurate. The general catalogues of the British Museum/British Library are significant bibliographic source for the century though the collections are nothing like so rich, relative to the total output of the century, as they are for the previous century. The practice of the New Cambridge bibliography of English literature in providing occasional notes of the locations of items known not to be in the British Library collections is a useful device which often refers in fact to eighteenth century books.

The development, in recent years, of microform catalogues available on general sale to many great libraries offers the chance of filling in some of the detail of eighteenth century bibliography accurately. The National Library of Scotland catalogue is an important example from among many. The Library of Congress National union catalogue is also rich in eighteenth century English language material.

In ninteenth century, there has been a continuous thread of current bibliographic control of varying quality initially, it must be admitted, somewhat tenuous in form. The English catalogue of books through a series of retrospective volumes published in 1914 has a continuous history since 1800. The British Library's General catalogue is a major source for the whole period. The major current bibliographies of British publications in order of their first appearance are:

The English catalogue of books 1864

Whitakers cumulative book list 1924

British national bibliography 1950

Books in English 1970

The first three services have been the subject of a detailed examination by D.K. Weintraub. Each has particular strengths and weaknesses. The English catalogue and Whitakers cumulative book list are most likely to list reprints and ephemera—especially local publications—whilst British national bibliography gives most attention to free publications. These findings doubtless reflect the fact that the former two items are principally book trade tools whereas British national bibliography is both a librarians' work and the official record of the country's publishing.

Both as a book trade bibliographic staple and a valuable stand-by cumulative bibliography for librarians The bookseller's twice yearly 'Export Numbers' have a special place in the structure of bibliographic control of British books. The bookseller is the weekly book trade newspaper which, amongst other things, forms the initial listing for Whitakers cumulative book list and produces a special number each February and August which lists new books expected from publishers during the subsequent six months. It is a reminder that individual publishers catalogues are a useful bibliographic aid. The 'Export Numbers' of The bookseller are nothing like so comprehensive as Publishers trade list annual produced annually by Bowker each October which cumulates the catalogues of 1500 or more United States publishers and indexes them comprehensively. Nevertheless the 'Export Numbers' are more topical and go a long way towards filling the gap between the publication of an item and its recording in a current bibliography which can cause difficulty. A library user sees the announcement of a forthcoming book somewhere and fails to notice it is, indeed, 'forthcoming' and asks for it at the library or in the book shop as if it were published. Much abortive checking of current bibliographies through many individual parts can be avoided by reference to the 'Export Numbers' which amongst other useful features actually indicates alongside notices of many books dates expected for publication.

Since 1950, the backbone of British current bibliographic control has been British national bibliography. The accent is upon the 'British' in the sense that the listing is of material produced in the British Isles rather than a comprehensive listing of books published in the English language. Although publications issued in the Reblic of Ireland are included there is no attempt to produce a 'whole language' record lines of the French Bibliographie de la France/Biblio 1811-(Paris, Cercle de la Library weekly cumulative) or Cumulative book index 1898-(New York, H. W. Wilson monthly cumulative). Even Books in cumulative frequently through each year to an annual definitive set) does not claim to be a complete English language record despite the title. This important bibliography records the British national bibliography and the Library of Congress MARC records which although considerable do not render such services as Australian national bibliography 1961(Canberra National Library of Australia weekly cumulative) irrelevant as it is not fully comprehensive.

It would have been a tremendous benefit to British retrospective bibliographic control had British national bibliography been as efficient a service over a hundred years or more as it has proved since its inception in 1950. Despite their longer range English catalogue of books and Whitakers cumulative book list are nowhere near as authoritative and accurate a record as that needed as a thoroughly sound basis. It is a great pity there seems to be no prospect of a British national bibliography retrospective coverage along the lines recently attempted by its United States nearest counterpart American book publishing record 1960-(New York, Bowker monthly cumulative) who have recently produced American book publishing record cumulative 1876-1949 in fourteen volumes.

A definitive bibliography of the history, development and applications of British national bibliography has been produced by Anne Lunn and a tape-slide sequence illustrating its achievements within the broader framework of the Bibliographic Services Division is also available.

SUBJECT BIBLIOGRAPHY

Subject bibliographies form the largest group of enumerative bibliographies. They are of two kinds:

1. Large-scale reference bibliographies
2. Small-scale reading lists

Subject Bibliographies for Reference: In theory there should be exhaustive subject bibliographies. Some large-scale bibliographies appear to be so. But, in fact, it is quite impossible to compile a subject bibliography which is absolutely exhaustive, recording every single publication on its subject, as so much is published which escapes advertisement and legal deposit, and the scattering of contributions to books and periodicals is a problem which defeats even the best bibliographers' vigilance. Also, it must be conceded that there comes a point when no purpose is served by listing a so-called 'contribution' to the literature of a subject simply because it has appeared in print. The large-scale subject bibliographies therefore only aim to be exhaustive within chosen limits, which should be made clear.

Large-scale bibliographies can be either ad-hoc with, perhaps, occasional revision or supplements, or serial bibliographies with the benefit of regular, sometimes frequent publication and time saving cumulations. Most of the familiar large-scale subject bibliographies are those published serially. They include the indexing and abstracting services. At their best, non-serial large-scale subject bibliographies are given cover-to-cover revision, but this can be dilatory, or supplements, although several of these can be tiresome to use. Two highly praised bibliographies which have lately been given a new lease of life, one by revision and the other with a supplement, are Leslie T. Morton, A medical bibliography (Garrison and Morton): An annotated check-list texts illustrating the history of medicine (4th edn., Aldershot: Gower, 1983) and George Ottley, A bibliography of British railway history (Allen & Unwin, 1965; reprinted HMSO, 1983; Supplement HMSO, 1983).

An interesting group of subject bibliographies which although mostly used for reference sometime encourage browsing when newly published, are the annual bibliographical surveys. The object of these is to provide each year classified bibliographies of the more important literature published during a year on particular subject. Two contrasting surveys of this kind deal with progress in English studies. They are the Annual bibliography of English language and literature, 1921-(Camebridge University Press for the Modern Language Research Association), a list of books and articles without annotations, and The year's work in English studies 1919-john Murray for the English Association), a narrative critical survey with the accent on books. For some. subjects annual bibliographical surveys are called 'Progress in....'

Large-scale subject bibliographies are important, especially when, they cover more than books. But they are not enough. Anyone who wishes to study a particular subject, at whatever level needs a carefully prepared select bibliography of it. 'Such a bibliography must be appropriate in scale and cautious in its inclusion of out-of print publications. It must be helpfully arranged and annotated, and reasonably up to date. The more suitable, and more usual name for this kind of bibliography is 'reading list'.

Although reading lists are quite common and produced by people who know or should know the literature they recommend the average standard of reading lists is low. The most lamentable aspect of this is that in the production of reading lists for students in universities, polytechnics, adult education institutes and schools, the subject knowledge of the teachers is seldom linked with the bibliopegically knowledge of the on site librarians. (It should be added that librarians cannot always be depended upon to be bibliographically literate, despite their bibliographical instruction at library school). When the inadequacy of academic reading lists was ventilated by Mike Cornford in the Library Association Record a few years ago, the comments published on his article were remarkably unhelpful. One correspondent said that students ought to know from their lectures what their tutors meant by the cryptic references of their reading lists. If not they should ask for clarification. In other words, if a reading list is worth doing, never mind if it is done badly. There are librarians and staffs in bookshops who wince every time they are presented with reading lists emanating from schools, colleges and universities. As I have discussed the need for what I call 'bibliographical literacy' , I will not deal with the all too common faults in reading lists here, although undoubtedly they waste millions of hours in libraries and bookshops. A simple fact of life is that teachers are the most difficult people to convert. What they do they do. To be fair; there are a few exceptions; general run of amateurish, uniformative, unimaginative and Generally Frustrating, reading lists which add to the burdens of, students of all ages, Althougn they are not beyond criticism, those distributed by the Open University are well above average.

So far I have had in mind reading lists prepared and distributed by tutors. But a further problem with reading lists is that many are provided by the authors of textbooks. They commonly appeal at the ends of textbooks under the heading 'Eurther reading'. These reading lists may not only be printing, probably the revision of the texts, they, too, are of doubtful value. Generally speaking, publishers are as little concerned with the aulity of reading lists in the textbooks they publish as they are with the indexes to them.

An interesting technical point about reading lists at large is that they can be produced in narrative form, like The year's work in English studies mentioned earlier in this chapter. This device is not ideal for quick reference (a good reading list is one which, having been read, will thereafter be constantly referred to) but it does encourage students to go through it and it helps the compiler, if he knows what he is doing, to link one publication with another. Good examples are the reading lists appended to the individual volumes of the Oxford history of England.

Universal Bibliographic Control

The approaches for universal bibliographic control have been concerned principally with author/title listings and the cumulative patterns of current bibliographies. As far as the subject approach has been present; it has been incidental to the main purpose of the works so far described. National library catalogues, general bibliographies and retrospective and current national bibliographies are the basic groundwork upon which a total bibliographic control system is erected. Their modes of arrangement are usually those which will facilitate the widest possible access to as great as possible a range of people. Inevitably this presupposes priority for the author/title approach.

The subject arrangement of some current bibliographies and the existence of subject indexes to many more is an important source for the generation of facilities to enable detailed subject searches to be made, the need for bibliographic tools which stress the subject approach as paramount is considerable. Such subject bibliographies exist in huge quantities with their scope as wide as 'The Social Sciences' or as narrow as 'Bagpipe Music'. The sum of all subject bibliographies collected together in some way into a coherent whole represents another way of evolving an approach to universal bibliographic control. The impression must not be given that all subject specific bibliographies are arranged in some form of classified subject order. Many subject limited bibliographies are arranged in author / title form or in some form of alphabetical subject arrangement. It will be recalled that such general current bibliographies as British national bibliography are arranged in a classified order as their primary mode of arrangement but they are not, 'consequentially, described as subject bibliographies. Neither, therefore, does the act of arranging a subject bibliography in alphabetical order disqualify it from being termed a 'subject bibliography'.

Primary Device

The primary device for the articulation of subject bibliographies into a coherent system of bibliographic control is the class of works known as bibliographies of bibliographies. The compilation of catalogues of available bibliographies as a means of achieving bibliographic control is an attractive proposition and it is a means which is extensively used. Bibliographies of bibliographies can only be as comprehensive as the available resources of published material will allow them to be. The 'available resources' are not always wholly adequate in terms of either coverage of the ground of all subject areas or in terms of quality of those materials which are available. Theodore Besterman's. A world bibliography of bibliographies' (Lausanne, Societas Bibliographica, 1965) is a five volume work and the best known example of the genre. It has been supplemented by a two volume work compiled by Alice F Toomey published by R.R. Bowker in 1977 and bringing the basic work down to 1974 in terms of coverage. H. W. Wilson's cumulative Bibliographic index (1938) is the most wide ranging current source which is published three times a year with the third part each year forming the permanent volumes cumulating the other two parts and adding to them. Index bibliographicus (Paris, UNESCO) is another well known source of current information. Whilst these are all general bibliographies of bibliogrilphers a large number of more specialized works exist listing bibliographies in specific subject fields.

The Categorisation. It is principally the bibliographic control of books which is being considered at this stage it must be emphasized that subject bibliographies are often much wider in their scope. They tend to cross physical format boundaries much more extensively than other types of bibliography. David Lee, in an excellent survey of the scope of subject bibliography copiously, illustrated with examples makes the following categorization of the field:

1. General retrospective and current bibliographies which have a subject approach, including guides to reference books, and general library catalogues.

2. Subject bibliographies (selective), including series, handbooks to literature, generally categorized by Roberts'as 'systematic bibliographies'.

3. Special library catalogues and guides to libraries.

4. Subject bibliographies (comprehensive)

5. Analytical indexes of various kinds; including those to periodicials, government publications and other materials.

The reference to Roberts which David Lee makes is to A.D. Roberts Introduction to reference work (London, The Library Association third edition 1965) which was an historic and almost-classic contribution to the literature of librarianship.

As Lee says the first dimension of subject searching is that provided by general and national bibliographies. It is, however, to specially produced bibliographies that consideration must be given. Photo and micro-reproduction facilities in recent years have made it possible for large numbers of special library catalogues to be produced for wide dissemination in the same way that many other catalogues have been produced. R.L. Collison has described many of these catalogues. In his introduction Collison takes great pains to justify the recognition of library catalogues as genuine bibliographies. As noted elsewhere in this volume not all bibliographers have been willing to concede this point. They would certainly be unwilling to concede that the sales catalogues of major publishers are useful bibliographic sources. R.L. Collison's other account of bibliographic activity should also be remembered.

Guides on Literature

A particular form of guide to available resources in specific subject fields is that called variously, literature guides, resource guides, source books or, indeed, other similar names. Terminological problems abound in the field and there is no standard form in which these guides are presented. Some restrict themselves purely to books, others include materials in other formats, details of relevant learned societies, libraries and research organisations for example. Carl M White defines the literature guide thus: Loosley used, this term refers to any work that helps somebody to use books. It is used here in the narrower sense to refer to the type of sources designed to map the way through the literature of a reasonably extensive area, the type which in doing so helps evaluate, organize and introduce the literature. This distinguishes it from ... the bibliographical list (whether annotated or unannotated) and the introductory treatise. It is more informative than the one, and, unlike the other, it introduces the literature, not the content of the subject.

White description indicates the important points to bear in mind when considering the function of a literature guide. A literature guide must show up the bibliographic structure of the subject and assist in the comprehension of the means of obtaining access to the materials. There are a very large number of guides of varying standards of scholarship. The principal problem encountered by the authors of literature guides seems to be that they confuse their objectives.

It is a worthwhile and informative exercise to compare and contrast the structures of some typical literature guides:

Bateson, F. Wand Meserole, H.T.A. guide to English and American literature London, Longman third edition, 1976.

Davies, J.H. Musicalia: source of information in music Oxford Pergamon Press second edition revised, 1969.

Morrill, C Computers and data processing: information sources Detroit, Gale Research, 1969. Reviews and progress reports.

An important aspect of subject bibliography is that encompassed by those works with titles beginning with words like Annual review of Progress in and Year's work in Such works exist to provide a regular means of critical examination of new contributions to the literature of particular subject fields and of making evaluative judgements to assist research workers to find significant materials in their fields. Most review surveys are international in their scope.

They take a variety of forms of compilation from simple selective listings to detailed state-of the-art surveys written as essays liberally sprinkled with reference to recently published work. Example of this valuable medium of bibliographic control are: Progress in stereochemistry (New York Plenum Publishing Corporation, 1970); Annual bibliography of English language and literature (Cambridge, Modern Humanities Research Association, 1920).

A bibliography of reviews and progress reports can be found in Ulrich's international periodicals directory and A. M. Woodward's has published a bibliography. Another convenient source of the bibliography of such works is the Institute for Scientific Information's Index to scientific reviews (1974) which has recognized more than 20,000 such works.

❐

2
History of Cataloguing

There was a time when it seemed important to arrange books and prepare Catalogue according to color or their binding. Authors were enterd under forenames. One of the oldest lists of books of which we have knowledge occur on a Sumerian tablets found in Nipper and dated about 2000 BC. 62 titles were recorded on these Table, out of which 24 are Currently known as literary work. The purpose of the list is knowing. This list shows that there was some method or lists. It is assumed that 'Egyptian' libraries were developed earlier than "Babylonian writings were listed on claytablets which were fired, while the Egyptian wrote on papyrus (c) material which is far from everlasting even when buried in the parched sands of the desert. Among some Amerna tablets of 1400 BC, some references were found. It was found that whole callection of clay tablets was addressed to king and queen of Egypt and mere written in Babylonian language. Tags (plaques) were used in fragment, the tablets in which the names of the king and queen were written. These were arranged in book cases. Colophon were used on tablets which is the evidence of bibliographical details to some extent. The tablets as excavated in capital city of "Hittetes" may be the evidence of using colophon to convey bibliographical information. The Script written on these clay tablets identify the tablets in a series, its, title and often the name of the scriber.

There were other 20000 tablets found in the city "Nineveh" (650 BC), which bears colophon. These are kept in library of Egyptian king. Details found on tablets were the title, Name of original, if copied, tablet Number, Name of the scriber, and king's Stamp. This period has been assumed as the period of evolution of catalogue. The other evidance was the well known catalogue found on the walls of the tample at EDFU in Egypt.

In ancient period, Greek literature was rich and several references given in the book Collection in School or private libraries. There were two famous libraries in Alexender period which were developed with the development of Greek Civilization, *i.e.* Alexandria compiled the 'Pinakes' in 250 BC. in which few quotations of other writers were cited. 'Pinakes' bears imprint, which shows it bibliographical work in addition to the list of holding.

The writings of the scholar 'Callimlchus" clearly indicates that:

1. Preference wás being given to Author,
2. Title was used afte.. the subject,
3. Greek writtings never used any classified system permanantly,
4. Alphabetical and chronological arrangement was not followed firmly,
5. Mostly works were edited as previous writing were recorded and completed.

Roma libraries were influenced by' Greek as the Greece scholars several trip to Rame and stay for some times. During his stay the scholar visited several libraries and took active interest in the development of the libraries there. It was noted from the Roman literature that Romans used some fixed locations on their writings.

Medieval Period. The medieval period was a period of religious. feelingss. There was a slagan to establish more and were tambles and monastries, which were having their own librarirs. In 8th Century the books were having fly leaf which was used as a list of brief to title with authors appended to a few of them. There was no system of arrangement neither alphabetical nor classified. The system applied may be said as a inventory type and it was used as shelflist.

In 9th Century. German library 'Reicheman' compiled some catalogues, which were classified and listed at one place for all its valumes. But there was no standard code. The system was very frequency changed. There was 110 one voice about a perticular system, *i.e.* Alphabetical or classified. But preference was given to classified arrangement.

English Monesteries contributed much in the development of catalogue. These monestries (13th Century) made some efforts to compile a union list of its holdings. Some numbers were alloted like wise a code. It shows that English Monesteries were very much interested in framing some rules for cataloging a union list. The system of union list was modified and shaped as a shelflist in 14th Century. Shelftists were compiled and arranged by several libraries in England. Cathedral library included the price of the book in it. This list was treated as a part of the general inventory of the monesteris. The main point noted was the absence of any location symbol (call numbers). There was no satifactory progress in 16th century except Mr. Konard Gesner of Zuric, who compiled author bibliography and subject list. This system was followed by several years. In 1560 Trafer wrote first book on libraries "A Treatise on keeping of a library". He advocated for the use of call numbers to represent the colour of the binding. He was also in favour of a suitable classification scheme and a fine part of catalogue, *i.e.* shelflist, a classification index to analytics, a list for extra books not kept with main collection, and a alphabetical author index. In 1995 Mr. Andrew Marsell also wrote a book "Catalogue of English Printed Books", and mentioned some rules of cataloguing in the preface of the books. The main rules were related to the entry in the pesonal name under surname rather christian names.

16th and 17th Century. 16th century was a age of evolution of printing, which caused a production of books in big quantity. The libraries, whether monasteries, or the Universities found inadequate for the demand because of inadequate and improper catalogue. Though some scholars prepared index to the collection in various libraries, but it was not according to demand. Thomas Bradley's countribution to the cataloguing field is unforgettable. In 17th century he personally dictated minutes of cataloguing procedures. His approach was progressive. He was the first librarian, who recognized the catalogue as a reference tool, and introduced a catalogue code and favoured a classified arrangement with alphabetical authors. This concept was followed by many other libraries including some French libraries.

18th Century was a set back to library catalogue. Freech Revolution puts the libraries 10 years back as the whole World was engaged in War. All resources (finance) applied to the libraries, were used in revolutionry activities. After the French revolution, the new French Government took the innovation move of libraries throughout the Country Govt. issued special memorenda to all libraries of the nation to implement a National Catalogue Code of Cataloguing and Catalogue each and every book accordingly. Govt. also approved the Card Catalogue and issued directions. But the after effects of the revolution effected the supply of the Catalogue Cards. There was a shortage of Cards. Libraries were advised to use playing cards as catalogue cards and the Playing cards were collected from military personnels. The procedure adopted for cataloging was:

(a) Title page to be transcribed on the card;

(b) Entry under author's surname underlining by the filing word;

(c) If there was no author, the key word of the title was to be entered;

(d) Use of collation (Number of volumes, illustrations, missing pages, and description of binding).

19th Century. Modern catalogue begins with this era. There were libraries well developed in Britain. There was a difference of opinion whether there should be a classified catalogue or the alphabetical catalogue. Reviser Thomas Hertwell tried to solve this problem and published both a classification scheme and *"a Code of Cataloging Rules"*.

He complied a classified catalogue for the library of Queen's college, combridge and suggestion for British Museum. But the suggestion could not be materialized for a long time. This work proved more costly. The main reason of the failure of this code was 'that it was 'not a revolutionary code. House of commons also discussed the cataloguing problems and readers in public were also allowed to participate in the discussion.

Sir Anthony Panizzi was one of the great cataloguer who followed the Anglo-American tradition. He was appointed as Assistant Librarian in British Museum library in 1831. He was a lawyer and a man of intellect, energy and of dominating personality. British Museum library was facing cataloguing problem as there was not a proper catalogue. House of commons appointed a select committee to go in to the affair of British Museum library. This committee was assisted by a sub-committee on cataloguing and classification, After a period of one year Panizzi was appointed as a keeper of Printed Books. In 1833 the Trustees decided to have prepared and printed a new catalogue of the printed Book. Panizzi was given the responsibility to formulate some rules. In 1839, Panizzi formulated 91 rules to govern the compilation of Printed book catalogue. These rules were approved by the trustees with some amendments. He was of the opinion that 91 rules may be proved useful if proper editing is done. Work is done in its own time, Printing is done when manuscripts finally checked. But Trustees were interested in its immediate printing. A part of the catalogue was printed. There were many errors. The Printing work was suspended in 1847 for want of proper guidance. A commission was set up to enquire the affairs. Panizzi was of the opinion that *(i)* catalogue should not be prepared for a individual or one generation, but for many generations, *(ii)* It should function as part of 'a greats National under taking' for the promotion in general. The code was later revised in 1936 and reduced to 41 rules. It was a first code of its kind and followed by other libraries also. This code is treated as the begining of modern cataloguing.

Following are the important features of the Panizzi's code of cataloguing.

(a) The code gives much importance to the title page.

(b) The code favours direct entries.

(c) The code made provision of form Headings as and when required. It is a occassional treatment. For example : entry of periodicals under the form heading PERIODICA PUBLICATIONS divided by place of publication.

(d) Entries should be based on the information found on the title page.

(e) The name used for entry purpose should be given on the title page.

(f) The code recognized corporate authorship and made provision to enter institutions and societies under ACADEMIES divided by the place.

(g) Psendonyms publications were entered under author's designated name.

Panizzi was aganist the "determining the subject matter" of books as no two cataloguer agree to one subject matter. According to him subject knowledge and subject judgement are not required to a cataloguer. He gave more emphasis on the preparation of "Indexe matters".

This code could not gain popularity because of many errors. It was bitterly criticised by many big librarians of the period. Though more of the mistakes were made as thorough analysis of the problems was not done. The code required a revision in full particularly the rules for corporate authership and the anonymous works. The code was mainly criticised by Mr. Collier on the following points:

(i) The preferred entry was in name.

(ii) Second choice was name of a organization.

(iii) The place of the title was last resolt when all other details fails to be found on title page. Mr. Comer proved the above criticisms after cataloguing 25 books with his over hand and the system.

In 1950 a new code was introduced by Charles C. Jewett for "Simth Sonion Institute" and it was the first code came with maturity. This code, consisting of 39 rules, was published in 1952 under the title "on the constructions of the cataloguer of libraries; and their publications by means of separate stereotyped titles, with rules and examples, published by Smith Sorian Institute. This code was the modified work of Panizzi's code with the new change that:

(i) The corporate body will be entered. directly under name like U.S., as the author of Govt. publications.

(ii) Pseudonym names were also to be entered under the real name.

(iii) Anonymous works to enter under the first word of the title than in form name as in Panizzi's code. Mr. Jerwett made provision of cross references from the subject of the biography. Jewett's books of 39 rules is a Slim little pamphlet. Besides giving rules for author entries, he included examples and a model subject Index. This code led to the development of the idea of an established code of rules.

Prior to 1876 there was no dictionary catalogue code. Previous codes were treated as the Author-Catalogue codes. Moreover, no attempt was made to set forth the rules in a systematic way or to investigate which might be called the first principles of cataloguing. Cutter compiled a dictionary catalogue code titled "Rules for a Dictionary Catalogue" in 1876. These rules formed part of a special report of the United States Bureau of Education on the history, condition and management of public libraris in the United States of America. It was the first code of complete cataloguing practice for every kind of entries needed in a Dictionary Catalogue.

Cutter's code was the first code which was adopted by majority of tbe libraries and become popular among the public libraries. It is evident from 70000 copies published for IInd edition of 1889. The code includes all problems relating to the auther, litle, subject.and also form entry for description purposes. There are also rules on filing of entries.

The following are the important features of the code:

1. Code is based on three principles:

   Specific principles, usage principles and syndetic principles. Specific principle requires a book to be entered under its specific subject, as distinguished from listing it under a heading for a class which includes that subject.

   Usage principle requires choice of heading as per terminology and from that users of the catalogue will expect. -

   Example. The Automobile-under MOTOR CAR.

   Syndetic principle requires a subjeet heading to be connected together by means of references in order to direct the reader from the heading.

2. Cutter had supported the principles of Panizzi and modified.
3. Enter the anonymous work under the first word of the title.
4. There is a provision of subject entry.
5. He made no use of form heading but transferred this type of heading to the area of subject.
6. Possibilities of grouping is recognized in cutter's rule No. 340 and 343.
7. Cutter felt free to make main entry under subject when thought of commonsense. He was of the opinion that catalogue should not point any individualized publication but a organized library unit. This concept was also accepted by Mansell in 1595 and Panizzi in 1841. Jewett further strengthen this thought by the use of real name rather than pseudonym.

Author entry is not merely to facilitate the finding of a given book by the authors's name.

8. Cutters another feature was that all libraries are not equal and material required is also different. Hence rules were framed to cover all type of libraries. He suggested small, medium and full cataloguing to meet the needs of various libraries according to their size and nature D.M. Norris remarks that Cutter's rules are a sound exposition of the fundamentals of the cataloguing and should be studied by all the cataloguers.

Cutter was presumed as a man of the Dictionary Catalogue. But recently, he was presumed as a man of Classified Catalogue. This view has arisen from cutter's remarks on the syndetic structure of the Dictionary Catalogue.

Cutter constructed rules principally by to Printed book catalogue, but also made notes of relevance the card catalogue occassionally. Most of the rules constructed by the Cutter are difficult to understand.

By the time of the publication of fourth edition of Cutter's code, a great change has come in the field of cataloguing. Cutter has clearly shown the difference between Library of congress catalogue code and his own:

1. Difference in trifles in punctuation, capitalization, the place of certain items on the cards. Cutter preferred Library of Congress rules in case one is commencing a new catalogue.

2. Difference relating to place of entry of the code in catalogue, or of choice of heading.

Cutter says that cataloging is an Art, not a Science. No rule can take the place of experience and good judgement, but some of the results of experience may best be indicated by rules.

Professor Karl Dziatzko, a university librarian in Germany, published some instructions for the alphabetical catalogue in 1886. These instructions were translated in to English by American librarian

K.A. Linderfelt in 1890 with the title "Electric card Catalogue Rules: author and title entries". The aim of Prussian Instructions was to provide a standardized system of cataloguing so that the contents of Prussian libraries might be entered uniformly and catalogue of their holdings complied. Its second edition was published in 1908 followed two guiding principles simplification and abbreviation of entries. Much attention was paid to the real title or that part of the title which really names or describes the works. It also provided the use of the first grammatically independent word of the title as the entry word, rather than the first word of the title not an article. Compound names and contractions had to be expended in headings.

Exp 1. Who's who in Trade Agreements becoming WHO IS WHO Agreements Trade.

P.I. did not accepted the principle of corporate authorship, as their work was regarded as anonymous if no author is given.

The main defect of P.I. is that this code was designed by grammarians for grammarians and whatever merit once decided by the grammatical structure is not suited to the present day catalogue and the material of the complex.

New Era (Revolutionary Period)

The year of 1876 was most important year. American Library Association was established in this year. Card catalogue come in to exhistance but not popularly practiced universally. There were several libraries using Printed and the card catalogue both. Card catalogue began to make its popular use in America and Britain round about 1976. Library Bureau with Melwil Dewey as its head, was established to supply the card catalogue. Both the British Library Association and the American Library Associations had already published their own cataloguing rules independently. Dewey wanted cooperation among both the associations and the uniformity of the cataloguing rules throughout the English-speaking world Other important event was that in 1901 Library of Congress started printing and selling of catalogue cards. This made great influence on the libraries. LC. code was also made popular. America was the first country where the system of card selling has started. Hence 'here were two parallel monuments in England and America. In 1893 both the associations joined their hands. British Library Association published the Anglo-American code in 1908. This code was constructed with him to fulfill the requirements of large libraries of a scholarly character.

OBJECTIVES OF A LIBRARY CATALOGUE

Since a Liberary acquires documents to serve users, a cataloguer must record them so that the user is able to locate material quickly. This record must be a complete one, providing a key to the holdings of the library, irrespective of the fact whether a given document is in the hands of the user, or on shelf, or on loan. In order to make this record an efficient one, it is essential to decide what should be its objectives. We shall examine these objectives in detail.

Basic Objectives

The objectives of a library catalogue were broadly described by Charles Ammi Cutter in 1876. These have been frequently quoted and criticized a great deal. The objectives are:

"1. To enable a person to find a book of which

(A) the author or
(B) the title or } is known
(C) the subject

"2. To show what the library has

(D) by a given author

(E) on a given subject

(F) in a given kind of literature.

"3. To assist in the .choice of a book

(G) as to its edition (bibliographically).

(H) as to its character (literary or topical)."

Objective 1 emphasizes that the library catalogue should serve as a finding list for specific documents. This would require provision for individual entries for each book, providing approach through author, title, and subject. Objective 2 emphasizes that the library catalogue should serve as a finding list for groups of documents. This would require provision for a uniform entry for each group. Objective 3 deals with document description in the catalogue. According to it, the description should enable a user to distinguish between different editions of a given document. Besides, it should assist in the choice of a document by providing enough information about its distinctive features.

Objective

(A) is clear enough, and an acceptable one. Author entries with necessary references are provided to serve this objective. Title entries are provided to satisfy objective.

(B) This objective is in practice usually adopted for works of personal authorship, possessing fanciful titles, or if the title contains a proper noun, or if the title is treated in usage as a proper noun. Works like periodicals, anonymous works, etc., where the main entry would have the title as a heading, also meet the objective.

(C) is a highly suitable objective. Subject entries and subject references are provided to meet this objective.

(D) is easily acceptable. Author entries with necessary references serve the purpose. But in order to achieve this, the codes have to provide a large number of rules to overcome the problem created by the fact that some authors write under different pseudonyms, change their names, etc.

(E) is satisfied by providing entries under given subject and lated subjects.

(F) is implied to cover form and language entries. The forms include dictionaries, encyclopaedias, yearbooks, etc. This is and sirable objective. Such entries are provided on selective basis in a dictionary catalogue, otherwise the list of material covered under each form can be enormous. There is no such problem in a classified catalogue.

(G) is meant to be covered by descriptive cataloguing for a given work. Cutter provided edition and imprint along with notes, when found necessary, to satisfy this objective. The fullness or otherwise of details within each entry are decided by different libraries on the basis of various factors.

(H) covers the provision for notes to indicate character of documents. In a catalogue of a large library, these are provided on a selective basis because the provision of these add to the cost of cataloguing enormously.

The objectives stated by Cutter have stood the test of time more or less. These have been criticized a great deal and quoted very often. However, "later statements are most usually restatements of them."

Besides the objectives described by Cutter, we can add one deeper purpose to be served by a library catalogue. According to Ranganathan, "if it is interest in a subject which takes him to the library, his wants will be better served if the catalogue can spread before him a full, connected, panorama of all the materials on his specific subject, all its sub-divisions, and all broader subjects of which it is itself a sub-division". The reason is that it is only a few readers who are able to express their subject requirements in specific terms. They think either of a narrower or broader subject than the specific subject they require. Ranganathan has raised a very important point. However, the additional purpose suggested by him can be satisfied only by a classified catalogue.

According to Cutter, "The convenience of the public is always to be set before the ease of the cataloger....strict consistency in a rule and uniformity in its application sometimes lead to practices which clash with the public's habitual way of looking a things. When these habits are general and deeply rooted, it , unwise for the cataloger to ignore them, even if they demand; a sacrifice of system and simplicity."

It would appear that "convenience of the public" would come in conflict with the objectives laid down by Cutter. Thus the basic problem is how to reconcile strict logic behind a code with "convenience of the public."

The dictum of "convenience of the public" cannot be wished away because public opinion is not constant and can reverse itself easily. It needs to be taken seriously notwithstanding the seeming contradiction between convenience and objectives which, in other words, is the age-old contradiction between theory and practice. In the ultimate analysis, theory is born of practice, which in turn obtains nourishment from the former. In fact, there can be no theory without practice and vice versa. All objectives of a library catalogue were born out of the practical necessity of retrieving documents expeditiously and economically.

In fact, the variation in CCC and AACR occurs owing to differing interpretations of the convenience of the user as seen through the eyes of authors of the codes. In both the codes we find a contradiction between the objectives and the public convenience. In the final analysis, any such difference between theory and practice is an essential concomitant of all progress.

According to Ranganathan, a catalogue should be designed as to:

"1 Disclose to every reader his or her document;

"2 Secure for every document its reader;

"3 Save the time of the reader; and for this purpose

"4 Save the time of the staff".

The above objectives are simple and deeply enough expressed in the light of the five laws of library science. However, these a general in nature. On the other hand, the objectives proposed by Cutter are more specific.

Lubetzky is of the view that a library catalogue should serve first, to facilitate the location of a particular publication, *i.e.* of a particular edition of a work, which is in the library. Second, to relate and display together the editions' which a library has of a given work and the works which it has of a given author.

The above objectives were formulated as a part of ground work being done by Lubetzky for the revision of ALA code of 1949. The two objectives do not present a problem if a given author is identified in his works by one name and also each of his works is represented by one title each, because author and title entries will serve the two objectives fully. On the other hand, if an author is identified by different names in his works and also each of his works is issued under different titles, then author and title entries would satisfy the first objective while the second objective would not be served. In order to serve the second objective, works (*i.e.* the literary units embodied in various editions, translations, adaptations, abridgements, revisions, etc., each being a distinct publication having characteristics of its own) must be entered under a uniform heading using a uniform name or form of name of the author or title.

The International Conference on Cataloguing Principles was held at Paris in 1961. This conference preferred to use the term functions instead of objectives. The Paris conferences resolved that:

LIBRARY CATALOGUE AS A REFERENCE TOOL

Some persons have suggested that a catalogue should be designed as a reference tool. Lubetzky considers this idea a misconception, "one born from a confusion of the potentialities of the catalog with its purpose, and that the question of the function of the catalog cannot be decided in terms of an ambiguous finding list or reference tool but in terms of the specific objectives which the catalogue should be made to serve as a guide to the library's resources Lubetzky is nearer to Ranganathan who thinks on the same lines and is farther away from the Library of Congress practice, which has a tendency to load the catalogue with much information.

AACR is more concerned with reference functions of the catalogue as seen in the elaborate instructions provided by it relating to descriptive cataloguing. The detailed rules for notes, for instance, give the impression of elaborate rituals that are a seeming concomitant of cataloguing practice. Similarly, title and author statements of AACR to some extent emphasize reference functions of the catalogue. However, CCC is less concerned with descriptive cataloguing; the result is that it goes to the other extreme. It must however be said to the defence of AACR that the reference functions of the catalogue can be useful per se. The asceticism of CCC can be irritating and this seeming advantage should not be made a fetish of.

The functions of a library catalogue should be decided in terms of what it should serve not on what it can do. If we expect a library catalogue to serve as a reference tool, then we will be overloading it, making it a costly tool to prepare and maintain.

LIBRARY CATALOGUING VERSUS BIBLIOGRAPHICAL CATALOGUING

Library Cataloguing

In library cataloguing, a cataloguer tries to distinguish one work from another. Each document being catalogued is considered identical with other copies of the same edition. However, a distinction is made between a given work and its various versions or editions. The amount of details to be given vary from library to library and also differ with types of material. Author's name as a heading, along with the title are generally found to be sufficient. For anonymous and pseudonymous works, extra information regarding the name of the author or imprint is required to enable the user of a catalogue to distinguish between works having the same title.

Bibliographical Cataloguing

There is no complete agreement about bibliographical cataloguing. It means different things to different cataloguers. It is supposed to provide sufficient information to enable a bibliographer to reconstruct an entry without actual examination of the work. The information includes title in the form of exact transcript of the title page, except mottoes and other non-essential items. Each item is identified, and enough description given so as to distinguish it from other impressions or other copies of the same edition. Minor variations in texts of various issues are included. Even slight peculiarities regarding a title page or other parts of a document are covered rigorously. A bibliographical catalogue may include price of publication, type of binding, channel of availability etc. Consequently, bibliographical cataloguing requires more attention than library cataloguing.

Comments

There have been cataloguers who believed that "a catalogue entry should be so designed as to enable a bibliographer to use it as a substitute for the actual examination of the book." This would lead to overloading of the catalogue unnecessarily. The above view existed mainly because in the first half of the 20th century some cataloguers became absorbed in developing the catalogue for its own sake, without taking into consideration the true functions of a library catalogue. If the above view is put into practice, then we will be led to the practice of bibliographical cataloguing. Bibliographical cataloguing requires detailed description of each document being catalogued, which will add to the cost of preparing a library catalogue and also overload the catalogue unnecessarily. We have reached a stage when librarians are thinking of ways to reduce the cost of cataloguing. Besides, many details included in bibliographical cataloguing would not be required in a service library catalogue. Therefore, bibliographical cataloguing should be avoided by a service library catalogue.

LIBRARY CATALOGUE VERSUS BIBLIOGRAPHY VERSUS PUBLIHER'S CATALOGUE

The library catalogue is a bibliographical tool. Other tools are the publisher's catalogue, the bookseller's catalogue, shelf list, accession list, bibliography, etc.

Catalogue is a general term.

The library catalogue is a list of documents in the holdings of a library or group of libraries. A library catalogue can serve as a bibliography to a limited extent but the reverse is not true. For instance, the catalogue of a special collection of a given library can serve as a subject bibliography in a particular field of specialization.

A bibliography is an organized list of documents which is not limited to a particular collection.

The publisher's catalogue is a list of publications published by a publisher.

Library catalogues serve both inventory (listing) and retrieval (finding) functions, while a bibliography and publisher's catalogue serve the inventory function. Thus these tools have different functions to perform but contain sufficient information to serve those functions. However, in actual practice, the functions of a library catalogue are decided in relation to other bibliographical tools.

The statement of principles adopted by the International of Conference on Cataloguing Principles held at Paris in 1961 is a landmark. The functions (objectives) to be performed by a catalogue finalized at this conference can serve as a guideline for the framers of catalogue codes and cataloguers. This will also lead to standardized practices. However, the basic aim of a library catalogue will remain to serve its users in a most efficient manner in a practical way. The scholars for their specialized requirements should be expected to depend on bibliographies. A cataloguer should feel satisfied, if the catalogue is able to meet the requirements of ordinary users.

❑

3

Document Description

Cataloguing Involves a sort of description of a document being catalogued. Descriptive cataloguing is that aspect of cataloguing which is "concerned with the information given in the body of the entry as distinct from the heading." It is used to identify and describe a particular document. However, it is to be distinguished from subject cataloguing.

Principles

Principles of cataloguing have been enunciated in AACR. These are supposed to provide guidelines to a cataloguer in solving problems, for which rules in AACR do not provide a ready made solution.

The following are the principles of descriptive cataloguing: "*Objectives of descriptive cataloging.* The objectives of descriptive cataloging are: *(i)* to state the significant features of an item with the purpose of distinguishing it from other items and describing its scope, contents, and bibliographic relation to other items: *(ii)* to present these data in an entry which can be integrated with the entries for other items in the catalogue and which will respond best to the interests of most users of the catalogue.

"**Description of a Perfect Copy.** An attempt is made to describe a physically complete copy.

"**Extent of Description.** The item is described as fully as necessary to achieve the objectives stated above, but with economy of data and expression.

"**Terms of Description.** The terms used by the author, composer, publisher or other issuing authority in or on the item generally form the basis of the description. Ambiguous or unintelligible statements used in the description are followed by explanations. Inaccuracie are indicated and corrected when necessary.

"**Organization of the Description.** The descriptive elements are given in the entry in the order that will best meet the needs of the users of the catalogue and will facilitate the integration of the entry in a catalogue with entries for other items.

"**Documentation.** The source of information contained in an entry need be specified only when the information is questionable or the source is unusual.

"**Style.** A uniform style is adopted for all catalogue entries, covering spelling, capitalization, punctuation, abbreviations, use of numerals, indentions, and for printed cards, type faces".

Elements of Descriptive Cataloguing

The basic problem is to decide which elements should be included and what should be the order of these elements. The elements usually consist of title, subtitle, alternative title, author statement, edition, imprint, collation, series, notes, and annotation.

Title is the most important feature of a document essential for its identification. In computerized catalogues, it is the principal element for identification. The title is usually given in full as found on the title page. The subtitles are also added, which are considered useful in identifying different editions and in individualizing the document. An alternative title, if any, is included because the document might become better known in future through the alternative title than the original title.

Author Statement, in AACR practice, is repeated after the title, if there are two or more authors. The names of translator(s), editors(s), illustrator(s), etc. are also added after the title. In Ranganathan's practice, if there are two authors, both names are put in the heading, whereby there is no need for repetition of the names of authors after the title; and in case of three or more authors, only the name of the first author is given in the heading.

Edition is a must for a' catalogue. However, information regarding impression or a reprint is ignored.

Imprint includes, place of publication, publisher's name, and date of publication. It helps in identification of different editions. Date of publication is the important item. AACR recommends inclusion of date of copyright, provided it is different from the date of publication. Information about the publisher sometimes helps to confirm the degree of reliability of the work. Place can indicate biases and differences in terminology, etc. Publisher and place of publication have little value from the point of individualizing element. It is suggested that in case the entries are typed or handwritten then imprint may be omitted, except in a research library. However, if the library has adopted a mechanical method of duplication, then imprint may be included. AACR recommends inclusion of imprint but in Rangana than's practice, imprint is totally omitted in. a catalogue of a service library.

Collation is concerned with pagination or number of volumes, illustrations, size, etc. The number of volumes and indication about illustrations, if considered significant are considered essential in an entry. AACR regards even size essential. On the other hand, Ranganathan in his CCC, recommends the use of symbols to indicate size, and pages are not to be indicated. For normal size, no symbol is to be used. In oversized books, book number is overlined and in undersized books, book number is under lined. Exact size as prescribed by AACR is hardly of any significance in most cases except for publications like atlases, etc.

Series is often referred by the users, especially casual readers. Sometimes it may give an indication about the level of the work. Information about series is helpful in the identification of an edition of a particular document. Series statement is very helpful to librarians checking the catalogue to find out whether the library possesses a complete set in the series or not. AACR and CCC consider series statement an essential element.

Notes follow the formal description (that is, after the body of the entry). "Notes amplify or qualify formalized description, either when the rules do not permit the inclusion of the needed information in any form other than a note or when the incorporation of information in the formalized description would be misleading, cumbersome, or inappropriate". These assist to identify documents and provide information, which may be found useful by the users of catalogue. These are prescribed generously by AACR, AACR suggests? notes on title, subtitle, alternative title, authorship, collaborators, edition. imprint, collation, series, and additional physical description, bibliographical history, relationship to other works, and to other editions of the same work, contents (or partial contents) title romanized, and literary form, etc..

Annotation may cover information about authorship, subject, relationship with other documents, etc. Very few library catalogues include annotation. The details regarding annotation will be found in chapter VIII. It may be added that an annotation falls outside the purview of descriptive cataloguing. However, certain notes-which provide necessary additional information relating to title, edition, imprint, collation sometimes list of contents fall within the scope of orthodox descriptive cataloguing.

Order of Description

The order of description of various elements usually consists of title, subtitle, alternative title, author statement, edition, Imprint, collation, series, notes, and annotation. The basic idea behind the order is to place the most important elements first cause it is thought that the users of a catalogue usually read the first few lines of an entry.

Amount of Information

Amount of information to be included in a catalogue entry depends on kind of library, availability of financial support, nature of the document, nature of catalogue, etc. If cost is a main consideration, then minimum details should be provided. If the document is an incunabula or a rare one, then more details would be required. In case it is decided to print the catalogue, considerations regarding space and cost would lead to provision of limited details. On the other hand, if the library is using a mechanical device to reproduce catalogue cards, then it may be possible to give more details without increasing the cost very much. If catalogue cards are handwritten or typed, then it may be economical to provide maximum details in the main entry, and added entries may be made as brief as possible. The kind of library is crucial in deciding about amount of information to be included in a library catalogue. In a research library it might be essential to provide information about imprint, collation, and notes. A public library catalogue can do without these, except size of the document.

A cataloguer who wants to restrict descriptive elements to a bare minimum will have to choose only those elements which assist in individualization of the documents. For this purpose, title, edition, and date of publication are sufficient. However, persons like Ranganathan are in favour of adding elements like series and notes. In American practice, based on A.A.C.R., all the items except annotation are added without any hesitation in library catalogues. British standard 1629: 1950 Bibliographical references suggests author, title, date, and series as the bare minimum.

AUTHOR AND TITLE CATALOGUING

Author is the supreme in cataloguing likewise Author catalogue or its variations, pure or simple, author entry in dictionary catalogue, or the author-index entry to a classified one. Author is important in value and supremacy. It is obvious that reader's first approach is author. He ascertain whether library has a particular book of a particular author, as authors name is undisputable. There may be a difference of opinion about the subject, but there may not be a difference of opinion about the author except few exceptions. There may be a little difference of opinion about form of names, compound names, pseudonym to a real name, family or best known name etc. Author catalogue is perhaps the oldest form of catalogue and fundamental to all other forms and combinations.

Author catalogue is a list of books in a collection, entered under the names of the authors of books, the entries being arranged alphabetically.

Author entry consists of the surname of the author, followed by, forename.

Choice and form of Heading. Personal author presents a number of problems before the framers of the catalogues. But the choice of heading of the main entry for a simple book by single author appears to be so simple, yet the codes have devoted considerable space and energy in dealing with it. Bhattacharya has very well compared and evaluated cutter's RDC (1904) and the different editions of CCC and AACR pertaining to choice of the heading for the main entry of a simple book by a single author. CCC (1964) has improvement over CCC (1958) in case of terminology and rules of choice. Fasana in his paper presented before A L.A. meeting of Jan. 1975 and reviewed the achievements of AACR, proposed changes in rules on choice of heading, application in retrospective catalogues and the mode of operation. Soper stressed that the concept of authorship, corporate and possibly, personal. will be retained for serials. Content is more important than format and that the same basic rules should apply to all serials. Hoffman gives an example to show the short of unhelpful entry for sound records which is strictly the application of AACR rules 250 B. Hall suggested 2 methods *(1)* strict romanisation from the original script; and *(2)* a Europeanised form, generally based on the pronounciation. He deals with 14 specific languages and highlighted the problems presented by each. According to Hall if catalogue spends an inordinate length of time searching for the best heading, it may take the reader the same length of time to find it; and that the reader should be helped by catalogue easily accessible to him even though he may be unfamiliar with them. Khurshid outlines the origins and structure of muslim names, particularly in Pakistan, stressing that although upto a different elements may occur in a name, there is no agreement among scholars as to the order in which they appear. He states that the order depends on local linguistic and cultural differences. These differences must be observed before cataloguing code can describe particular orders for these elements.

Author catalogue have some drawbacks as it cannot provide information about the subject or the title of a book. There have many efforts to correct the criticism. The result is Alphabetical subject index.

Barbeti says that the code does not prescribe for old books, manuscripts. A permanent committee should be set up to study the interpretation of the code and to formulate rules for special catagories of material.

Anglo-American Cataloguing Rules

The term 'author' is defined in the Glossary and footnote 2. The person or corporate body chiefly responsible for the creation of the intellectual or artistic of a work. Rule 1 B deals with cases where the publication attributes the authorship erroneously or fictitiously to some one who is not the author. may be classified by comparison with 16 (writer or nominal author). In Lubetzky's 1960 code of cataloguing Rules a single rule (CCR 2a) covers two cases (1) A work prepared by one person for another person in whose name it is presented is entered under the person who is reportedly responsible for it. (2) A work fictitiously or erroneously attributed another person.......is entered under the person who prepared it.

Edgen deals with the revised edition of the AACR due in 1977 and states that major innovations in the code will probably effect most libraries. He comments on the AACR revisions by the author and 3 other cataloguing experts-C. summer spelding, phillip A. Richard and Ronald Hagler. Areas discussed are: How the A.A.C.R., was developed; who is responsible for revising; the significance of the standardisation of the ISBD for monographic publications: some of the problems that will be resolved and some that will not; changes that are recommended; and obvious advantages of the revision.

Buchinski presents a paper at the annual conference, Canadian library Association, falifax, June 1976.

Joint Steering Committee took major policy decisions in the following areas: General International Standard Bibliographic Description; Corporate authorship; subordinate corporate entry; form sub-headings; mixed authorship; diffuse authorship; fullness of name;

pseudonyms; uniform titles, related works; additions to headings; and names in non-roman alphabets. The committee suggested strategies that might be developed to assist libraries in adopting the new code. Garman and Winkler writes that the AACR II edition which is an attempt to reconcile in the single text of the North American and British texts of 1967 edition and to incorporate in the single text all amendments and changes already agreed. The revision has been prepared by the American Library Association; the British Library; the Canadian Committee on Cataloguing; the Library Association; and the Library of Congress. Mckinlay in one of the papers Presented at the seminar 'Cataloguing in isolation' held by the Victorian Group, Special Libraries Section, Library Association of Australia, Melbourne, Oct 1977 and outlined events leading to the 2nd ed. of the A.A.C R. and the 19 the ed. of the Dewey Decimal Classification. The author made comments on changes, new features and their expected effect on Australian librarianship. The Library of Congress and the national libraries of Australia, the U.K. and Canada have agreed on a joint strategy for implementing A.A.C.R. 2 and DC, 19 from 1 Jan. 80. Briefly considers the Librery of Congress Subject Headings and PRECIS which the author hails as the first intellectually satisfying and demonstrably practical method of regorous subject analysis. Garman notes the importance of 'real life' cataloguers in the formulation of the rules. A.A.C.R. 2 is divided into 2 parts bibliographic description and choice and form of headings. I.S.B.D. (G) was used heavily in the rules for bibliographic Descriptions. A.A.C.R. 2 is a comprehensive statement of the best current cataloguing practice in the Anglo American tradition. Anderson discusses the features of the A.A.C.R. in the light of Universal Bibliographic Control (UBC) and emphasised that A.A.C.R. is the basis for the development of UBC International Standards, and it should be agreed and accepted so that the bibliographic records prepare in each country are accepted by other countries. There is no international cataloguing code, but most national codes, have the 1961 Paris Principles as their basis. There are also multi-national codes such as the A.A.C.R. Current trends in preparing international cataloguing tools, *e.g.* the International Standard Bibliographic Description. ISBD (M) and ISBD (S) indicate that even if there is no international code the existing codes will be offering the same solutions.

Cole proposed the two changes to the North American Text of the Anglo American Cataloguing Rules which are: the adoption of the British text of 6 B; and the deletion of 6 C. With the deletion of 6 C serials would be entered only under title or corporate author. Gorman examines critically the 'Paris Principles' adopted by the International Congress on cataloguing Principles (Paris, 1961) and the A.A.C.R. (1967) in the light of the changes to entry and heading which will be brought about by the 2nd ed. of AA.C.R. (1978). In particular, the de-emphasis of the main entry is very important because it creates an environment for the ultimate abolition of this outdated concept. It was found necessary a racial re-evaluation of post and current practices and mean in practical terms, the 'revision of the Paris Principles by international agreement and the constant review of A.A.C.R.

Flowers gives the concept of corporate authorship in the context of periodicals. He argued strongly in favour of title entry and suggested that, because by far the most common title variation is a change in the order of the title, *e.g.* 'Bulletin of the Society' and '.....Society Bulletin; and also to avoid over crowding at the 'Bulletin', 'Transactions', etc. entry points a standardised title-form be adopted. This would consist of corporate body first followed by 'Journal', etc., and would also abviate the need for an added corporate body entry.

Accroding to conochie. There arises many difficulties in cataloguing government publications including collaborative publication, establishing the correct title of the body producing the publication, whether the body should be entered directly or as a sub-heading under the name of the country or state. These problems should be resolved by consulting the A.A.C.R. The most important point to remember in cataloguing, most particularly in cataloguing government publications, is to provide access points where ever an enquirer might start his search. Many changes will take place in the philosophy of the rules, punctuation patterns develop for consistency and in the organisation of the text. The absence of a separate rule for serial entry, new rules for serial description, a change in what will be entered under corporate body, no form sub-divisions, and no 'dash' entries are among the aspects of the 2nd ed. which will have implications for serials librarians. Entry for serial publications needs re-examinations in view of recent developments and proposals and possible solution may be made to take into consideration the compatibility between A.A.C.R., and international standards for serials as well as the integrity of the catalogue. New rules that particularly effect serials statements, and first issue descriptive cataloguing.

According to Flinterman the new-rules for the descriptive part of the entry are based on the I.S.B.D, where as the rules for cataloguing and the choice of headings are based on the precepts embodied the Statement of Principles of the International conference on Cataloguing Principles (I.C.C.P) For this reason the new rules differ in many aspects from the old rules, although there are instances where the new rules follow the old rule instead of conforming to the I.S.B.D. or the Statement of principles Gavin gave a brief notes on the principles by which the 1977 Swiss cataloguing rules were drafted. As far as possible the work was based on the 1961 I.F.L.A. Paris Principles, with Anglo-American rules, French standards and the German R.A.C., also considered. The rules are primarily intended for activity, special and cantonal libraries.

Author and Title Cataloguing

The new Finnish Cataloguing Code. 'Suomalaiset luettelointisaannot', based on A.A.C.R., the cataloguing codes of Denmark and Sweden, existing draft or published, and early drafts of A.A.C.R. 2; was published during the period under study.

Corporate Author

The choice. rendering and form of corporate authorship present baffling problem before the framers of the catalogue codes as well as before the practising cataloguers. Since cutter, the catalogue codes were much concerned about the problems and solutions of

'Corpotate Complex'. The wellknown categories of corporate authors are: Government, Institutions and Conferences. Hanson has added a new category 'societies' and created the actificial distinction between institution and society. Ranganathan was pioneer to have recognised the unhelpfulness of this distinction and he raised voice against this. Lubetzky and others become fascinated over this and propagated the same. Through their efforts this distinction was eroded in the I.C.C.P. (1961) and finally in the A.A.C.R. (1978) this century old controversy came to an end.

The application of sections 601-695 (1973) and 401-487 (1974) of the new Rules in relation to Corporate bodies are categorized:

(1) organisations institutions and undertakings which by virtue of their names constitute individually identifiable units; and

(2) Territorial units (regional corporate bodies), such as countries, provinces, etc., had their organs, such as parliaments. ministries, courts.

The individual contributions should receive individual subject cataloguing.

Conference publications may be handled either as monographs or serials. The current practice in the U.S.A. shows a lack of standardization in this matter. A.A.C.R. gives no guidance, I.S.B.D. (M) I.S.B.D.(S) contradict one another. There is a great need for standardization, specially with the current trend towards increased library co-ordination and recommends the monographic approach.

Bourg and others, describe a systematic approach to the design of fixed length. derived, truncated search keys for corporate author records. Reports of experiments using record samples from the Ohio College Library Centre (O.C.L.C.). data base to (1) investigate various procedures for the constructIon of efficient truncated key types as derived from corporate author records; (2) evaluate the effectiveness of a representative key type for a growmg file. They concludes that the performance of a variety of conventional O.C.L.C. type truncated corporate author keys is extremely poor in distinctness and relative entropy, and that use of a stop-list results in significant increases in performance for all key types. When limits of 3 to 5 words are used in key collstruction only a short stop list is required to achieve substantial enhancement in key performa..ce.

Psendonym

The false or fictitious names assumed by authors have the problems of choice and rendering in the catalogue entries. Different codes have specially provided for their treatment. The Classified Catalogue Code, perhaps, is the only code which provides for such names in a helpful and systematic manner based on the Canon of Ascertainability. A.A.C.R, on the other hand, leaves practising cataloguers to use their discretion and judgment in dealing with pseudonymous authors. They have to exercise lots of extra bibliographic efforts, which in turn become time consuming and inconsistent catalogue entries in identical cases.

Purohit suggested the amendments in Rule MD 4 of the Classified Catalogue Code and give analogous new rule MD 4 for the choice and rendering of pseudonymous works as suggested by Ranganathan. Specifications ring in the author statement of a title page should not be taken as try heading. The terms like 'Pseud' or 'Pseud of' are superfluous attachments and they should not be given place in the heading.

Title As Main Entry

The recent development in the field of cataloguing, specially the Mechine Readable Cataloguing and the proliferation and mushroom growth of authors, have rendered it unhelpful to enter the works under their authors as main entry headings.

The most sensible approach to cataloguing is to abandon the concept of 'Principal authorship' as used by the A.A.C.R., in favour of title main entry with added author entries. With unit cards, the main entry and tracings can be printed on the title card and this would fulfil the basic requirements of a library catalogue that is be a finding list, not a bibliographic tool. Computer cataloguing would be simplified, books would get to readers more quickly and the number of cataloguers required could be greatly reduced. Readers wanting author entries could still get them.

Following the Eighteenth Century Short Title Catalogue Conference June, 1976 and a subsequent 6 month pilot study by the British Library, a commitment was made by the library in June, 1977. to recatalogue the Reference Division's 18th century holdings. These makes evolved over several months whilst the recataloguing took place, and they endeavour, where possible, to incorporate the pres criptions of the revised text of the A.A.C.R., and to meet the requirements embodied in the British Version of the M.A.R.C., manual. and cited 6 sample titles and text pages from various 18th century works with filled out input sheets and notes on points to watch.

Responses received by the Library of Congress to a query on display of uniform titles showed that a clear majority (80 percent) of those expressing views favoured the display of all uniform-titles when A.A.C.R., 2 is implemented.

Kaula and Singh tracing briefly the genesis and development of the concept of author as main entry heading since Cutter, describe the reasons for the dominance of author entry in the Anglo-American Cataloguing Practice. The shift-in emphasis on title main entry in different bibliographical sources like bibliographies, abstracting and indexing periodicals and book reviews have been presented by them. They point out the irrelevancy of author main entry due to advent of computer and machine devices and mention the various advantages. of the title main entry system.

❐

4

Forms of Document Cataloguing

INNER FORM OF LIBRARY CATALOGUE

The Inner Form of library catalogue has undergone many changes which have kept pace with changes in the concept of service to users. The following account about evolution in the internal form is based on description provided by Ranganathan.

There was a time when libraries were regarded as mere depositories where books were kept for preservation. Library catalogues were prepared to serve as inventory of the library for its holdings. The catalogue was made of the title-a-line type, in which books were listed in the accession order. Books on the shelves were also arranged according to accession order.

Next, the library began to be regarded as a service institution. Thus the idea of preservation was replaced by the spirit of service. As a result of this, title-a-line entries began to be arranged in the alphabetical order according to the names of authors.

Next, the importance of the subject approach of the users began to be realized. Thus, the single alphabetical order was replaced by as many sequences as the number of broad classes into which the universe of knowledge was divided-one sequence corresponding to one broad class.

This was perhaps followed by adoption of the shelf register approach. Here the title-a-line entries were listed in an order parallel to the order of the books on the shelf.

The next development was that of dictionary catalogue, consisting of entries of various kinds in a single sequence, so as to satisfy the various approaches, including the subject approach.

According to Ranganathan, the next stage of evolution of the library catalogue led to the splitting of the catalogue into two parts on the basis of the differences of function, with one part containing all the entries arranged by call number and the second part consisting of the rest of the entries arranged alphabetically like a dictionary.

CHIEF TYPES OF CATALOGUES

The following are the chief types of catalogues based on the internal form of the catalogue:

1. The alphabetic catalogue:

   (a) Author catalogue; *(b)* Name catalogue; *(c)* Subject catalogue; *(d)* Title catalogue; *(e)* Dictionary catalogue.

2. Classed catalogue or classified catalogue.

3. Alphabetico-classed catalogue.

Alphabetic Catalogue

Author catalogue consists of author entries arranged alphabetically. It is the oldest and the most important type. This type of alphabetical catalogue tells what works of a given author are possessed by the library and whether the library has a particular work of a given author. Author is a comprehensive term which includes editor, compiler, illustrator, translator, etc.

Name catalogue consists of author catalogue and subject catalogue mixed in one sequence arranged alphabetically. The subject catalogue is restricted to the subject entries for the names of persons occurring as subject of books (*e.g.* biographies, diaries, memoirs, criticism, etc.), that is subject headings consisting of names of persons treated as subjects.

Subject catalogue consists of subject entries arranged alphabetically. This satisfies the approach of the reader from any subject aspect dealt in the document.

Title catalogue consists of entries for books under their titles arranged alphabetically.

Dictionary catalogue is a "catalogue in which all the entries are word entries". AACR defines dictionary catalogue as "a catalog in which all the entries (author, title, subject, series, etc.) and their related references are arranged together in one general alphabet. The subarrangement frequently varies from strictly alphabetical". Such a catalogue is called a dictionary catalogue because it is easily usable as a dictionary.

Classed Catalogue or Classified Catalogue

It is a catalogue in which subject entries are arranged according to some scheme of classification. Strictly speaking, it is a subject catalogue, in which the entries are arranged according to some scheme of classification. In practice, a classified catalogue is not sufficient by itself because it fails to satisfy author, title, and subject approach of a reader. However, the subject approach can be met if one knows the layout of the scheme, which is too much to expect from an ordinary user. Thus an alphabetical index consisting of author, title, and subject entries is a must. Therefore, Ranganathan rightly considers the classified catalogue as a "catalogue in which some entries are number entries and some are word entries". Thus, according to Ranganathan, a classified catalogue is one which has two parts one containing number entries and the other containing word entries, called classified part and alphabetical part respectively. The classified part will contain main entries and cross reference entries arranged according to a scheme of classification. The alphabetical part contains added entries arranged alphabetically.

Alphabetico-Classed Catalogue

In it, either the major subject divisions are arranged in a classified order and subordinate subjects within major division in the alphabetical order, or the major subject divisions are put in alphabetical order with subordinate subjects arranged in classified sequence. Suppose major divisions are Mathematics, Chemistry, Botany, Zoology, History, Political Science, Law, etc.

These would be arranged in a classified pattern. Within each major division, its subordinate divisions will be arranged alphabetically.Thus, within Mathematics, subordinate divisions like algebra, calculus, geometry, etc. will be arranged alphabetically. In order to locate books on algebra, one must know that algebra is a branch of Mathematics. In practice, it needs to have an alphabetical index. In this form of catalogue, the combined advantages of both alphabetical and classified form are aimed at. One can get all the related material in a collection in a logical manner. Similarly, the alternative form of alphabetico—classed catalogue can be obtained. Alphabetico-classed catalogue has not been fully experimented. Therefore, much can not be said about this form.

Divided Catalogue

A dictionary catalogue may be divided into two parts, an author and a subject catalogue. This simplifies the arrangement but introduces certain complications. Entries for the works by an author are included in the author catalogue and works about him are placed in the subject catalogue. Also, extra cross references, subject cards for autobiographies, are required. Of course form headings like Laws, statutes, etc. have no logical place in a divided catalogue.

Shelf List

It is a catalogue of books in the order in which they stand on the shelves. Each title is represented by a card usually giving the author, title, edition, number of volumes (if more than one), number of copies, call number, and other essential items. It is a very important record of the location of all the copies. In case the library adopts a dictionary catalogue, it is not generally used by the public. Only parts of it are consulted or duplicated to furnish a classified catalogue. In a library it can also serve some of the functions of an accession register.

COMPARISON OF DICTIONARY AND CLASSIFIED CATALOGUES

Out of the various types of catalogues, the classified and dictionary catalogues are the most important. Therefore, both types have been compared to bring out advantages and disadvantages of each.

Classified Catalogue (CC)	*Dictionary Catalogue (DC)*
1	*2*
Preparation	
From the point of a librarian, it is simple to prepare because it utilizes the work already carried out in classifying the documents and its indexing proves easier as the collection grows.	Is equally simple to prepare but subject indexing gets complicated with the growth of a collection.
Arrangement	
Arrangement of entries in the classified part is the same "as", that of books on shelves. Arrangement in the alphabetical part is like a dictionary, which is easy to understand. Arrangement of multilingual entries does not present difficulties in the classified part but in the alphabetial part, multilingual entries can present difficultiys.	Arrangement of entries is alphabetical like a dictionary, which is easy to understand. Multilingual entries can present difficulties.
Logical and systematid order	
A logical and systematic order is achieved "in the classified part because the order is based on a scheme of classification. The order of the scheme of classification used in bonks and the classified catalogue being the same, users are likely to become	Owing to the natural order of alphabets, entries relating to the same subject would get scattered. For instance, subjects like heat and magnetism are related ones but in the catalogue, subject entries relating to these would get scattered.

1	*2*
come more familiar with the shelf order of books, in case the library adopts the classified catalogue rather than the dictionary catalogue.	
Subject approach	
In case a user approaches through a specific subject he has to consult the alphabetical part first, then is directed to the classified part where he can find entries on the specific subject together at one place, thereby requiring double action As regards answering enquiries on various aspects of a subject, CC is certainly superior to DC because it brings together the material on a specific subject as well as on various aspects of a specific subject in its classified part.	It provides a direct approach to those who approach through a specific subject. Thus it is most suitable for answering enquiries under a specific subject and serves specific subject enquiries better than CC. It is difficult to consult for information on various aspects of a subject. In this type of enquiry it is slow as well as unsatisfactory in yielding information. For instance, material under various aspects of physics, like electricity, heat, magnetism, nuclear physics, etc., would get scattered due to the very nature of alphabetization. As a result, a user would find it difficult to know about material on all aspects of a given specific subject.
Deeper function	
Most readers are not able to name exactly the specific subject of their interest. They are wont to name a broader or nar-	In it, there is an inevitable scattering of subjects and see also directions, which will virtually tire out the reader.

1	*2*
rower subject. A reader first consults the alphabetical part and then goes to the classified part where he finds the fullfield of his interest spread before him in a logical manner, becoming vaguely conscious of what he wants. The CC collates all material, on a given topic and displays relationships between subjects in a way more useful to the user than any other kind of catalogue.	
Consultation	
The CC is not really as difficult to consult as it appears to be. It does not require deep knowledge of the scheme of classification but it does sometimes set a psychological barrier in the mind of the users. Use of a large number of guides within and outside the catalogue, and training the users of the catalogue by the reference staff can be extremely helpful. In fact, once the basic structure of the catalogue has been understood, its use is likely to present very few difficulties. Users who have used published bibliographies and catalogues will usually not find it at all difficult to use.	Easy to consult and outwardly simple to use, because it is usable like a dictionary. The complex system of subject entries creates hindrante in use, which at times can prove frustrating.

1	2
Role of classification	
Usefulness of CC depends upon the qualities of the scheme of classification though indexing and guiding can overcome the weakness to some extent. The scheme should be able to individualize each specific subject at book level, provide filiatory sequence and individualize various books.	Its usefulness does not depend upon a scheme of classification.
Role of cross references	
The number of cross references is less. Owing to the presence of the classified arrangement, the role of cross references is limited to referring from rejected headings to selected headings.	For its ultimate success, it depends upon an elaborate scheme of references. References can often prove to be tiresome and there is always a possibility of missing one or more vital headings. They also multiply at a fast rate, making the catalogue difficult to use.
Language barrier	
In case an international scheme of classification like the Univeral Decimal Classification is used with its multilingual indexes, then literature searches for foreign-language literature become easy. Thus international cooperation is possible.	International cooperation is difficult to achieve.

1	2
Printing of a subject catalogue	
Any class or subject catalogue can be printed at any time easily.	Subject catalogue is more difficult to print.
Rate of growth	
Overall rate of growth is slower.	Subject entries and references increase at a higher rate than in CC. Rate of growth of the catalogue is high, making it difficult to use.
Maintenance	
The maintenance of subject entries in the alphabetical part is easier because replacing of old subject terms by new ones is easier as compared with DC.	Replacing of old subject terms by new subject terms is a tedious and time-consuming process.

Both catalogues have their advocates who cling strongly to their favourites. While the opponents of the classified catalogue argue that it was an estoric instrument difficult to decipher by users, its votaries have held the view, which they constantly propogate, that there is no substitute for it. There is a lack of objectivity on the part of both groups because very few people are familiar with both types of catalogues.

In a survey conducted among users of the Sapru House Library, New Delhi, on a sample of 136 respondents, it was discovered that 85 per cent asserted that they were able to consult the classified catalogue of the library with ease. 15 per cent were unable to, of which four persons mentioned that they were not always able to consult with ease. It was also found on the basis of the same survey that 105 (76 per cent) of the 138 respondents claimed to use the classified catalogue frequently. If the above-mentioned statements are to believed, the widely held assumption that the classified catalogue comes in the way of improving service in Indian libraries cannot be sustained, I unless it can be established that statistics, as in other instances, lie in this case also.

This shows that the classified 'catalogue is not as difficult to use as made out by its opponents. Further, the impression that may linger in the mind of anyone looking into the above table comparing the advantages and disadvantages of classified and dictionary catalogues will be that of the overwhelming superiority of the former over the latter. The working experience of two catalogues tells us that this is not exactly so.

The theory that the classified arrangement brings together related classes in a filiatory sequence, and hence is of considerable importance to the user, is not exactly borne out by experience. A majority of readers are interested in a specific subject or a document and to them related fields are of limited interest. The very fact that the subject approach to the classified part of the classified catalogue is through the completion of two steps, by consulting the subject index first and the classified part afterwards, may be irritating to a user. In a large library, the amount of walking to be done may mean an extra amount of time spent by him. The success of a classified catalogue greatly depends upon the qualities of the scheme of classification used. The scheme should be kept up to date, otherwise the resultant catalogue would be a poor substitute. Many of the classified catalogues in existence are poor examples mainly due to the use of outdated schemes of classification and because they are provided with poorly compiled subject indexes.

As pointed out earlier, the dictionary catalogue has certain weaknesses, but a carefully worked out net-work of cross references can help to mitigate the inconvenience resulting from the absence of a strictly classified arrangement. However, there is no doubt that very often careless use of cross references can prove irritating to users.

Thus there is scope for a case being made for either type of catalogue. It will be interesting to make a comparison between the two types of catalogues in statistical terms, which may decide the issue ultimately.

Choice of a catalogue by a library would depend upon certain factors-type of library, availability of printed catalogue cards, type of the catalogue used by neighbouring libraries, kind of training of the chief librarian, and attitude of authorities.

It is generally accepted that school and public libraries find the alphabetical form more suitable; and college, university, and research libraries prefer the classified catalogue. However, in practice a large majority of libraries use the dictionary catalogue, mainly because of lack of good schemes of classification.

MARC (MACHINE-READABLE CATALOGUING)

Theoretically it could be possible for an individual library to maintain its catalogue solely in Machine Readable form, integrative, computes directly to answer quaries. In any case it would require permanent access to the computer developments in computer cataloguing accruing with a such rapidity that any detailed account of the changes now taking place with quickly date.

Following the King Report on antomation in library of congress a programme aimed at the aventual proouction of cataloguing data in Machine Readable Form, *i.e.* Mark (Machine-Read able Cataloguing) was established.

It was decided to produce weekly tapes and issued to cooperative libraries. The first tapes were issued in Oct. 1966. 16 libraries participated. This experimental project MARCI came to an end in 1968.

Brunt States about the seminar held at Laughborough, University of Technology, Sept. 76 which has brought together not only existing users of MARC but also those considering its introduction, and library school lecturers. The aim was to discuss the more recent developments in automated cataloguing and to chear of proposed developments. Papers were given on BLAISE, LOCAS (local cataloguing system) MARLIN, LASER. BLCMP (Hirmingham Libraries Cooperative Mechanisation Project) and its on-line derivative BOSS, the use of MARC and related systems in the book selling field, SWALCAP (South West Academic Libraries Cooperative Automation Project), and SCOLCAP (Scottish Libraries Cooperative Automation Project).

Nose deals mainly with the National Diet Library's treatment of foreign Publications. The system for books is based on the MARC tapes received from the library of congress. These are converted to NDL formate to provide output on cards or in list form. The system use 10 programmes and now contains more than 500,000 records. Scientific and technical literature is recorded in 'Monthly list of foreign Scientific and Technical Publications,' which 15 compiled be selecting records from the US government reports, announcements, and tape service.

Smirnows recommends that CLANN catalogues should be as compatible as possible and that the LANN data base should be fully acceptable by other networks. The main difficulty is in the differing cataloguing practices found in U.K. Library of Congress and Australian MARC records. CLANN should use LC subject Headings; difficulties with American terminology can be over come by means of 'see' references. He discusses problems raised by AACR rules 42 and 98-99, *i.e.* treatment of Psendonyms LC subject Headings; *i.e.* treatment of Pseudonymys and provision for entry of certain corporate bodies under place. Undy points out that an assential subject of facilities which a cooperating library should expect from a processing centre includes: access to all current and retrospective National MARC data base records, central control of additions, rationalisation of records in accordance with Australian practice, feedback and cost levelling devices.

UNIMARC, the Universal MARC format developed to facilitate the international exchange of bibliographic data in machine readable form, was published, with notes on the scope of the format and the international standards on which it is based, definitions, principles used in design and guidelines for use. The British Library plans to implement UNIMARC in 1980, as does the state library of South Africa, while NCL and the National Diet library are working toward complementation but have set no date.

XMARK, this system provides students with a simplified means of writing programmes for the automatic indexing of an experimental collection of MARC records. The indexes so created then become part of an on-line data base. XMARC also provides means for searching such a data base. They system therefore can serve as an aid to inventing and designing new MARC-based indexes and other bibliographic products and as an instructional aid in the design and use of on-line information services.

Ballots

BALLOTS opperates from Stanford University Centre for Information Processing and was begun in 1967. There are 120 users world wide; 26 share the system and the rest are search users only. The data base comprises 5 files. The MARC file is composed of library of Congress records dating from 1972 which are updated weekly. In Process File contains Bibliograpbic and occession records of material on order or in process. When a title is catalogued, it is deleted from this file and moved to the Catalogue Data File. The Reference File has the features 'see also' and explanatory/historical references. The Standing Search Request File enables a library cataloguing backlogs to institute a weekly search against the MARC file of updated entries.

In an effort to encourage uniform usage of MARC tags in the various bibliographic formats, LO and BALLOTS began jointly to build an on-line data base describing the U.S. MARC data elements used in LC MARC records. The data based represents an expansion of the BALLOTS Data Elements Dictionary maintained by BALLOTS in machine-readable, text editing form.

BALLOT. revised its pricing structure, decreasing shared cataloguing rates, offering special rebates for original cataloguing and increasing charges for searching witbout cataloguing. A California State Library cost/benefit study showed BALLOTS to be no more expensive than previously used systems and to be more effective in several aspects of service. Other developments at BOLLOTS included: *(1)* changes in its service hours to accommodate East Coast Users; *(2)* a new tape service, the Catalogue Data File Tape, which reflects for a shared-cataloguing library all of its cataloguing records as they exist in tbe BALLOTS data base; *(3)* a new terminal the ZMS.90; *(4)* Network File Design, a new project to restructure the data base to support all MARC records distributed by the Library of Congress, including authorities, serials, films etc.; and *(5)* the second videotape in the BALLOTS series, "A Librarian's view of IBALLOTS." Standford associate provost Edward E. Shaw was appointed interim director of BALLOTS, reflecting the "importance BALLOTS has to the University, and the University's commitment to guide the BALLOTS center to independent non-profit status. BALLOTS and the BCR entered into a contract for BALLOTS to serve more than twenty five clients of BCR, with four using BALLOTS as their primary system. The University of California chose OCLC to supply technical processing services for the libraries in its nine-campus system, while the eastern Research Libraries Group (RLC) chose BALLOTS.

Following the three-to-one vote for BALLOTS, Harward with draw from RLC, noting that its continued participation was not the most effective course for Harward or RLG. Harward library director Bryant explained that the "idiosyncratic nature of Harvard" was responsible for the difficulties experienced by that institution as it attempted to participate in RLG. Skipper expressed regret at Harvard's withdrawal but asserted that the insident did not "imply that complex research libraries can't cooperate." There was speculation on the effect that the BALLOTS choice would have upon the highly developed automation efforts of another RLG member, New York Public Library.

Micro Cataloguing

Com Cataloguing

Meyer states that based on the experience of the University of taxes at Dallas, Compares the Ohio College Library center's online system and Blackwell North America's B/NA Title Index on microfiche as sources of cataloguing copy. The Ohio College Library Center (OCLC) and Backwell North America (B/NA) have data bases used by many libraries to produce catalogue copy; OCLC is an online system, and the B/NA data base is accessible via a Computer Output-Microfiche Title Index. The experience of the University of Taxes at Dallas is used to compare the data bases for availability of cataloguing for English language books although OCLC provides cataloguing for a larger percentage of titles, the B/NA data base produces a high enough percentage of hits to be very valuable. The greater number of titles available through OCLC is attributable to the larger group of contributors, not necessarily to quality of the data base. The difference in cost between the 2 systems and the comparable-peripheral services available make utilisation of the B/NA data base appealing.

La Trobe University Library decided to evaluate the Title Index marketed by Blackwell North America (BMA Index) which contains all LC and Canadian MARC records as well as these input by BNA, to discover how cost effective use of the Index might be. The test involved searching a sample of order requests and books and collating the results. The Index is quicker to search and more effective than the NUC. A large number of British impints were not found. He discusses the effect if U.K. and AUSMARC records were contained in the Index and the value of these improvements for processing efficiency. This value has some components; savings from increased coverage of computerised cataloguing with MARC records. The Australian library community needs a comprehensive, sound index to the major existing Machine-readable bibliographic data bases.

Cataloguing on Microfiche

Indexing of microfiche can help to overcome 3 problems, finding the correct microfiche; finding its specific sections, and finding the exact location of the information required. Figures show: *(1)* a suggested array for microfiche titles to ensure standardisation; *(2)* an example of block letter identification between sections of a given report to ensure the microfiche is found; *(3)* a conventional micro-fiche grid index; *(4)* the layout of universal COM index. A decimal continuum is needed both in the vertical and horizontal direction applicable to any 105 mm x 148 mm fiche. In the com index a series of dots is inserted at mid-point to indicate the position of conventional 132 character columms under 42 x reduction.

Green provides examination of the Georgia Tech. Library remote access system LENDS provided an opportunity to study faculty attitude towards microforms and faculty use of microforms. He illustrates the methods and the findings in tables: *(1)* faculty responses to microform attitude statements; *(2)* the relationship between microform attitude and the frequency of microform use is not storing since the samples were constituted of 50 LENDS users and 50 LENDS non-users; *(3)* microform attitude is not related to subject area, teaching or research responsibility, but is to age; *(4)* microform use frequency is not strongly related to teaching or research responsibility but seems to be related to subject areas.

The need to use equipment for cataloguing inevitably slows down the cataloguer and often there is no introductory frame equivalent to a title page. Some U.S. libraries do not catalogue individual microforms when dealing with a set, *e.g.* a report set from NASA. The subject approach trends to be even less fatisfactory; analytical entries are often for author and title only. The important factor is the treatment of microforms for storage, since interfield material will probably receive the same treatment as the main collection where as separate runs of microforms often receive a running number. Decisions defend on the quality and type of material received and the user population.

Computerised Subject Indexing

Alley discusses Canadian on-line use, trends, implications and policies. They explores the Canadian use of online data bases through examining trends and attitudes, and finds confusion created by the public enterprise approach and the impact of competition. They discusses the implications for national information policy and suggests that there are three options, a government controlled system, or a mixed one, and that only the mixed, is feasible. Future decisions.

must consider the Canadian information industry, and databases International cooperation, the use of government subsidies and the balance of payments.

Conditions in Hungary make Online connections to international systems easy. It need not be expensive and technical difficulties can be overcome, On-line connections and the use of IAEA/INIS and ESA/SDS databases in Hungary is very useful for information retrieval.

The commencement of Euronet's operations will increase the number of on-line services from abroad available in Germany via network links in Frankfurt. German subject information systems are now in competition with those from abroad; the resulting wide range of products and methods can only prove beneficial to the consumer. In general American services are more advanced technically than German services, although some German retrieval systems are more sophisticated than their American counterparts. Germany has sometimes tended to develop products identical to those already on the international merit. Comparative studies of all available services should be made. Information marketing in Germany has been unsatisfactory until now due to insufficient broken services and a lack of data collections catering specifically for the German consumer. Detailed market analysis is required.

The start up of Euronet in 1979 eventually resulted in increased hourly charges to U.S. On-line users. This would arise from a drain-off of European business; access for Europeans to U. S. Data bases bas been made artificially expensive by the telecommunication charge established by the PTTS of the countries in the European. Economic Community. Since the major data bases on the Euronet system will be U.S. produced considers that concerted effort by U.S. data producers and users would assure competitive communication rates in Europe. Euronet is the SBC'S own on-line retrieval system which will link 29 data bases, and provide a document delivery service.

Potential use and social impact of viewdata systems—Viewdata is a convivial tool particularly in comparison with on-line bibliographic data bases. Viewdata should make information more readily available to more people, enabling more effective use of time and money. Secondary social impacts wilt include fragmentation of the culture and the encouragement of active pursuits.

The EDITOR facility on Blaise and the Blaise/Locas interface are now operations. Complete cataloguing operations can be processed on-line to the Blaise network. The average response time on BILISE is 1-8 seconds with the use of 218M 370/158's. New MARC format data bases planned are; ISDS Serials databases; EMMA cataloguing from the SRL, and non-copyright language material acquired by the Department of Printed Books. A further source of cataloguing records in the EMMA cataloguing produced by subscribers to Locas, presently stored off line, which lacks a uniformly regulated input standard. An online interlending service is now possible by an interface between tbe Blaise network and BLLD. A customer support team of 16 liaises between BLAISE HO and customer libraries. The original idea of making available weekly BNB issues on Viewdata was dropped in favour of a select list of references on topical subjects.

The ARDIS.EC information retrieval system—It was conceived for application with computers produced in the COMECON countries, the productivity of information searches was improved considerably. But there arises problems connected with the application of DUC as the index language for the automated processing of information. In the majority of cases UDC is applicable, in some cases it has to be combined with samples taken from natural language. A polythematic thesaurus is at present not available in Ozechoslovakia.

On-Line Cataloguing

A mere few years ago the Paris Principles. entry forms, authority files, and cataloguing rules were things with which only cataloguers were much concerned. These terms and many others related to cataloguing have become more commonly used by all kinds of librarians. Time has changed, and cataloguing has come out of the closet.

OCLC raised our collective consciousness. Although there were other significant developments in the use of computers for processing and displaying bibliographic records before the emergence of OCLC. It was OCLC that spread the advantages of shared cataloguing throughout the country and made librarians more conscious of descriptive cataloguing rules and standards.

Formerly, many libraries with relatively small catalogues did not have a requirement for through and accurate bibliographic descriptions—a requirement that is strongly felt by libraries with large catalogues unusual collections, and/or demanding clientele. These more stringent requirements were forced into all member libraries of OCLC, who are in fact contributing their cataloguing to a much larger file.

Other more recent development have caused attention to be focused on the authority control aspect of descriptive catalogue. among these developments are the prodigious growth of the OCLC file, the implementation of shared bibiiographic files that are under authority control, the plan of the library of Congress to change a substantial number of its established entry heading forms, the prospect of totally replacing card catalogs with on-line catalogues, and the prospect of some kind of national computer based authority file system.

It is important in a discussion of library cataloguing to distinguish among the various components of a cataloguing record. Though cataloguing data can be grouped and categorized in various ways, for this discussion the followmg components should be distinguished:

1. Basic bibliographic description.
   - (a) Title through series statement traditional catalog card.
   - (b) Notes.
2. Access headings.
   - (a) Names.
   - (b) Titles as they appear on the item.
   - (c) Uniform titles.

(d) Topical subject terms.

(e) Classification and call numbers.

Recitation of the Paris Principles, followed by an exegesis thereon, has become de rigueur in exposition on cataloguing. Nevertheless the ritual does serve a purpose. The Paris Principles state that "the catalogue should be an efficient instrument for ascertaining whether the library contains a particular book, which works by a particular author and which editions of a particular work are in the library." There are two kinds of access specified in these principles. One is the finding function, or the location function the catalogue should serve as a location tool for an item known to the user before he or she approaches the catalogue. The user wants to ascertain whether or not the item is in the collection, and if it is, how it can be obtained.

The second kind of access is usually called bibliographic access. The catalogue should serve as a tool for identifying in a library collection all the works of a particular author and all the versions of a particular work. To provide this bibliographic access, consistent forms of entry headings are used. To link together the various versions of a work, a uniform form of its title is established, and all the versions are brought together under this title. In this way, translations are usually grouped under the title in the original language. To link an author's works, a unique form of name for each author is established, and this name heading is used for all the author's works in the catalogue. In additions to identifying other versions of a work and other works by the same author, library catalogues also identify groups of items that are related in other ways: other works in the same series or multivolume set, or works that are related to an item as supplements, appendices, indices, concordances, etc.

Providing a unique description of a bibliographic item is a relatively straight forward task. The more complex part is a identification of relationships among items and linking the basic bibliographic descriptions to one another. This activity can not be automated. Because of the variations in ways of rendering the same names and titles, a human being must perceive the relationships and establish the links. Descriptive cataloguing is partially a process of building bibliographies of authors' work-accurately attributing authorship and compiling the records related to a particular author, never mixing the works of what are actually separate authors and never separating the works of an author under more than one form of name. Uniformately, forms of names and titles are not static. Established headings and references must be modified as new knowledge is gained about relationships and about identities of people and corporate bodies.

Ideally, with the addition of each item to a catalogue, necessary research would be conducted to identify relationships of the item to other items already in the catalogue and to provide references from variant forms of names and titles. Since most libraries can not afford such thorough research and do not have the highly specialized staff to do it, they rely on the wor k done by the library of Congress and try to use heading forms that are used by LC. Of course: as most cataloguers know, followiug LC and keeping up with their changes is not always a straight forward matter.

Even if they do not authority work locally, libraries that use Library of Congress catalogue a large position of their collections will have an implicit authority structure—a little rough around the edges perhaps, but still. The library of Congress has one of the largest collections and one of the best maintained authority control structures in the world. Using LC records assures a modium of consistency in a local catalogue.

This vision has been imagined since the 1960s when computers were first applied to library processing. It seems we are almost there. Systems very close to this ideal have already been developed. Commercial vendors of circulation systems are adding into on-line catalogues. The questions of the necessity of authority control in on line catalogues for individual libraries may be passes. There are complications, however, related to automated authority control in shared bibliographic files. To extend the above description of the on-line catalogues, imagine that the library is a member of a group of libraries, sharing an on line catalogues. The user at a terminal could begin with a search restricted to records of the local institution, and then extend the search to other collections perhaps regional then national. It is in this extended search capability that technical and administrative problems relating to authority control arise.

The problems are minimised if the sharing libraries agree to follow one set of authorised headings, and are almost eliminated if the cataloguing is done by a central cataloguing agency. If, however, cataloguing is performed by multiple independent units, it is difficult to maintain the authority structure, Although on line access to a shared common authority file and to the related bibliographic records makes such an arrangement possible, there remains a requirement for some sort of bIbliographic governing and editorial board to monitor quality. Cataloguers in such a system must identify relationships among bibliographic items and provide connecting. links even when items are not held in a cataloguer's local collection. It is instructive to note that the library of Congress is maintaining editorial control over headings being established and entered into its authority file by other libraries as part of an experimental project in sharing the maintenance of an authority file. Another approach to a charod on-line catalogue is a system that allows for multiple sets of authority files and differences. In choice of heading forms. Though this approach may in some ways ease the burdens of administration and coordination, it seems to preclude bibliographic searches of the total catalogue that is, searches for all the works of a single author, all the versions of a particular work, etc. If heading forms are not consistent from collection to collection, or if related records have not been identified in some way, there is no way that records from the various collections can be combined in a single coherent display, and one might argue that there is no need for such a capability.

On-line union list file for periodicals currently being developed by Pittsburb Univusity and other libraries in the Pittsburgh Regional Library Centre (PRLC). The file is part of the OCLC on-line data base. Regular production of printed lists of holdings for each library was required and encouraged on-line development. Work with serials in the on-line system has been in progress since November 1974.

Freedman explains the distinction between the act of cataloguing and the products which is created and through which it is expressed and than concentrates on the automation of the cataloguing process rather than providing merely a review of different systems and products. These are computer printed catalogue cards, COM catalogues, searching capabilities. The operation of the CCLC and a different automated bibliographic control system, the Washington Library Network incorporates the quadraplanar data structure originated by the University of Chicago and the New York Public Library's long-term plan for on-line authority control, as well as the sophisticated search techniques built into the BALLOTS system.

BALLOTS is an integrated on-line technical processing system designed to handle all types of library material except manucripts. The prototype system has operated since 1969. A major guiding principle was to define system requirements in advance; a System Book fully describes all functional aspects of the system. The BALLOTS effect in 7 major areas: acceptance testing; training; supervision; organization and management; staff morale and attitude; employment; concenas about the future of the card catalogue.

In a meeting held to discuss the design of BIBDATA, the Australian on-line cataloguing system proposed by the National library of Australia. The discussions were made on the issues regional participation: the use of the OCLC as an alternative of BIBDATA; Costs; standards and quality control. The meeting unanimously adopted a motion supporting the general aims of BIBDATA. The meeting decided the aims of BIBDATA *(1)* to reduce the rate of increase in the cost of cataloguing and increase the ability of libraries to respond to readers; *(2)* to provide the means for the development of efficient resource sharing by Australian libraries.

In a paper presented at the Library Association of Australia 'Cataloguers' Section's national seminar '1876 and all that' held at Medlow Bath, Sept. 1976. Love describes the differences between shared cataloguing and centralised cataloguing and between access by batch systems/or on-line. Considers what is most appropriate for Australia, starting with what the very basic Australian MARC Record Service Officers, a national part of the longterm operation. The national system as proposed envisages a central data base with centralised processing in the early stages, but with provision for user owned and operated computers to be attached. It is proposed that the system provides access to a data base of records prepared by several national agencies as well as local input. He discusses the effect on user procedures and the maintenance of authority files.

Joint Annual Conference of the Aslib Midlands Branch and Northern Branch, Llandudno, 4th-6th May 1978. discussed BLAISE. It came into existance in April 1977 when the MEDLARS databases were mounted on an IBM 370 series computer which made files available without the need for a transatlantic link. The MARC files were added in Oct 1977. The files now available on' BLAISE, TOXLINE, CHEMLINE and the MARC files. Other BLAISE users besides information retrievel are discussed: reader services; acquisitions; inter-library loans. The use of MARC tapes may also be extended to allow for automated circulation systems within local systems. Details of how to subscribe to BLAISE and the cost as well as plans for future development are provided.

Current cataloguing networks, such as ODLC as and UNICAV (Ontario University's Union Cataloguing system) do not, as hoped for, offer the user substantial cost raductions. On-line cooperative system of automation cataloguing UNICAT/TELECAT is now its 7th year of operation. It has 17 users including university, government and public libraries. The objectives of this plan are to dovelop this into a local system of library management. IBIS, a software package based on the concept of an integrated system to cover all library activities. The requirements established for IBIS are as under. SAFRIS aims to provide an on-line cataloguing and information retrieval system for books and non-book material using computers and microforms. Its main purpose is to save time otherwise spent in cataloguing by teacher-librarians. Activities open to automation include: catalogue processing; preparation of cataloguing; current awareness service; assistance with acquisition; circulation control. Adoption of MARC has been recommended. By the end of 1977 the School Libraries Branch Master Catalogue was used on computer complete with subject, series and publisher authority files. The catalogue then appeared annually on microfiche. Non-book material is to be brought into the scheme.

On-line acquisition and cataloguing are now fully operational in the London-on Borough of Button and COM cassetted microfilm catalogues are availablcp for public use, with a switch to COM fiche under way. Originally 3 categories of record comprised the main bibliographic file: on under, catalogue: potential requirements. (PER); each record being on fixed field, with 277 characters in upper case. The PRF records have recently been deleted in order to make the file more manageable. Each record field is discussed. MARC records are no longer taken and all acquisitions are catalogued locally. The main routes for on-line enquiry to the system, each of which are described are. *(1)* by title number, *(2)* by accession number, *(3)* by Author query. The system has resulted in a greatly improved service to readers. Once the two on-line systems currently operated by the library service are integrated, it is hoped to extend the enquiries to title and subject searches.

KINDS OF ENTRIES

A LIBRARY CATALOGUE is a record of the holdings of a library. In order to meet the requirements of users, it is prepared to consist of various unit records. These unit records are called entries. Each entry is designed for satisfying a particular approach of a user. In this chapter we shall describe the various kinds of entries recognized by AACR and CCC.

AACR

AACR is a code meant for a dictionary catalogue. The dictionary catalogue is "a catalogue in which all the entries (author, title, subject, series etc.) and their related references are arranged together in one general alphabet. Subarrangement frequently varies". Thus, in a dictionary catalogue, all the entries and concerned references are arranged in a single file.

AACR recognizes the following kinds of entries in a dictionary catalogue:

Main entry

Added entries

Besides main entry and added entries, AACR also recognizes references or cross references.

Main Entry

AACR regards the main entry as "the complete catalog record of a bibliographical entity presented in the form by which the entity is to be uniformly identified and cited. The main entry normally includes the tracing of all other headings under which the record is to be represented in the catalog". The main entry is the basic entry. Each document gets one main entry. It is usually an author entry, with sometimes title occupying heading of a main entry. The last section contains the tracings, which indicate headings under which added entries have been prepared for a given document.

SAMPLE MAIN ENTRY

E198

N59 Gaudefroy-Demombynes, Maurice, 1928-1968.

Noxious gases. Rev. ed.2. New York, Reinhold, 1959.

5427 x, 415p. 18cm. (American Chemical Society. Scientific monograph series, 7)

1. Gases, asphyxiating and poisonous.

2. Nitrogen gas. I Title. (Series)

Unit-Card

A unit card is, "a basic catalogue card, in the form of a main entry, which when duplicated may be used as a unit for all other entries for that work in the catalogue by the addition of the appropriate headings". A unit card provides us a very simple way of preparing added entries of various kinds. Sample entries given in the next section are based on the unit card system. However, printed and mimeographed cards are more suited for unit cards. It is considered economical to have brief added entries when cards are handwritten or typed. The examples of such entries prepared according to CCC are given in section 2 and 3.

There are obvious advantages in using a unit card. Each added entry will provide adequate information to a user. It will be easier for a cataloguer to give directions for the preparation of added entries. Printing or mimeographing of the added entries will become mechanical, which will make it easy to obtain; multiple copies. This will make it possible to go for cooperative; and centralized cataloguing. The examples of added entries prepared according to unit card are to be found in the next section.

Added Entries

An added entry is "an entry, additional to the main entry, under which a bibliographical entity is represented in a catalogue". The additional entries supplement the main entry by providing an additional approach to documents listed in the catalogue. Sometimes, added entries are called secondary entrie's. These have their own importance. These are prepared for subordinate authors like joint authors, editors, translators, and illustrators. These are also prepared for title, series, and subject. However, a reference is prepared for editor of a series. AACR has provided rules for their preparation. Sample added entries based on unit card practice are given below:

SAMPLE ADDED ENTRIES

B6:7 Kelly, Paul J joint author.

J3 Busemann, Herbert

Projective geometry and project metrics, by Herbert Busemann and Paul J. Kelly. New York,

798 Academic Press, 1953.

viii, 332p. 2lcm.

I. Geometry. I. Kelly, Paul J joint author.

II. Title.

Noxious gases.

Gaudefroy-Demombynes, Maurice, 1928-1968.

(Rest as in the main entry)

American Chemical Society.

Scientific monograph series.

Gaudefroy-Demombynes, Maurice, 1928-1968

(Rest as in the main entry)

GASES. ASPHYXIATING AND POISONOUS.

Gaudefroy-Demombynes, Maurice, 1928-1968.

(Rest as in the main entry)

NITROGEN GAS, p. 50-60.

Gaudefroy-Demombynes, Maurice, 1928-1968.

(Rest as in the main entry)

References

Reference is "a direction from one heading or entry to another". A see reference directs the user from the name of a person or of a corporate body or the title of a work or subject or name of series under which the user might be reasonably expected to look, to the form that has been chosen by the cataloguer as a heading or as uniform title. A see also reference directs the user from one heading to a related heading. Refcrences play a very important role in the success of a dictionary catalogue. AACR has given detailed rules for the preparation of references (except subject references). Sears list of subject headings provides directions with regard to subject references.

SAMILE REFERENCES

McGregor, John P ed.

see American Chemical Society.

Scientific monograph series.

Libra

see Ranganathan, S R

U.S. State Dept.

see U.S. Dept. of State.

Persia

see Iran.

ASPHYXIATING AND POISONOUS GASES.

see GASES, ASPHYXIATING AND

POISONOUS.

Paris Peace Conference, 1919

see also Treaty of Versailles, 1919.

LIBRARY CATALOGS

see also CATALOGS, CLASSIFIED.

Ccc

A classified catalogue is one in "which some entries are number entries and some are word entries". Thus it consists of two parts, namely, the classified part and the alphabetical part.

CCC recognizes the following kinds of entries in catalogue:

Main entry
Book index entry
Class index entry
Cross reference entry
Cross reference index entry

Classified Part

The main entry and cross reference entry are number entries. Therefore, these form part of the classified part.

Main Entry

The main entry is a basic record for a given document. It is a specific entry, which provides maximum information about the document. Each document gets one main entry: The tracing of the entry given at its back, indicates which other entries have been prepared.

SAMPLE MAIN ENTRY

E198 N59

GAUDEFROY-DEMOMBYNES (Maurice) (1928).

Noxious gases. Rev ed.2.

(American Chemical Society,

scientific monograph series. Ed. by

John P McGregor. 7).

5427

SAMPLE FOR TRACING OF MAIN ENTRY

50 P50-60 Gas, Chemistry.

Nitrogen, Chemistry.

Chemistry.

Gaudefroy-Demombynes
(Maurice) (1928).
Noxious gases.
American Chemical
Society, scientific
monograph series.
Demombynes (Maurice Gaudefroy-) (1928).
McGregor (John F), Ed.

Cross Reference Entry

It is a number entry which is entered under one of the classes other than its dominant focus or class. The class number given in the leading section also contributes to class index entries.

SAMPLE CROSS REFERENCE ENTRY

E150

See also
E198- NS9
Gaudefroy- Demombynes.
Noxious gases. P 50-60.

Alphabetical Part

Book index entry, class index entry, and cross reference index entry are word entries. Therefore, these are included in the alphabetical part.

Book Index Entry

Book index entries are provided under author(s), collaborator(s), title and series of a document. The number of entries to be included varies. These are specific added entries which satisfy the approach of the users through author(s), collaborator(s), title and series.

SAMPLE BOOK INDEX ENTRIES

GAUDEFROY-DEMOMBYNES (Maurice) (1928).

Noxious gases. Rev. ed.2. E198 N59

NOXIOUS GASES.

By Gaudefroy-Demombynes. Rev. ed.2.

EI98 N59

AMERICAN CHEMICAL SOCIETY, SCIENTIFIC

MONOGRAPH SERIES.

7 Gaudefroy-Demombynes: Noxious

gases. Rev.ed.2. EI98 N59

Glass Index Entry

Class index entries are provided under subject headings derived through chain procedure from the class number in the main entry or cross reference entry. These satisfy the subject approach of the users.

With the help of rules for chain procedure, out of class numbers El98 and E150, we may derive the following class index entries for the sought headings:

SAMPLE CLASS INDEX ENTRIES

CHEMISTRY.

For books in this Class and its Subdivisions see the Classified Part of the Catalogue under the Class Number

E

GAS, CHEMISTRY.

For books in this Class and its Subdivisions see the Classified Part of the Catalogue under the Class Number

E198

NITROGEN, CHEMISTRY.

For books in this Class and its Subdivisions see the Classified Part of the Catalogue under the Class Number

E 150

Cross Reference Index Entry

Cross reference index entries are prepared under headings which have not been already covered by any of the earlier class index entries and book index entries. These are prepared under headings which are likely to be referred from by the users. Referred from headings refer him to referred to headings, which further lead him to bibliographical entries.

SAMPLE CROSS REFERENCE INDEX ENTRIES

DEMOMBYNES (Maurice Gaudefroy-) (1928).

See

GAUDEFROY-DEMOMBYNES (Maurice) (1928).

McGREGOR (John P), Ed.

See

AMERICAN CHEMICAL SOCIETY

SCIENTIFIC MONOGRAPH SERIES.

ANALYTTCAL ENTTTRES

An analytical entry is an entry of a part (like articles in periodicals, contributions to conference proceedings and collections, etc.) of a document referring to the document which contains it. In other words, an analytical entry is "an entry for a work or part of a work that is contained in a collection, series, issue of a serial, or other bibliographical unit for which another, comprehensive entry has been made. Analytical entries may be either separate, self-contained entries or added entries that are part of the cataloging of the larger work."

There are three kinds of analytical entries, namely, author analytical, title analytical, and subject analytical. The sample entries are given below:

SAMPLE MAIN ENTRY (AACR)

2

p7N53 Chandrasekharan, K ed.

Library science in India.

Madras, Madras Library Association,

5962 1953.

xii, 203p. 18cm. (Madras

Library Association, publication series, 21)

1. Library science 2. Libraries

U.S.I. Fitzgerald, William A American.

II. Title. III. Title: American librarianship.

(Series)

SAMPLE AUTHOR ANALYTICAL (AACR)

Fitzgerald, William A

American librarianship, p7-13:

Chandrasekharan, K, ed.

Library science in India. (Rest as

in the main entry).

SAMPLE TITLE ANALYTICAL (AACR)

American librarianship, p7-23:

Fitzgerald, William A

Chandrasekharan, K ed.

Library science in India. (Rest as
in the main entry).

SAMPLE SUBJECT ANALYTICAL (AACR)

LIBRARIES-U.S.

Fitzgerald, William A p7-138:
Chandrasekharan, K ed.

Library science in India. (Rest as
in the main entry).

SAMPLE MAIN ENTRY (CCC)

2 p7N53

CHANDRASEKHARAN (K), Ed.

Library science in India.

(Madras Library Association,
publication series. 21).

5962

SAMPLE AUTHOR ANALYTICAL (CCC)

FITZGERALD (William A).

American librarianship.

Forming part of

Chandrasekharan, Ed. Library
science in India. 2 p7N53

SAMPLE TITLE ANALYTICAL (CCC)

AMERICAN LIBRARIANSHIP

By fitzgerald.

Forming part of

Chandrasekharan, Ed. Library

Science in India. 2 p7N53

SAMPLE SUBJECT ANALYTICAL (CCC)

2.73

See also

2 p7N53

Chandrasekharan, Ed.

Library science in India, P7-13.

By preparing analytical entries, the subjects, authors, titles of the part of whole document analyzed are brought to the attention of the users, which otherwise would not have been noticed by the users of the catalogue. These also satisfy the laws of library science.

The number of analytical entries depends upon their need and usefulness to the users. The smaller the resources of a library, the greater their need and importance.

Some of the cases, in which analytical entries are prepared are given below:

(a) Author and title analyticals are made in the case of composite books. Subject analyticals are prepared for multifocal books (*i.e.* for those parts of books in which the subject dealt with is other than the subject of the book taken as a whole), especially when the library does not possess a book on the subject covered in the part.

(b) Sometimes a part of a document may contain original, or controversial, or new information which may be important as well as of sufficient length. In such cases subject analyticals should be prepared.

(c) If the biography of a person is published as the chapter of a book and it may be the only available biographical account on the person, then it is considered useful to prepare a subject analytical. The same would be the case if the given part of a work represents the only copy of an essay, play, poem or the only material on a given subject.

(d) If a document provides a good bibliography on a topic, then by means of a subject analytical we can indicate to the user about the existence of such a bibliography.

(e) Analytical entries can also be used to point out to the reader the existence of an extra copy of popular material, which may also be available in the library as a separate work.

There is no doubt that analytical entries serve a useful purpose. However, these increase the bulk of a catalogue, making its use more difficult. Therefore, weeding of these entries from time to time is suggested.

Ultimately, the requirements of users, availability of personnel, and existence of printed guides decides the question of preparation of analytical entries. It is thought that printed guides can be helpful, provided these appear in time. However, it is doubtful whether these guides can be very helpful. This is because these have limitations of their own and cannot meet the special requirement of different kinds of libraries.

❐

5

Cataloguing Technologies

A common attitude to the mechanization of library technical services is that the machine can be used to accomplish many of our current practices more quickly. In my opinion this approach is incorrect, and the use of computers to speed up and of perpetuate outdated systems is a perversion of technology. The best use of mechanization will be founded on a complete reconsideration of all of our systems, an examination of what we are doing and why we are doing it. If this process leads to radical change, so be it. If it means the abandonment of cherished ideas of the past, then let us abandon those idea. We must emphasize that this does not mean a supine acceptance of temporary technical and financial limitations of the present stage of automation. In this country it is scarcely necessary to point out that what human beings can imagine, human beings can do.

We should think of the eventual possibilities of machine systems and what they can achieve, and not be diverted by short-or medium-term problems. First, let us took at the physical nature of the end product of our work: the catalogue. Too often the prevalent attitude towards the physical form of the catalogue is that expressed by a student of mine in an essay which began of "As well as normal catalogues there are book and microfilm catalogues." We will divide these forms into what we call the old forms (that is, the card and the book catalogues) and the new forms (that is, the microform catalogue produced from machine-readable records and the on-line computer catalogue). If we contrast these two categories, certain qualitative and quantitative differences become apparent.

The old forms are either unique (that is, located in one place) or, in the case of the book catalogue, expensive to duplicate and heavy to transport. The new forms can be made available in many places, both inside and outside the library. The old forms are perpetually and inescapably out of date. The new forms are capable of speedy updating and near complete currency. The old forms are inflexible in that they allow limited and highly structure access to information. The new forms, either because of their nature (as with the on-line computer catalogue) or because of the cheapness of the material on which they are produced (as with microform catalogues) allow the possibility of many more points of access to information. The old forms arise out of previous technologies, and have the restrictions and limitations of those technologies. The new forms arise out of our current and emerging technologies, and do not suffer from those restrictions and limitations. These changes in the pnysical form of the catalogue have implications which go far beyond changes in form or even in improvements in speed and convenience to the catalogue user. They should be seen as changing the nature of what we are doing, or, at least, as forcing a reconsideration of our cataloguing practices. To take an obvious example, in a new catalogue how does our old friend the main entry fare? As with all emerging technologies, the computerization of catalogue records has had to develop both technically and conceptually. It has had to go through various stages, each of which is both a prerequisite of, and paradoxically a hindrance to, the next stage. It is only now, after 15 years, that we can see the shape of computer records of the future.

The developed catalogue record that is emerging is multilayered and multidimensional. It uses computer technology to achieve far more than the mere mechanization of catalogue entry production. To take a fairly simple example, we can imagine a user who is searching for information about a particular edition of Dante's Divine Comedy. The user can approach the system by mane, by title, by subject, etc. In this instance, let us imagine that the approach is by one of the forms of name by which Dante is identified-ALIGHIERI. This name would give access to the package of information relating to Dante. This package will include two important pieces of information First, that the standard form of citation for Dante is DANTE ALIGHIERI. Second, that name is linked with a number of works, among which is one sometimes identified as the DIVINE COMEDY.

The work package contains the information that the standard title for the work is DIVINA COMMEDIA. It also contains links with packages describing particular manifestations of the work. The user would then be presented, on a screen or in a print-out, with the information about the standard citations of the work and descriptions of those editions which were English translations entitled the DIVINE COMEDY. This process of assembling and presenting information is done automatically within the machine system by programme and it is done extremely quickly. The user is only aware of the way in which the assembled information is presented to him or her. The example I have used is extremely simple. Other packages relating to the work and its manifestations are also present in the system. For example, there will be links to individual parts of the DIVINE COMEDY (INFERNO, PURGATORIO, etc.); to series in which items have been issued; and to the subjects, names, and titles of the work, its parts, and of the series. We do not wish to discuss the mechanisms by which this developed record works, but to concentrate on it conceptually.

Because of the way in which the developed record is structured, it is possible to approach information from any level, and by way of any access point within one of those packages. For example, if a series package is associated with subject package, information relating to that series will be retrieved in a subject search. It is here that the multi-dimensionality of the developed machine system lies. We embarked on this somewhat lengthy description of a system with a question about the main entry. In fact, we believe that the idea of the main entry as a particular physical entity in the catalogue arose out of our previous technologies. What remains of the main entry idea of the main entry idea is the fact that the developed machine system, if it is to be capable of carrying out all its functions, allows for, and indeed demands, an indication of the standard manner of citing the name of each person and each body and the title of each work. In the example, there is a standard citation for Dante and a standard citation for the Divine Comedy.

As the link between them will contain an indication of their relationship (in this case, that of primary responsibility or authorship), the standard citation for the work emerges as DANTE ALIGHIERI. DIVINA COMMEDIA. The enables the machine system to fulfill all the remaining useful purposes of the main-entry idea. Individual items can, however, be equally accessed by any variant forms of that name or of that title. What has happened is that we have been released from the tyranny of the idea that there is only one place in which full information is to be found, and that there is only one way in which an item should be approached. We are left with the concept of standard citation.

The likely contents of two of the packages of information are: *(1)* a name package and *(2)* a work package. The replacement of the main-entry idea by that of a standard citation can readily be seen. In the name package there is a place for the preferred form of the name. In the work package there is a place for the preferred form of the title. Each package will contain links which not only connect one package to another but also define precisely the nature of the relationship between them. It is evident that the work of the cataloguer in preparing these packages is very different from the work involved in preparing conventional catalogue entries. A complete aggregation of related information is presented, rather simplistically, as a set of building blocks. Using this analogy, the task of the cataloguer can be seen as that of constructing new building blocks and fitting them into an existing structure. These new modules will be standard descriptions of items newly acquired, new subject packages, new name packages, and new work packages. Once these are created, the cataloguer must perceive the links between new and existing packages, and build them into the system. Familiar injunctions such as "Enter under..." seem to have been lost. In fact, in many applications the choice of main entry (or standard citation) is unimportant. A standard description will be accessible by a number of characteristics, each of which has equal validity. As far as the user is concerned, all access points are main access 'points because they all provide an equal amount of information. In other applications the choice of standard forms is very important, so this task remains when constructing multipurpose records. The multidimensional nature of the developed machine record.

The user can approach information either horizontally, that is, at one level containing subject name, and descriptive information; or vertically, that is, by category of information irrespective of level. The catalogue no longer has to concentrate on one level of information to the complete or partial exclusion of all others. We have seen that the work of the cataloguer is different in that such work demands as must, if not more, professionalism and commitment to standardization as before. There is one more, professionalism and commitment to standardization as before. There is one further important difference between such work and conventional cataloguing; this lies in the fact that the element of repetition that our present system demands is all but eliminated.

Once a package of information is established and its links to other packages are made, it remains as the package for that name, subject, item, etc., and subsequent work connected with the same data consists simply of citing the control number for that package in the appropriate field. Thus the machine system can be used to eliminate busy work and to leave the cataloguer with the task of establishing new information in a standard manner, that is, the truly professional task. To return briefly to the quotation from Morris, we believe that this aspect of technological change goes a long way towards the realization of the ideal of "useful" work. Another change that technology can bring to cataloguing is the possibility of resolving what have hitherto been considered irreconcilable problems. Take, for example, Russian names. No one has yet come up with a satisfactory solution to the problem of whether one should use a romanised form of name or the popular English form of name. Another instance is the difference between the English and North American practices in adding dates to personal names.

An other instance is that of the choice between pseudonyms and real names of persons. Other instances of unresolved or partially resolved conflicts of this type abound in our precomputer cataloguing codes. Using a developed machine-readable record these problems can be resolved. First, the question of whether one uses the systematic popular form of name for a Russian: In the developed machine system, each of these forms will be present, and each will be accompanied by an indication of the type of name. A particular printed catalogue using that record could select, by programme, the form which is preferred for that catalogue. Even within one library one could use the systematic form for a general catalogue and the popular form for a reading list. The other example, that of dates added to personal names, is resolved by the fact that, in the name package is created (or subsequently) and remain in the package only to be printed when conflict occurs. In that way, the irreconcilable problem in our premachine systems—the necessity to record dates and use then or not to record them at all is overcome. They are recorded in all instances, but only used in instances where they are relevant and necessary. Again we see that the impact of technology is to alter the cataloguing task and to alter the nature of the decisions that the cataloguers have to make.

An impact of computer technology which has already occurred is the system atization of the description of library materials. This was brought about by the introduction of International Standard Bibliographic Description (ISBD). We do not wish to discuss the merits or demerits of this particular way of systematizing description, but to make some deductions from its occurrence. The ISBD has been through a lengthy process of development. It will be seen that the second edition of AACR contains complete scheme for the description of library materials based on ISBD.

A fundamental aspect of ISBD is that the description is formalized in two ways. First, in the standard order in which the elements of the description are presented. Second, in the formalized punctuation that is used to separate one element of the description from another. This formalization was intended to have two purposes. The first was to enable the automatic translation of human-readable data into machine-readable data. Fairly simple programmes can be used to recognize the various elements of the description. The second, and to my mind, much more important, purpose was to aid the human comprehension of descriptive data. Here we can see the interaction of machine systems and cataloguing standards. The desire to make information more understandable to the user meets the necessity in the machine system for pieces of information (in this case elements of descriptive data) to be clearly delimited. Some people have said that this implies some kind of sacrifice of standards and the imposition of alien conventions on cataloguing. Both of these assertions as it seems to me that the systemization arises from an increased desire to communicate and from an enhanced understanding of the interaction of cataloguing and machine and human readable systems. This interaction is entirely desirable and furnishes a good example of the sort of cooperation and growth that should take place in the future. English speaking cataloguing community. No such universal system exists for the formulation of headings and uniform titles, though there has been much discussion of the possibilities of such a system.

The most important reasons are that the differences between different codes are far greater as far as access points are concerned than they were as far as description was concerned; and the fact that the question of the choice and form of headings is perceived to be far more important in its implications than the question of description. Arrived at a point where many of the differences regarding access points are either resolved or on the point of resolution because of the introduction of machine systems. In a developed machine system a name package can carry a number of preferred forms of name, each of which is accompanied by an indication of the environment in which it is preferred. For example, the name package for the government of the U.S.A. can include the forms United States, Etats-Unis, and Estados Unidos with an indication that these are the preferred forms in an English language, French language, and Spanish language environment, respectively. Thus the machine can be used to resolve a fundamental problem in international standardization. There still remain certain problems that cannot be resolved by the manipulation of name packages. One problem which is representative of these is the question of standard entry element for persons with family names that include a prefix. Some codes enter all such names under the part following the prefix, others (as in the case of AACR) base the decision on the language of the person bearing the name, and others base the decision on the nationality of the person. There are two ways to solve this problem. We can either aim at complete international agreement on entry elements or we can use the computer to arrive at a solution acceptable to all. This second solution presupposes that there is no one way to .enter such a name.

The cataloguer's task is to recognize and code each element of the name, and to add other necessary indications. Programmes can then be used to cite the name in the form appropriate to a particular output. If we take the example of the name VINCENT VAN GOGH, we find that it consists of three elements: a forename VINCENT, a prefix VAN, and a main element of surname GOGH. The cataloguer would add codes to each of these and an indication of the language of the person, the nationality, etc. An AACR programme would use the indication that the person's language was Dutch to assemble the name for printing in the form GOGH, VINCENT VAN. Other systems would use different programmes to achieve different results.

The implication of all this is that we no longer need an international code of cataloguing rules, whether based on the Paris Principles or not, because of the introduction of machine systems. We no longer need a single of options, in a standard and controlled manner, and permits these options to be selected by programme depending on the purpose for which a particular record is used. To return to a prevailing theme of this chapter the impact of technology on the work of the cataloguer the cataloguer is then entrusted with the task of analysing data and ensuring that alternative treatments are possible. He or she is no longer required to decide on one solution, and is therefore no longer presented with the kind of invidious choice that our present rules demand. Our last instance of the changes being brought about by technology is that which is commonly, though inaccurately, known as alphabetical filing. Library Filing Rules Committee, are much simpler than their predecessors. This simplicity depends, to a great extent, on a principle which states that one should file a character as it is and not as if it were something else. For example, the number 3 occurring in a title is filed as a number, in with other numbers, and in an order dictated by its numerical significance. One does not file it as if it were t-h-r-e-e or d-r-e-i or t-r-o-i-s. This change has resulted from a reconsideration of all our filing practices which itself resulted from the use of the computer in filing. This does not mean that it would be impossible to file 3 as if it were a word, in fact such a thing is perfectly simple. What it does mean is that the use of the computer in filing has made it necessary to look at our filing practices and to ask ourselves why we file one thing as if it were something else.

Most of us have come to is that such a practice may have had some validity in the past but has no validity now. It now seems a manifest absurdity to say that if this elephant were an orange, it would file in such-and-such a place. This is an illogical premise upon which to base an agreement. An elephant is not an orange, it belongs with the elephants and not with the oranges. Why, again, have we chosen to file names beginning with Mc as if they began with Mac? The answer is that they (almost) sound the same. Why base an aberration in arrangement on sound? These are awkward questions which the process of mechanizing filing poses. We do not wish to argue for one filing arrangement or another, though we do believe that the simpler the arrangement and the fewer the rules, the more chance users have of finding information speedily. We wish merely to point out that the reconsideration of filing practice which was necessitated by the introduction of computer filing has been a healthy and fruitful process. It has made us examine every aspect of the process, to stop doing things out of habit, to retain those principles which are logical and comprehensible and to discard those which are simply the accretions of the years. Technology can bring three important benefits. The first of these is an improvement of the efficiency of our service to library users; for example, the user of a developed machine system can approach information at many levels and from many access points.

The second benefit is that we are able to use our limited resources more sensibly; for instance, using a machine to arrange entries is more efficient and more cost-effective than using people to carry out that task, also the elimination of redundant and repetitive work of all kinds is something that tends towards efficiency and cost-effectiveness. The third benefit is the improvement of the nature of the work of those engaged in cataloguing and other technical services.

Any composite may be metaphorically separated into its component parts by the use of surrogates in the cataloguing while the whole to which the parts belong stands intact upon the shelves. A particular chapter in a book, a single monograph in a series which has been regarded as a bibliographic entity, an article in a periodical, one piece of music in a collection, a single work in a microform publication that may contain many different works in fact, and item that has an individual author, identifying or subject that could usefully be brought to the attention of readers, can have its own record in the catalogue, with a reference to the volume, series or other publication within which it will be found and a directive where to find that publication. Such a record is called an analytical entry.

Analytical entries essential components of subject bibliographies. They comprise almost the whole content of indexing and abstracting publications. They may appear selectively in national bibliographies. The Canadian national bibliography, Canadian, for example, includes analytical entries for Canadian topics that from a substantial part (at least one third) of the contents of works published outside Canada, and also far Canadian composers, performs, and others whose work is represented in sound recordings and sheet music.

The *Australian national bibliography* makes similar provision for recording material of Australian interest originating outside the country. The indexing and abstracting journals have their own conventions for content and style in their entries, derived of course from what has evolved and been codified as the necessary set of data for identification and characterization of bibliography cannot immediately be item described in a subject bibliographical description may be produced by the inspection he bibliographical description may be enhanced by the addition of such elements as a translation of a foreign-language title, a note of the author's affiliation annotation or an abstract keywords, and so on.

Abbreviations for journal titles are widely used. An international standard for word abbreviations in serial titles is available but it is not universally employed. In libraries analytical entries that are to be integrated into a general cataloguing must have headings that can be interfiled with headings already established and must refer to other entries in the catalogue in the form in which they will be found there. Where the entry for a whole composite publication contains a contents note, it may be sufficient to creat an analytical entry by superimposing on a unit entry for the whole publication the heading under which the part might be sought.

Library science students, as well as practitioners whose experience has not included managing a copy cataloguing operation, should find the discussion helpful as a primer and over view of the major components and issues involved with setting up and managing a copy cataloguing unit. Experienced copy cataloguing managers may also find the discussion of alternative organizational structure useful when considering ways to improve productivity and to adapt the copy cataloguing operation to local needs. The chapter also includes a final section devoted to a discussion of emerging trends and the impact of automation.

The chapter will explore five basic topics.

1. Copy cataloguing procedures and workflow
2. Staffing and training
3. Organizing the copy cataloguing operation
4. Productivity and performance standards
5. Impact of automation and emerging trends

Simply stated, the purpose of copy cataloguing is to provide bibliographic access to books and other library materials and to get those materials to the shelves and available for use in a timely fashion. The final product of the copy cataloguing process is a bibliographic record, the final form of which is either a catalogue process is a bibliographic record, produced through the adaptation of an existing catalogue record ("copy") to local standards.

Access to existing records is made possible through computer terminal connected to a bibliographic utility. Records in these huge database may appear in various levels of completeness and are contributed through two primary source: *(1)* The Library of Congress ("LC copy"), and *(2)* individual libraries representing members of the bibliographic records through such utilities has made possible the practice of "shared cataloguing" and has made revolutionized cataloguing for an item is replaced with the more streamlined task if reviewing and modifying existing records.

While many variations exist, the typical copy cataloguing operation includes the following basic components.

(a) Staff: copy cataloguers, supervisors, and so forth.

(b) Terminals for access to a bibliographic utility.

(c) Agreed upon criteria for judging acceptable or usable copy; that is, which types of catalogue records can be accepted without review and which require a more through review to verify the accuracy and appropriateness of the various record components.

(d) Procedures for searching and identifying the various types of copy.

(e) Policies and procedures for the dispensation of materials for which usable copy cannot be found: for example, route material for original cataloguing, or store material in holding are for processing at a later date.

(f) Optional procedures for simply copy cataloguing (*e.g.*, procedures for editing and adapting LC contributed copy) and complex copy cataloguing.

(g) Cataloguing priorities: which types of material will receive priority attention and which can be deferred until a later date. For example, materials destined for a course reserve or reference location are often catalogued before other material.

(h) Cataloguing standards and others support documents: for example, Anglo American Cataloguing Rules-2nd edition (AACR2), international standard Book Description (ISBD), Library of Congress subject Heading (LCSH), Cataloguing service bulletin (CSB), training manuals. Local cataloguing practice manual, OCLC/LC MARC formats, Library of Congress (LC) class schedules, technical bulletins, and so forth.

(i) Materials to be catalogued: the copy cataloguing operation is supplied books and other materials from several source- new purchases, gift collections, temporary "holding areas" (materials awaiting the availability of catalogue copy), and backlogs.

Optional activities often associated with the copy cataloguing operation include: catalogue maintains; processing and final shelf preparation of materials *e.g.*, property stamping, call number labelling, etc.); and procedures for the processing of added copies, added volumes, withdrawals, and transfers.

Detailed procedures for recorded editing and criteria for evaluating acceptable or usable copy vary local policy and practice. While local variations exist, a typical workflow sequence for the copy cataloguing of library materials is as follows.

(a) Conduct search for copy on bibliographic utility. This step can be done at the library's options either in the acquisitions department (per-order searching) or the copy cataloguing unit at one of several points in the cataloguing workflow.

(b) Distribute materials to appropriate units and staff. The routing of materials is often based on the nature and complexity of the available copy.

(c) Check local catalogue / shelflist, if necessary, to identify current holdings and to avoided call number duplication. (Checking for call number duplication is often not done when using LC copy; rather, bibliographic records are checked for duplicate numbers at the time of filing or during the loading of tapes in to the on-line catalogue.)

(d) Check local authority file, if necessary, to verify headings and access points.

(e) Edit record on-line: verify and/or complete descriptive cataloguing, subject cataloguing and classification, assign accession numbers (*e.g.*, OCRs barcodes), produce cards and/or machine readable records (distributed by the bibliographic utility).

(f) Route material to appropriate unit for physical processing and shelf preparation.

(g) Receive catalogue/shelf cards or machine-readable tapes from the bibliographic utility. Verify records against input records (*e.g.*, purchase order, work form, tag-sheet) and spot-check for errors while filing in the catalogue/shelflist. Verify machine-readable records as they are loaded in to the on-line catalogue (generally accomplished through a computer programme).

(h) Route material for which no usable record could be found to a temporary "holding area". Search one or more times, at predetermined intervals, for usable copy.

If copy can still not be found after a predetermined interval, route the material on for original cataloguing.

On a procedural level identifying the type of copy becomes somewhat more complex. Examples of sereral basic type of catalogue copy include: LC/AACR2,LC/PreAACR2, CIP (LC Cataloguing in publication), member contributed, UK-MARC, minimal versus full level cataloguing, and similar edition ("close copy"). Copy cataloguers must be trained to recognize these and other variant forms of catalogue copy. Procedures are designed, are designed to handle general classes of copy based on the relative complexity of the editing process and degree of expertise required on the part of the cataloguer.

Various criteria determine the acceptability of each type of copy and prescribe the procedures for adapting the record for local use.

The criteria which define "acceptable" or "usable" copy vary among libraries and are depend on local cataloguing standards/ practice, on-line catalogue capabilities, and network regulations. Often, locally established criteria are a function of the library's perception of the relative quality (accuracy and completeness) reflected in records of different types and forms various sources. For example, full-level/LC AACR2 records are often accepted virtually as is, while member-contributed copy is subjected to closer scrutiny.

The final judgment as to what constitutes acceptable copy often boils down to how much "quality" the library can afford; verification and editing of records increases both the time and cost associated with cataloguing materials and getting them to the shelves. While judgments concerning acceptable copy are often subjective, some libraries have taken a more empirical approach. For example, a list of likely source of copy is drawn up and a random sample of records from each source of copy is drawn up and a random sample both as to the type and number of cataloguing errors. Each source is then ranked in order or overall record quality.

Although such statistical techniques offer useful objective data, the process of setting local policy continues to require considerable judgment and considerable judgment and consideration of local needs and conditions. Particularly relevant are the capabilities of the local catalogue. Many on-line catalogues now offer a vast improvement in retrieval capabilities over the conventional card catalogue. With such powerful features as keyword searching, Boolean searching, and the ability to search virtual all components of a bibliographic records, errors or omissions that would have rendered the record irretrievable to the patron using the card catalogue may be not at all critical in the on-line environment. Copy cataloguing policy should attempt to find the optimal balance among cataloguing efficiency, retrieval capabilities, and the usefulness of the information contained in the bibliographic record. In addition to defending the criteria for usable copy, procedures must be implemented for handling materials for which no usable record can be found. A common practice is to hold materials until cataloguing copy (usually LC) becomes available. Among ARL libraries, holding periods of three to twelve months are typical. This is particularly true for non-English language material. The advantage of this practice is that expensive original cataloguing is avoided.

The disadvantages are that the materials are not available for patron use until months later when it is eventually catalogued, and that material in holding areas must be balanced against the cost and the feasibility of performing original cataloguing. Libraries may choose to shelve metrical for which copy can not be found by date of receipt and to retrieves such items from the holding areas upon patron request. This presumes that the patron has some way of determining that the library owns a particular item-perhaps through access to an automated acquisition system that identifies new receipts. Alternatively, brief bibliographic records can be keyed in to becomes available, a full-level record can be adapted and used to replace the interim record. The practice of creating less than full-level bibliographic records is fairly controversial. Proponents argue that materials can be made available to the patron via on-line access to minimal-level records until such time as these records can be upgraded, generally through a machine match and overlay process typically possible with on-line catalogues. After materials are received from acquisitions and the search for usable copy has been performed, materials are distributed to the appropriate cataloguing units and staff. While the criteria for distribution vary among libraries, it is essentially the perceive level of cataloguing difficulty which determines the appropriate destination. The relative level of difficulty is often determined by the following:

1. Source of the cataloguing copy.
2. Language of the material,
3. Material type (*e.g.*, audio-visual, music, microform),
4. Presence of a usable call number,
5. Degree to which copy requires editing of descriptive cataloguing and,
6. Degree of subject analysis required.

The editing of copy varies widely with local practice and represents a process which can become quite complex. Dowell's Cataloguing with Copy provides an in-depth analysis of the process and can offer the reader complete coverage of this fine art. The basic steps in a typical copy editing process might be as follows. The item in hand is searched on a bibliographic utility (*e.g.*, OLC, RLIN) and a matching record displayed. This step may be simplified if the item has already been searched by acquisitions or a searching unit. In such cases, a numerical search key (LC card #, OCLC #) would have been recorded on any slips (*e.g.*, purchase order) accompanying the item. The record is examined carefully to verify that the records does indeed match the item in hand and to item the source and type of record. For example, a full-level/AACR2/LC record can be identified by verifying that the fixed field element "encoding level" = "blank", the "description" = "a," and the 020 field = DLC/DLC.

Depending on the source and type of copy, and the local policies regarding such, a predetermined list of specific record fields and elements are examined for accuracy and completeness. For instance, if a full-level AACR2/LC record (not in series) is found, abbreviated procedures involving a minimum of checking can be followed. The copy cataloguer will quickly verify the fixed element "language code" and date of publication" to ensure that they match the piece in hand. Next, the cataloguer will check the 050 (LC call number) for accuracy of format and then scan the IXX field (author), 245 field (title), 250 field (edition statement), and 260 fields (place and data of publication) for typographical errors, accuracy, and completeness. Any discrepancy in edition is detected at this point.

Finally, the 049 fields is edited to reflect local holding and, optionally, a 949 field added to provide item specific information such as OCR/barcodes number (accession number for circulation), branch location, media code, price, and so on. The cataloguer completes the process by invoking the "produce" function. Shelf/catalogue cards and/or machine-readable tapes containing the edited records are sent by the bibliographic utility to the library generally more library generally within a week or two.

The process is generally more complex for member-contributed copy or less than full-level records. For example, the 300 fields (physical description) must be completed for LC/CIP records; the subject heading fields (6XX) may need to be require additional attention, and so on. A question often asked is how much of a bibliographic record can be accepted without checking? There is no single answer to this. The answer depends on the source and type of copy, the library's perception judgment as to the accuracy and completeness of the copy, the level of staffing and other resources the library can afford to devote to copy cataloguing, the patron population served and their particular information needs, the library's definition of the minimal acceptable level of service and access to information, the storage and retrieval capabilities of the local catalogue, and the "local culture" and its philosophy regarding the broader issue of bibliographic control. The subject remains a hotly debated issue and has led many to rethink conventional wisdom regarding traditional access points and record content. Research is underway examining the usefulness of the various access points and the information content of the typical catalogue record.

Cataloguing priorities are established to determine the order in which different categories of materials will be catalogued. Such priorities are perhaps the major determinant of copy cataloguing workflow and are often influenced by interest external to those of the cataloguing department. Cataloguing priorities may be based on such considerations as the following.

(a) Imprint (*i.e.*, the timeliness of the publication). New material is often given top priority. Material from backlogs may be done only after all other types of material have been catalogued.

(b) "Rush" materials, patron requests and "notifications", as well as cataloguing for a branch library or a reference location are often given special consideration.

(c) Relation of the item to the collection (*e.g.*, as determined by collection development subject specialists).

Whatever the basis for the cataloguing priorities, they should be clear, will documented, and communicated to all interested individuals and departments that allows the copy cataloguers and other staff to easily recognize the treatment and priority that specific items should receive. This is typically achieved through the use of coloured 'flags" or specially designed forms that are clearly labelled as to the intended treatment and which include any additional information required to process the item accordingly. A well documented and publicized policy regarding cataloguing priorities becomes critical when the volume of material exceeds the cataloguing capacity of the department. Under such conditions, the issues involved can become quite sensitive politically as various interest groups attempt to win priority attention for their materials; very few individuals want to see their new receipts relegated to a backlog. It becomes very important to negotiate mutually acceptable priorities which are perceived by all interest groups as being, if not ideal, at least rational and equitable.

A certain amount of flexibility must be built in to the system in order to allow the copy cataloguing manager to adjust workflows around changing conditions. The inflow of materials will vary over time, not only in volume but in the relative composition of material type and the sources of cataloguing copy. For example, a recently received collection donated as a gift may include many items for which only member contributed or pre-AACR2 copy is available. In order to avoid flooding the unit responsible for this type of material, items from the collection may have to be fed gradually in to the workflow, while others remain in a temporary backlog. Last but not least, things should be kept simple. While it is tempting to try to accommodate all interests when negotiating priorities, too many exceptions and special treatments introduced in to the workflow can degrade the performance of the entire operation and in the end, result in poor service for all parties involved.

Copy cataloguing is done by the full range of staffing levels ranging from student assistants and clerical staff to paraprofessional and professional staff. As with other aspects of copy cataloguing, the level of staff deemed appropriate for a given level of cataloguing complexity varies among libraries. Generally, clerical staff and beginning level paraprofessionals are thought by most to be well equipped to handle abbreviated copy cataloguing procedures, such as those used in adapting LC copy. Intermediate and higher levels of paraprofessional staff are thought more appropriate for working with member contributed copy and with more complex problems of yet higher complexity, such as those associated with classification or the establishment of subject headings are often reserved for professionals or the highest level paraprofessional staff. In a typical arrangement, the copy cataloguing department is headed by a professional, with individual units supervised by high level paraprofessionals. Because the definition of staffing levels oil essentially an arbitrary local distinction, perhaps the more relevant issue concerns the level of knowledge and expertise required. Depending on the relative complexity of the cataloguing task at hand, staff require varying leave's of familiarity with such codes and standard as AACR2 (as well as earlier codes), International Standards Book Description (ISBD), LC/MARC formats, library of Congress Subjects Headings (LCSH), and LC classification schedules. At the simplest levels, staff with little exposure to the full breadth of these codes may be able to do an acceptable job of copy cataloguing if provides with clear and simple decision rule-based instructions. These instructions allow minimal latitude for judgment on the part of the cataloguers and limits their actions to those prescribed by specific "if-then" rules.

Any situations that fall outside of the prescribed decision-rules are referred to staff members of higher expertise. As the level of cataloguing complexity increases, so too do the requirements for expertise and familiarity with the various code and standards. The managements challenge then is to match knowledge requirements with specific levels of task complexity. Dowell's Cataloguing with Copy includes a chart and checklist relating just such specific knowledge requirements with the various tasks associated with copy cataloguing. Both the level and number of staff should be matched to local cataloguing volume and workflow patterns. Variables to consider include the relative frequency of various material types (*e.g.*, books, microfilms, serials), the ratio of acceptable copy to adaptable copy (*e.g.*, the percent of materials with full-level LC copy versus member contributed copy), the language of the material, the presence of any backlogs, the total volume of material to be catalogued, and the degree of fluctuation in the receipt of materials. For example, a department with a separate unit for cataloguing with LC copy and another for member-based cataloguing, will want to adjust staffing so that the capacity of each unit marches the relative proportions of LIC and member copy associated with incoming materials. If such coordination is not made, one unit is in danger of being overwhelmed while the other units is searching for materials to catalogue.

Of course, the problem here is that non of these variables remain static-equation budgets fluctuate, spending on new receipts is generally heavier at the beginning of the fiscal year than at the end, backlogs shrink or are eliminated, unexpected gift collection may be donated, changes in approval plan profiles are made, a change in collection development emphasis may change the proportions of English and non-English receipts, and so forth.

Most libraries employ a one-one training programme that moves from simple to more complex copy cataloguing over a period which varies from three to twelve months. Usually under the tutelage of a high-level paraprofessional or professional, the trainee is first taught the basics of searching the bibliographic utility (*e.g.*, OCLC, RLIN). After mastering the art of moving about in the database, the trainee is then taught to recognize the various types and sources of cataloguing copy-first and foremost, to recognize full-level/AACR2/ LC copy. The next step is to begin to learn the steps in editing simple LC copy and saving the results in a "save" queue for review by the instructor at a later date (usually the end of the day). This process, known as "revision" continues until the instructor is confident that the trainee has mastered the concepts and procedures involved.

A similar process of training, practice, and revision is then followed for more complex cataloguing such as CIP, pre-AACR2 LC, and member-contributed copy. Such training is quite time-consuming. Following periods of heavy staff turnover, the cataloguing instructors may find themselves doing nothing but training new staff, with little or no time to perform their own cataloguing. A few libraries have developed accelerated programmes for training a large number of new staff for such occasion or during the start-up of a new department.

Several basis choices are available for organizing a copy cataloguing department or unit. Among ARL libraries, the following are the most common dimensions by which organizational structure vary.

(a) Centralization or decentralization of cataloguing operations.

(b) Organization by either "form" (*e.g.*, separate units for monographs and serials) or by "function" (*e.g.*, acquisitions, cataloguing).

(c) Separate or integrated cataloguing operations. Original cataloguing and copy cataloguing can be combined into one department or organized separately.

(d) Separate or integrated procedures for variant types and sources of copy. Simple (*e.g.*, LC copy) and complex (*e.g.*, member copy) cataloguing can be integrated in to one unit with each cataloguers performing both levels as required, or separate units can be established.

(e) Interface with other departments such as acquisitions, processing, original cataloguing, catalogue maintains. (Interdepartmental communication is important. For example, policies need to be coordinated with the circulation department regarding procedures such as catalogue before or after the binding process).

(f) Procedures for finding usable copy. For example, pre-order or post-receipt searching can be then be "flagged" to identity the matching record before reaching the copy cataloguing department, separate search and distribution units can be set up specifically for verifying the availability and identifying the nature of cataloguing copy.

A major that governs the choice regarding the letter dimension is to avoid duplication of effort in having to search and re-search the same item at multiple stages in the cataloguing of an item. A related workflow variable concerns the disposition of materials for which no usable copy can be found.

A common practice is to send lower priority material to a backlog and routinely re-search them at periodic intervals. Such practice have involved out of the need to reduce the volume of material requiring original cataloguing.

(a) Authority work may be integrated in to normal copy cataloguing routines or handled by separate units (*e.g.*, original cataloguing, catalogue maintenance, or an authority control unit).

(b) Input and edit. Some libraries prefer to separate the intellectual function of reviewing and adapting a catalogue record from the actual inputting and outline editing. Copy cataloguers will adapt usable copy and record the necessary changes on a workform which can then be passed on to clerical staff for input in to the database. Other libraries seek to avoid the redundancy inherent in this practice by having the record called up only once and edited immediately by the cataloguer.

The choice of organizational options discussed above will differ from library to library and is influenced by a variety of local needs, resources, and considerations. First among these variables is the library's definition of "copy". While variables such as library size, number of branches, number of volumes, staff size, and budget are often cited as bases for overall organizational design of cataloguing operations, the organization workflows and individual processing units is influenced most by how a library defines the various types of copy and the relate complexity involved in adapting each type of copy to local standards. A distinction is made between LC and member contributed copy. Either separate procedures, or in some cases separate units are then designed to process each type of cataloguing one for processing LC-based copy, the other for adapting member contributed copy. Establishing separate units has the advantage of allowing the less complex cataloguing to be done without delay; that is, materials for which LC copy is available is not held up by the more the time-consuming member-based cataloguing. This is consistent with the traditional production-line maxim the asserts that "the entire process can go only as the slowest step". By eliminating the bottlenecks created by the more time-consuming cataloguing, materials for which readily usable copy available can be catalogued and sent to the shelves with minimal delay. An additional advantage of establishing separate is that different staffing levels can be employed. For example, entry level paraprofessionals may be trained to perform the LC-based cataloguing, while the more highly paid intermediate and upper level paraprofessionals are reserved for more complex cataloguing. Staffing costs, as well as training time, can be minimized.

Such a separation of units, however, is not without certain drawbacks. The efficiency of this arrangement hold up as long as materials representing both types of copy (LC and member) are readily available and the cap of each unit is well matched to the existing workflow. (The existence of large backlogs is deal for this arrangement. As fluctuations in new recipes result in shortage of LC copy, the backlogs can be tapped to keep the units adequately supplied). If either class of copy (usually LC) falls off, the result will be excess capacity and idle staff in one of the units. A single integrated unit, with each cataloguers doing all classes of copy, has the advantage of greater flexibility in adapting to fluctuations in the number and nature of incoming material. Thus, if separate units are employed, it is important to build flexibility in to the procedures and to identify alternative activities for staff during such fluctuations.

Other variables that come in to play when considering alternative organizational designs, staffing needs, and required resource include the following.

Format of Material. Will the copy cataloguing department process only book-format monographs? Or, will the workflow include music. Audio-visual materials, microform, and so on?

Language or Alphabet of Material. Are non-English language or non-Roman aplhated materials catalogued or sent on to other special units? What priority do these materials receive?

Library Collections. What special interest must be served? Will cataloguing be done for departments such as special collections, reference, or branch libraries? What special needs and turnaround times are involved?

Other Produces. Will the copy cataloguing department have to perform transfers, withdrawls, added-copy or added-volume routines?

Subject of Materials. Should separate units or staff designated to handle different subject areas such as Humanities, Science, or Literature? All of these variables must be considered in light of the availability of staff—staff with the background or training to work with foreign languages, specific areas, and the various MARC formats.

While the organization of the copy cataloguing operation varies among libraries, the general components and principles involved can be seen in several variations on a common theme.Components of a typical organizational model appear below.

Search and Distribution Unit. Searches bibliographic utility for copy, identifies nature of copy (*e.g.*, LC/ AACR2,CIP, member), and routes material to appropriate processing unit based on locally establishing criteria.

Maintenance/bibliographic Support. Performs support functions for the units such as typing and filling in the public catalogue, shelflist, and authority file; maintains the local catalogues and files (both on-line and manual) through the addition, deletion, and correction of bibliographic and authority records.

Copy Cataloguing Unit(s). Many libraries have their abbreviated procedures or separate units for cataloguing materials for which full level, AACR2 LC copy is available (typically called "fast" or" rapid" cataloguing).

Added copy/added volume, withdrawals, transfers: often performed either in the catalogue maintains unit or the copy cataloguing units.

Marketing and Physical Processing. often part of or closely associated with the copy cataloguing units. (Error in call numbers are often detected during the marking process; this step may serve as an additional quality control mechanism for the copy cataloguing units). As with all organizational decisions, there is no one best structure. The choice of structure depends on many interrelated variables including the personnel and expertise available.

Automation offers the potential for improved statistical reporting function for better management decisions and control. Whether manually or through the local automated system, data should be collected and analysed as a means of providing the manager with relevant feedback on the efficiency of various operations. Data typically collected includes the total number of titles/volumes catalogued by each cataloguers, unit, department, and so forth. The record count might also include a breakdown of materials catalogued by class number (*e.g.*, for collection development use). On-line capabilities may also include a management report utility capable of generating a variety of statistical summaries and analyses. In addition to raw counts of performance data, the report may include various numerical analyse (*e.g.*, the ratio or percentage of LC to member copy, average titles catalogued per fulltime equivalent staff, average titles catalogued per hour, etc.).

If the local on-line system cannot provide such management reports, data can be recorded on specially designed forms and later input in to a microcomputer-based speradsheet (*e.g.*, Lotus 1-2-3, Super Calc). Typically, individuals cataloguers record their production statistic at the end of each month. The cataloguing data are then keyed in to the spreadsheet programme for summary and analysis.

Performance is not measured only in terms of total titles catalogued. The accuracy and completeness ("quality") of the bibliographic record should also be of significant concern to the copy cataloguing manager. Finding and maintaining the optimal balance between cataloguing productivity and cataloguing quality is one of the more challenges aspects of maintaining the cataloguing operation. The means of monitoring cataloguing quaiity very among libraries.

A typical methods is to match each newly produced shelflist card against the record of original input (*e.g.*, purchase order, workform) and to revise (make corrections) during the filing of cards in the shelflist or catalogue. In an automated environment, records can be reviewed on-line and on "error reports" produced during the loading of each new tape of catalogue records. These methods tend to be rather informal and focus primarily on catching highly noticeable errors.

Libraries may also purse a more systematic approach to quality control. For example, libraries may require cataloguers to revise the filing in the public catalogue on a periodic basis (*e.g.*, weekly). Other approaches involve taking periodic random sampling of the catalogues/ shelflists or of the records produced by individual cataloguers. The sampled records are then thoroughly reviewed for accuracy and completeness. These more systematic approach require a significant investment of time and expense. The costs involved should be weighed against the marginal increase in cataloguing quality. The copy cataloguing operation can be quite complex, making it difficult for the manager to identify ways in which procedures or workflows can be improved. While improvements can be made through a more intuitive approach, formal system analysis techniques can help identify bottlenecks radiance that might otherwise go undetected. Among these techniques flowcharting is perhaps the most popular and useful. Through the flowcharting process, each individual action (task) and decision is identified and placed in precise sequence to other steps in the process.

The flowchart's graphic depiction of the steps in the cataloguing process make it easier for the manager to spot weakness in the workflow design. Systems analysis techniques such as flowcharting also offer an excellent way to document the copy cataloguing operation and should be included with any textual material such as procedure manuals. Training of new personnel can be enhanced through the clear picture of the cataloguing process that the flowchart provides. In addition to the finished product, the flowcharting process itself can be an invaluable exercise in that to forces one to thoroughly examine and understand each step in a process. Flowcharting enthusiasts, in fact, are found of claiming that "if you can't flowchart it, you don't understand it". The flowcharting process should be repeated at regular intervals or whenever a major changes is made in the workflow. Often, seemingly insignificant changes in a procedure can be revealed to have an impact on other points in the process once seem from the enchanced perspective of a flowchart. The availability of thousands of bibliographic records through the large database of the bibliographic utilities that made copy cataloguing possible. The impact on library operations has been tremendous and has wrought many changes in local procedures and practices. Among the more significant effects of large-scale shared cataloguing has been the impact on staffing levels. For many libraries, the availability of adaptable cataloguing copy has reduced the volume of materials requiring cataloguing.

The streamlined procedures used for copy cataloguing do not require the extensive expertise needed to do original cataloguing. Thus, the least decade has seen a shift in support of copy cataloguing operations. Ironically, while bibliographic utilities were created initially to provide printed catalogue/ shelflist cards, the availability of machine readable records and outline catalogues has led to a reduction in the number of card files maintained by modern libraries. This, in turn, has greatly reduced traditional library activities such as card typing and card filing. Staff are now being reassigned to tasks such as reviewing and maintaining records on-line or reviewing printouts (error reports) produced following the periodic loading of bibliographic records in to local on-line databases.

Not all aspects of shared cataloguing have led to time or cost savings. Along with the benefits of having access to the catalogue records of the bibliographic utilities comes the responsibility for maintaining the integrity of the database. Records contributed to the database are not the exclusive property of any individual library and, therefore, must adhere to agreed upon standards for accuracy and completeness. In this sense, a library's cataloguing becomes more closely scrutinized and subject to even greater, and more time consuming, quality control measures. Libraries must also make sure to consider the various legal restrictions (*e.g.*, copyright) which may be imposed by the bibliographic utilities on the use of catalogue records.

Along with the development of shared cataloguing the increasing implementation of the on-line catalogue has had a major impact on library operation practices. Library scholar and practitioners are by no means agreed on the implications of the new technologies for the future of bibliographic control. The debate stems from the powerful indexing and retrieval capabilities of the newly developed on-line catalogues. At one end of the spectrum are those who argue that traditional access points and cross-references are less critical given the on-line catalogue's ability to perform searches based on keyword, boolean operators, would proximity, and search key truncation. Other, more conservative opinions, argue that the extremely literal manner in which the on-line catalogue performs indexing and searching makes to more, not less, important to ensure that access points, records tags and indicators, and filing characters be closely examined for accuracy.

On-line catalogues have also impacted the nature of bibliographic record maintenance. With the capability to access local catalogue records on-line, separate maintenance operations can be established to enter records and record modifications directly in, to the local on-line database. This is particularly true for such procedures as added copy at these would have precisely been done through the capabilities of the bibliographic utility, which changes to the records appearing only when the library loaded the next tape of the on-line catalogue, these operations can be performed immediately and in real-time.

The extreme precision with which the on-line catalogue performs searching and indexing has introduced new problems in to the maintains operation. As catalogue records new are loaded in to the catalogue via tape, or on-line via direct transmission, the system performs a number of checks on the validity of the content and format of the incoming field tag, subfield, and indicator against a stored table of valid values: any discrepancy is noted (usually in the form of a printout identifying the records and the source of the problem). Due to the literal character-by-character can result in a rejected record and a maintains transaction that must be reviewed manually.

The manager of the copy cataloguing operation, therefore, face a trade-off. As copy cataloguing procedures becomes more streamlined, and the review of individual record lements less through, the likelihood of generating a future maintenance problem increases. Thus, the efficiencies and economies realized through the abbreviated copy cataloguing produces can be partially offset by an increase in maintains transactions. The management challenges is to find a balance of cataloguing and maintenance procedures that makes optimal use of staff time, ensures adequate record quality, and minimizes total processing costs. Recognition of the workflow trade-offs described above, along with other similar phenomenon, have led to the claim that the staff time-saving promised with on-line catalogues is largely a fallacy. While libraries have experienced any reduction in total staffing requirements. When comparing the costs of maintaining manual versus automated library systems, however, it is important to recognize that we are in a sense comparing apples and oranges.

The on-line catalogue has opened up a whole new range of capabilities and represents a quantum leap in terms of improved library services. Although staffing requirements remain the same, or have increased somewhat, the ,level of service and potential for further improvements has been greatly enchanced.

Among the more powerful features of the on-line catalogue is the capability to perform a systematic machine-based matching process by which large numbers of bibliographic records can be quickly reviewed element by element. A familiar example of this process is the "global" search and replacement feature often associated with on-line authority control systems. Such machine-based operation not only facilitate the catalogue maintenance function but also offer the possibility of performing certain aspects of the cataloguing process after the bibliographic record has been created. For example, by integrating the LC name and subject authority files in to the on-line catalogue, it becomes possible to perform a verification process as bibliographic records are loaded in to the database. Headings associated with incoming catalogue records can be checked against heading in the stored authority file. Should an incoming heading match a cross-reference, the system can substitute the authorized from of the heading before allowing the bibliographic records to pass in to the database. Some aspects of catalogue records creation and maintenance lend themselves to such machine processing operations while others do not. The computer is a relentlessly literal device that can operate only according to precisely defined decision rules. Only those operations that can be reduced to a finite series of logical steps and lend themselves to well-formed machine algorithms are appropriate for such processing. In such, the highly labour-intensive process of manually reviewing a particular record element during the adaptation of catalogue copy can be replaced by a post-processing machine operation that is quicker, cheaper, more efficient, and more accurate. These new post-processing capabilities suggest a trend and catalogue maintenance function. Cataloguing procedures must be reviewed and possibly resigned to take advantage of these post-processing opportunities and to increase the efficiency of the manual review process. By relieving the copy cataloguers of those tasks that can be done more efficiently through machine-based processing, the manual review process can concentrate more effectively on those elements of the catalogue record which have a more critical impact on record retrievability. Thus, the management challenge becomes one of finding the optimal balance of manual review and post-processing maintenance.

The rate at which new technology is developed makes it difficult to anticipate the direction of future library operations and procedures. Certainly, an increasing number of libraries will implement on-line catalogues and other automated systems. These systems will also continue to be improved with new, more powerful retrieval capabilities. These developments will further fuel the discussion over the nature and content of catalogue records.

The improved capabilities of the on-line catalogue do not necessarily mean an easier time for library operations. The improved retrieval capabilities, more readable screen (record) formats information access, but make more conspicuous the errors and imperfections in the catalogue records. Much of what may have gone unnotices in the card catalogue may become glaring errors in the automated environment.

Expert systems represent another technology on the horizon with the potential to dramatically affect the copy cataloguing operation. These systems, originally developed to facilitate medical dances, may prove ideally adaptable to the highly codified, rule-based structure of the cataloguing process. While most researchers are agreed that such systems can never replace cataloguers, both original and copy cataloguing may be greatly facilitated through the assistance of such systems.

The precursor to such systems can already be found in the increasing use of microcomputer-based workstations such as the "smart" terminals developed by the bibliographic utilities. These workstations have already taken advantage of prepackage software that allows records to be downloaded, edited off-line, and updated in batch model. Some libraries have taken this basic concept a step further and have developed local microcomputer programmes to allow them to perform increasingly sophisticated record maintenance operations, including, for example, the processing of non-Roman character sets and diacritics. Libraries are also making increasing use of outside vendors.

❑

6

Evolution of Catalogue Codes

1. DEVELOPMENT OF CATALOGUE CODE

Dr. Ranganathan has given a new phenomena of the development of a code (classified). He has explained few stages of development.

1. Endless Spiral. There is never ending spiral in scientific method.

(a) From individual experiences, through generalisations to emperical laws derived from them, with the aid of induction and normal equations;

(b) Through their deduction to a few normative principles, with the aid of imaginations and/or intuition;

(c) Through deductive lawe or canons derived from the normative principles with the aid of methods of inference and semantics;

(d) Through fresh individual experiences not conforming to them;

(e) Back again through another cycle; and

(f) So on, without end.

2. Establishment of Cycle. Such a cycle of development has now been established in cataloguing and framing a catalogue code. Normative principles help in this process, New types of reading material may be catalogued by a proper interpretation of rules. If rules donot fitin, there may be amended or extended with the aid of normative principles. When needed old normative principles may be replaced by new one.

3. Dictionary Catalogue Codes. Like other branches of librarianship cataloguing is one of the important branch having allround development in the field. It has developed in many wings such as sectiốns, sub-sections, laws, principles, canons governing the choice and rendering of various elements in the entry, author and title component in the catalogue and the subject approach of information and other sections like descriptive catalogue, centrlised catalogue cooperative catalogue and mechanised catalogue, techniques and systems.

In ancient India, we used palm leaves, bamboos. Egyptians, Chinese and Indians used like the similar things to write. In the period of the Ashoka the great pillars were used as the source of cataloguing. Chinese traveller Huenshiang writes that there was no proper and systematised catalogue during that period. Some old catalogues were found on clay tablets called as Sumerian tablets. Catalogue is a work in which the contents are arranged in a regional way according to a set plan, There was a time when it seems important to arrange the book (catalogue) according to the colour of their binding and authors were entered under fore names. It was proved by the clay tablets found at Nippur dated about 2000 B.C. 62 titles are recorded on the table out of which 24 are well known literary work. It clearly shows that there was some cataloguing methods. It is assumed that Egyptian libraries developed there so called catalogue earlier than babylonion. Egyptians used papyrus. Papyrus is a material. It is far from everlasting even when buried in the parched sands of the desert. Some references were found on the collection of clay tablets about the Kings and queens. The tablets were fragments of small plaques (tags) on which the name of King and queen was written. Even than there was no basis of claiming any thing like catalogue enteries for them. The tablets as excavated in capital city of *Hittites*, may be evidence of using colophone to convey bibliographic information. Some 6000 years later (650 B.C.) about 2000 tablets bears colophon. These tablets were excavated in a archives of Aryan King in city Ninevehe. These tablets have the details *i.e.*, vol no., name of the owner, name of scriber, King's stamp. This period is more important for the evolution of catalogue codes. The other evidence is of later period of third century when the course of civilisation had made its way to Greece from middle east. There is well known catalogue in the walls of the temples at EDFU in Egypt.

During the period of Greece civilization was spread out side. A scholar of Alexandria compied his pinakes in 250 B.C. The scholar recorded the number of lines in each work but no imprint is given. The work of scholar specified the fact that few general categories were considered to be the sufficient subject approach to the literature. After subject the author was considered second and title third. No proper sequence or the way of cataloguing, classified then chronological and then alphabetization, was followed; most of the work was of Editorial nature.

So far the cataloguing system is concerned Romans also adopted some type of catalogue code. There is a well known story that scholar of Greek (Pergaman) made a trip to Rome. He suddenly suffered injury and forced to stay. He Visited Roman libraries and found that Romans adopted cataloguing methods.

During the medieval period religion given importance and monasteries established which were having their own catalogue at 8th century. It was not fly leaves. These were titles but in certain cases author was taken. In 9th century Germany adopted catalogue system prepared several catalogues between 822 to 844 One of the catalogue was classified but there was no standardisation of code during 10th, 11th & 12th. Century. No improvement was noticed. By the end of 13th century one librarian started a project which was a mile stone in the history of catalogue code. This was the compiliation of Registrum librarium and Anglian. It was union catalogue of English monastery. In 1560. Trefler wrote first book on libraries and discussed inadequacy of library system. He advocated five types of catalogue:

1. Alphabetical author catalogue,
2. Shelf list,
3. Classified Index,
4. Analytical index to classifled index, and
5. List of books not kept with the main collection.

It indicates that there were several approches to catalogue. In 1585 an English book seller Mannsell compiled a catalogue of English printed books kept in book-shop. The sir name was used as entry form for the author. In 16th century it was the age of printing. Monasteries broken down. With the dovelopment of book trade and literacy, many scholars contributed to the development of the library catalogue. During 17th century thomas Bodley appointed Mr. James as librarian and directed to work for catalogue codes. He used catalogue as reference tool. He introduced a catalogue code and insisted, for a classified arrangement with alphabetical authors and analytical references. Few other manuals of librarianship brought out and many showed progressive views about catalogue. 'Mr Naude a French scholar emphasised importance of catalogue as a funding tool and a tool for identification of books. By the begining of 18th century catalogue was seen as final list than inventory. These were classified-alphabetical. Indexes were considered useful but not compulsory. Author arranged by sir name and chronologically. The title page was assumed respectively and literary transcribed in catalogue entries. Imperints were included. Cross references were quite common and some analytical entries were used. This state of affair remained through out 18th century and no other development till 1780. In the end of 18th century and during the Frence revolution all librares were nationalised. France libraries were instructed to prepare catalogue. A frame work was finalised for all the libraries of France. It was like a code. Playing cards were used for cataloguing entries During 19th century modern cataloguing begins. British libraries were more developed. The dispute was whether the catalogue was to be classified or alphabetical. Every citizen took part in controversy. One Italian Sir Anthony "Panizzi" was appointed as Assistant Librarian in British

Museum library. He convinced the committee about the catalogue procedures and prepared the first catalogue code called as "Panizei catalogue code" 1841 (91 rules). It was British Museum code and followed by the other important libraries of the world. It had great impact. His code advocates only one entry that is author entry. He was first librarian who accepted the concept of corporate body not fully but partially. He was convinced that alphabetical author catalogue was more useful. The reason was that subject was not sured. He transcribed title page of the catalogue.

By this time the American library came in picture. Mr. Charles C. Jewett was librarian in Smith Sonian Institute having big museum and library up to this time. Americans were following Britisher's catalogue code. Jewett extracted the principles and prepared a catalogue code known as Jewett code in 1852. It has 39 rules. He recommended subject entries in brief form which was an impovement in concept of catalogue. Jewett had in mind that union catalogue should be adopted in America. In 1876 Cutter's code "Rules for a Dictionary Catalogue" came in practice. It was a modern catalogue adopting more than one entry for a author. Cutter made provision for all types of libraries. He has also stressed some functions of catalogue:

1. To enable a person to find a book through author, title and subject,
2. To know what the library has by a given author on a given subject, in a given kind of literature,
3. Choice of book in edition and character.

Cutter carried out an pragmatic research and concluded "'For a dictionary catalogue as a whole and for most of its parts, there is no manual whatever nor have any of the works, attempted to set forth the rules in a systematic way or to investigate what might be called the principles of cataloguing."

He took up the work of compiling the catalogue of Boston Athenaeum published in 5 volume between 1874 to 1882. Appreciating the contribution of Cutter, S.R. Ranganathan said that Cutter was a genious and his code have been the chief source of later course in the English language. He called "R.D.C. as a whole as an egg."

In 1890 the Royal library of Berlin brought out changes in some of the rules of Dziotzko's Instruction and modified it twice. In 1896 Prussian government incited for Union catalogue and Royal Library of Berlin Catalogue was adopted as the basis. A committee was appointed to simplify the catalogue rules and made provision for bibliographical details. The new form was the Prussian instruction, 1899.

During 20 century in 1901 a draft code was printed by the Library of Congress known as A.L.A. rules—advanced edition. Both the library Association of UK and USA taken up research work in cataloguing. They formulated their own catalogue rules. Melvil Dewey's contribution to the research of cataloguing has been very important. He suggested that both the associations might unite to establish to uniform catalogue code for english speaking countries. Both the associations agree to cooperate, It was further suggested by John Minto that code should be prited in two editions—English and American. The result was two editions of "Anglo American Code" in 1908. It was the combined effort of Library Association, Great Britain and American Library Association).

The Vatican Code

This code came about as part of the re-organisation of the very-extensive Vatican Library in the 1920's, when it was decided in 1927 to establish a new (Dictionary) Catalogue. There had been a Italian Code, of 1911, and this was added to from AA 1908. With the help of mainly American libraries, the whole was reworked and consolidated, the first edition was translated in to English, but the translation was not published because of the Second World War. Meanwhile, however, a second edition was produced, and published in 1939. The work used was the English Translation of this, but it is out of print now.

The code is note-worthy as being the only really Complete code in one value for printed books of the Twentieth Century. It includes *(a)* Author/title entry; *(b)* Description; *(c)* Subject entry; *(d)* Filing, and *(e)* Appendixes dealing with early printed books, abbreviations, glossary, transliteration and sample cards. It also has a very detailed index. The English language version has been adopted to some extent to English Language needs particularly important for subject heading work; although the examples are often not typical of English speaking Countries' Library Stocks, English translations, are usually included.

In the 1950's one would have pleaded for a serious considerations of the whole code by English Speaking countries, especially for libraries using Dictionary Catalogue. However, all of the main components have since been overtaken by events: *(a)* We have a new author/title and description code, entering also for many special materials not included in VATICAN; *(b)* There has been considerable new thought and practice in the alphabetical subject field; and *(c)* There has emerged a redically simple view of dictionary cataloguing filing, in the second edition of the 'ALA' rules for filing catalogue cards. Therefore, one must regretfully leave the Vetican Code with this brief mention as not being directly relevant in this work, but in the hope that in the future it will be possible to compare it in detail and at leisure with its more recent rivals. So we must be contented with the following brutally generalised conclusions.

(a) Author/title rules correspond approximately with ALA 1949,

(b) Description rules correspond approximately with the part LCRDC which deals with printed materials,

(c) Subject entry rules represent a 'case' codification of LC subject heading practice.

Code Revision Committee

ALA Committee on catalogue code Revision was set up immediately after the publication of the Lubetzky report and its first statement, published in 1956 emphasized the following eight objectives.

1. Consistency;

2. Comprehensiveness;

3. The amount of recataloguing involved should not be considered if changes are desirable.

4. Economy.

5. The code should cover of author-title entries only, though rules for subject entry may be included to clarify the rules for author title entry or as added entries for special types of material.

6. The need of practicing cataloguers should be emphasized.. but the use of the code in library education should also be considered when there is no conflict with the primary purpose.

7. The British Library Association should be informed of all the steps taken in the revision of the code.

8. The standard rules should meet the minimun cataloguing needs of general research libraries. Alternatives rules may be provided, suggesting simpler or more complex rules where necessary.

Mr. Seymour Lubetzky was appointed as general editor of the proposed new code of cataloguing rules. This change has been a revolutionary step of ALA as it altered the work schedule of the Americans.

British and Canadian committees jointly engaged on the formulation of the new rules, and resulted in a steadily increasing output of draft rules, minutes, memorandam and comments from the participating bodies. The British sub-committee decided, therefore that the appointment of a part-time editorial assistant was an immediate necessity, and in the following month Phillip Escreet was appointed to the post. He was subsequently to be elected a member of sub committee

Lubetzkey's Draft

British Cataloguing Rules Committee had been kept informed of the progress of the 1919 ALA rules, but took no active part in their preparation. A sub-committee was formed in 1951 which was to examine the 1949 ALA rules. Shortly after Lubetzkey started examining the rules, that eventually found expression in his book, he concluded that a rationalisation of over cataloguing will require not a revision of any particular rules, but a complete reconstruction of our code in accordance with deliberately adopted objectives which should define the aim of our rules, and well considered principles which would outline the pattern and character of the code.

Lubetzkey's code of cataloguing rules, author and title entry: an unfinished draft' (CCR) appeared in March 1960. It was incomplete but it gave some idea of what could be achieved with a drastic eduction in many rules and accompanied with commenteries by Paul Dunkin, which could draw attention to the rules which had been eliminated by basing the code on conditions of authorship instead of specific cases. It was appreciated by many. But on the other hand it was disapproved by people. Dewton was the main critic. He criticised its permissive nature and occasional lack of clarity. He supported his criticism with examples of titles which had been catalogued under different headings by different cataloguers using C. C. R. Dewton advised that a more detailed code with sufficient examples is needed in the field of cataloguing, He further explained that a less complex code (with full details) is better rather than suitable one.

Lubetzkeys code-faced much criticism:

(1) Dewton wanted greater uniformity between catalogues and published bibliographies, which the code lacks.

(2) A survey was made by Mrs. Elizabeth Tale. She examined bibliographical citations of 606 titles and compared them with draft headings chosen according to ALA 1949 and CCR.

In her survey she found that C.C.R. would link the citation more directly with the work than would ALA, but she concluded that there is a problem in using 'one' catalogue to accomplish simultaneously 'three' objectives-Locating a given document, collecting the work of an author, and assembling the literary unit.

Mr. Tale's criticism or so called recommendations were no doubt based on some logic and citations, but it needed a observation and investigation of how far the catalogue is used to locate all the works of an author and all editions of a work, acceptence of the entity mentioned on the title page as the author of the book for the main entry, preference of an individual to a corporate body for the main entry in every case, and use of title main entry when three or more authors are involved.

The another criticism was that it will cost more if changes are made in library catalogue. Main entry may also be effected. But on the other hand Mr. Lubetzkey replied that any change may no effect more cost as it is based on the same principles. Moreover, main entry is a unit card entry. It has three or more cards. Hence, any change in main entry may not confuse tbe readers as it has various approaches.

International Conference on Cataloguing Principles

The International Conference of Library Associations sponsored an International Conference on cataloguing principles, which was held in Paris, 1961. The principles worked out by Seymour Lubetzkey vertually formed the basis for the discussion and evaluation of the principles which emerged from the conference.

The most useful mension of the principles for the present purpose is the statement of principles... annotated edition with commentary and examples', by A.H. Chaplin assisted by Dorothy Anderson. Most of the principles themselves may seem quite so obvious as not to be worth stating, to the more sophisticated student of today. But it should be remembered that they did in fact effect the structure of heading decisions in AACR to a great deal, and they were internationally agreed. There were all 'Possibilities of its reflection in future cod), particularly the Pruision 'Instructions'. Principles are must and basis of a catalogue, code, but it should not be a skeleton on which a complete code be hanged. Principles are confined to the another (or title) heading for printed books or similar materials in large libraries.

When we go through the 'statement of principle', the first important statement is that a catalogue's fun tions are to ascertain: *(a)* if a library has a book when specified by author and title or their equivalent; and *(b)* the range of works and their editions by an author. The inference is that the first function is more important. Chaplin pointed out that Paris conference was only the begining as its scope was restricted to choice of headings for all author-title catalogue. The next step of development of internitional cataloguing was the "international meeting of cataloguing expert's and its International working party under the chairmanship of Mr. A. J. Wells. The committee was setup to evalulate a standard order and content for the description of books. It was an important effort in the field of descriptive cataloguing.

Paris conference has been a landmark in the history of cataloguing, It resulted to many standard publications, IFLA started a "Newsletter" giving details of Paris Conference. There was "IFLA Committee on Uniform Cataloguing Rules."

The Anglo-American Cataloguing Rules, 1961

In March 1961 the Henorary Secretary of the "Library Association Cataloguing Rules Sub-committee," the late H.A. Sharp, resigned from the Sub-committee, and the post of Honorary Secretary was abolished. But the appointment by the American Library Association, in 1956, of Seymonr Lubetzkey, as General editor of the proposed new code of cataloguing rules had significantly altered the work schedules of the American, British and Canadian Committee jointly engaged on the formulation of new rules, and resulted in a Steadily Increasing output of draft rules, minutes, memoranda and comments from the participating bodies. The British sub-committee appointed Phillip Escreet as editor.

Lubetzkey resigned as editor of the new Anglo-American code in 1968 and was replaced by C. summer spalding, who began a complete reappraisal based on the work already done by Lubetzkey based on the Paris principles. Lubetzkey has provided a priliminary review of A.A.C.R. in 1964 summerizing its aims as being "designed to streamline intellectually the cataloguing process' to make the operation, of cataloguing more purposeful rational and meaningful, and resulting catalogue a more intelligible and helpful guide to the resources of the library."

It is unfortunate on the part of A.A.C.R. that two separate texts, British, and American, had to be produced. The main difference the provision of some different rules for corporate bodies. Other differences are in the rules for serials, court rules, and treaties and inter-governmental agreements. The problem of implementation loom less large in this country than in the United States, since the British National Bibliography has adopted the British text of the code almost in its entirely, so that any library using B.N.B. cataloguing, whether in the shape of cards, entries in the weekly parts of B.N.B. and their successive cummulations, or M.A.R.C. tape, has to take positive steps not to adopt the new rules, so far as cataloguing of recently published accessions is concerned.

The two texts for descriptive cataloguing are quite different in some respects, though the philosophy behind them is the same. In general it may be said that British Text is closer to the Paris principles and to Lubetzkey's ideas than the North American Text. The fundamental difference between the two texts of A.A.C.R. is the British Text based on "conditions of authorship, in accordance with Lubetzkey's suggestions, while American Test based on "Type of work". Thus one looks in vain for rules for encyclopaedias, dictionaries, directories, almanacs etc.

A.A.C.R. is based on four general principles:

(a) The work should be entered under its author or principal author when one can be determined.

(b) A work should be entered under its edition when there is no author or principal author and the editor is primarily responsible for its existence.

(c) A work should be entered under a compiler named on the title page in the case of collections of works by various authors;

(d) A work whose authorship is diffuse or unknown should be entered under its title.

The arrangement of A.A.C.R. is much more logical than that of most previous codes. Garman has illustrated the processes described in various chapters of A.A.C.R, and draw a decision flow chart.

Basic Rules for Entry

Chapter 1. The first Chapter starts with a page and half of introductory notes. These notes are essential to a proper understanding of the rules. It includes-Relationship between the general rules for added entries and the instructions for making added entries; Bibliographical entries, rules, added entries for displaying bibliographic activities; sources for determining main entry heading.

The Rules in Chapter 1 falls in three main groups. General rules (rules 1-19), special rules for certain legal and religious publications (rules 20-32), and added entries (single rule 33) broken down in to 14 sub-rules.

We can very well describe them in a chart:

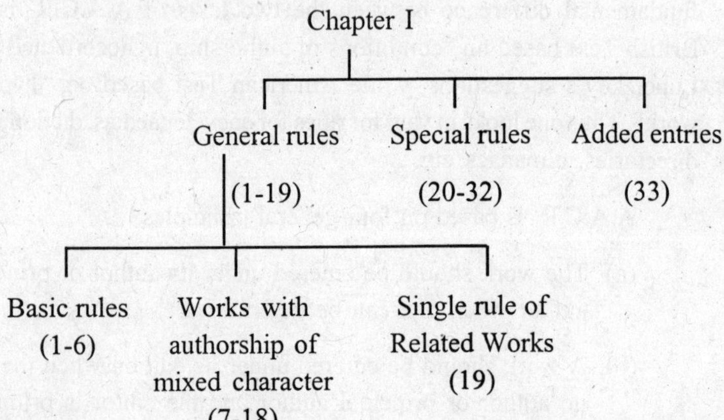

In this Chapter it is essential to bear in mind the principle underlying the structure of the rules. In the Section headed "Structure" it is set out that "This principle is that each rule dealing with a specific problem is to be understood in the context of the more general rules. This does not mean that there are no specific rules that completely cover specific problems, nor does it mean that aspect of more general rules are never repeated in specific rules. It does mean, however, that the relevent general rules apply to any aspects of a specific problem that are not dealt within a specific rule".

Chapter 2. This chapter is more influenced with morphology language, and custom upon the form in which a personal name is to be entered than with influences derived from the relationship between the name in question and other names.

Chapter 2 is divided in two main sections: General rules, and special rules. General rules will ordinarily suffice for persons whose names are not written in the Roman alphabet or whose names are in a non-European language that is written in roman alphabet. 'Special rules are confined to Arabic, Burmese, India, Indonesian, and thai names.

Chapter II

General rules (Ruels 40-51)

Special rules for names in certain languages (52-54)

Basic rules (40)

Choice and form of names(41-45) and entry of names (46-61), and Additions to names (52-53)

Chapter 3. This chapter is divided in two main Sections, consisting of general rules and special rules. The special rules of this chapter differs with from those in other chapters.

General rules (60-98) consists of a basic rule (rule 60). These are followed by two groups ef rules—choice and form of names, and subordinate and related bodies.

Rule 61-General rule for choice and form of name.

But it is subject to serious limitations in cases where the form of name used in the body's over publications varies. Rule 62 of varient forms in publications deserve careful study. The rule is concerned solely with varient forms of a single name. Library of congress pointed out that the published text of chapter 3 made no specific provision for varient spellings of the name of a corporate body.

Rule 63 (conventional names) is divided in two parts. Normally the conventional name is to be established in the language of the body. Rule 64 (language). It embodies the spirit of principle 9.4. of the Paris principles. It is worth noting that the first sentence of rule 64 makes the first choice the form [of the name] in the official language, but does not specify that it shall be the official form of the name in that language; the choice appears to be, rather between different language forms of the body's name as it appears in its, publications.

Rule 65 (additions to names). It covers not only two or more bodies with identical names, but also bodies with names so closely similar that they are likely to be confused.

Rule 66 (omissions from names).

Rule 67 (modifications of names)

Rule 68 (changes of names)

Rule 69 (Bodies with names implying subordination)

Rule 71 (Type)

Rule 73 (Additions)

Rule 75-77 (Government)

Rule 78-86-(Govt. bodies and officials)

Rule 87 (General rules)

Rule 89 (Number)

Rule 92-97 (Spl. rules for religious bodies and officials)

Chapter 4. On Uniform titles.

The need to apply rules vary from library to library. It is mentioned in the introductory note that any library adopting the code will well to consider the needs of the users, Mr. Lubetzkey in his code of cataloguing Rules mentions two objectives:

1. To facilitate the location of a particular publication, *i.e.*, of a particular edition of the work, which is in the library.
2. To relate and display together the editions which a library has of a given work and the works which it has of a given author.

This chapter follows the general pattern of being divided in to general and specific rules.

Rule 110 (basic rule)

Rules 101-103 (choice and form of title)

Rules 104-107 (Other General rules)

Rules 108-114 (Bible)

Rules 115-118 (other sacred spriptures)

Rules 119 (Liturgical works)

Chapter 5. (Reference) (Rule 120-126)

This chapter is largely concerned with consolidating and bringing together in one place, the instructions for the making. of references. It presents few problem, a part from that of securing effective implementation.

Rule 120 (basic rule) which calles for the making of a reference from any form under which 'the name of the person or corporate body—is or may reasonably be known'.

Rule 121 (Names of persons)

Rule 122 (Names of corporate bodies)

Rule 123 (special headings)

Rule 124 (Uniform titles)

Rule 125 (Collective titles)

Rule 126 (References in lieu of added entries)

Chapter 6. (Rules 130-156) deals with the description of monographs. The chapter of North American Text is a minor revision of the Library of congress 'rules for Descriptive cataloguing'. In the British Text the trend towards simplification is followed.

But there are a number of interesting variations from the North American Text. For example, plates are considered to be part of the pagination statement instead of the illustrations statement and the British prefer the date of 'edition' in the case of new impressions rather than the imprint date.

Chapter 7. (Serials). In the introductory note it is clear that some works appear in the catalogue as serials because a library decides to treat them as serials. There are, of course, some serial publications that even the laymen would think of as periodicals or Journals. rather than as books, if forced to make the distinction, but the point to bear in mind is that rules for the descriptive cataloguing of serials, like rules for the entry of serials, have to be judged with reference to their success in treating all serials, not just those that leap to the mind as soon as the word is mentioned. Rule 163 (holding's in North American Text) (Volume designation and dating, in British Text).

Chapter 8. (Incunabula).

Rule 184 (Bibliographical references).

Rule 185 (Notes).

Chapter 9. (Photographic and other reproduction).

Rules 190 and 191 requires extremely careful reading. As the 'Introductory note' points out, the fact that a work, or rather a publication or a copy of a work, is a photoreproduction or a fascimile is not always 'of significance for cataloguing purposes.'

Rule 190 (Facsimile editions),

Rule 191 (Photoreproductions to be described as such).

In general A.A.C.R. embodies the objectives stated by the American Committee on Catalogue Code Revision in 1956. The rules are consistant and comprehensive. They emphasize economy in cataloguing, and they cater for both the needs of practicing cataloguers and library education.

An Eye-view on A.A.C.R.—No doubt the A.A.C.R. is a large code. But once it is familiar, it is easier to apply than previous codes. This is because it is more consistant in principles than other codes' However, the great details deplored by Osborn and Lubetzkey in the past still persists. In addition to examples already mentioned, one should mention the minuteness of the rules for description. Nevertheless, these rules result in more useful information put in a more useful way than in past codes. *e.g.*, 'operative date of work is brought in to the imprint. Some cataloguers donot agree and deslike the degree of permissiveness allowed. However, apart from the alternative rules, this is a matter rather of allowing cataloguers to work towards an acceptable solution using their own initiative, and it is unpair to assert that this will result in more deviations than resulted from A.A. 1908 and AL A 1949. But if many deviations do result, this could indeed be unfortunate in these days of closer international co-operation in shared cataloguing and similar activities.

Sometimes the splitting of the bibliographical unit may have been taken too far, as already exemplified. Index includes some 'cases' but not others. Solutions in examples do not always show actual form of heading. The relation of unnecessary case enumeration has already been commented upon.

Filing rules would have been useful, specially with formalisation of the uniform title for say works, and similar collections.

Association published the final second edition known as A.L.A. Cataloguing Rules for Author & Title Entries. The entry part of 40 pages had increased over 200 pages in 1949. Mr. Seymour Lubetzkey, a consultant Library of Congress was assigned the task of reviewing and analysing the A.L.A! rules. He published a analytical-study of A.L.A. in his book "Cataloguing Rules and Principles, a critic of A.L.A. Rules for Entry" and a proposed design for their revision. It was published by Library of Congrcss in 1953. He clearly reviewed the necessity and irrelevancy of many of the rules of A.L.A. catalogue. This controversy led to a Code Revision Committee of A.L.A. and several sub-committees. These efforts emerged the new code 'A.A.C.R.'

Classified Catalogue Code. According to Dr. Ranganathan his Classified Catalogue Code is a institution which enabled him to design a catalogue code on scientific lines in 1924-25. Ranganathan said "The classified catalogue code owes itself to the sense of revolt induced in the mind where learning cataloguing in 1924-25 in the school of library science of the University College of London."

The main reasons of drafting a classified catalogue code are many 1—Dr. Ranganathan was annoyed with the teaching methods and the style in which A.A.C.R. was taught, 2—Each rule of Anglo American code was to be put into rote memory, 3 - Rules were not present as a system, 4-No other code was taken for comparison.

According to Dr. Ranganathan there should be a theory behind practice. The skeleton nature mixing up the author entry and subject entry, lack of unity in many of rules was the main draw backs in the drafting of the A.A. code. Ranganathan was felt that nothing could be discussed about classified catalogue and its difference with the dictionary catalogue in his class. There was also mention of bibliographical details about for made collation and imprint. All these reasons compelled Dr. Ranganathan to declare in the campus of University college of London "I will think to draft a classified code when I go back home."

Ranganathan drafted his Classified Catalogue Code in 1934. The rules were based on canons of cataloguing. He applied normative principles in a systematic manner to the rules of cataloguing in his second edition of C.C.C. 1945 and with more few modification in 1964. C.C.C. has several distinguishing features like normative principles, chain procedures, canons, descriptive portion of the entry etc.

A.A.C.R.—2

A.A.C.R.-2 is a modified version of A.A.C.R. The rules are framed having in view large libraries and research and special libraries. The small and medium size libraries have to resort to considerable amount of local variation to work with this code. The rules are Oriented to Machine Readable cataloguing and there is an open question before the libraries in resorting to manual cataloguing" practice as together the rules of the A.A.C.R.-2 with all its irrelavant bibliographical descriptions and peculiar punctuations would be a workable preposition.

Features of A.A.C.R.—2

A.A.C.R.—2 Published in 1978, is a culmination of three decades of research work in author, title and descriptive cataloguing. The points raised by Semour Lubetzkey in 1953 followed by the agreements reached at the International Conference on cataloguing principles 1961 and A.A.C.R. I are said to have been translated into practice. Not only this, about a century old controversy of Society and Institution and other such non standardised practices in Anglo American Cataloguing code, is said to have been removed in A.A.C.R.-II and thus an attempt is said to have been made to have a true Interational Catalogue Code acceptable, in entire English speaking area of the world, Some of the special features of A.A.C.R.—II are as under:

There has been definite impact of Ranganathan for we find that the rules for choice and rendering and description have been given separately.

There is a supremacy of descriptive cataloguing over the rules for author and title cataloguing, In 1974 the 'International Standard for Bibliographic Description for Monographic Publications' published followed by I.S.B.D. (S), I.S.B.D. (Maps), I.S.B D. (G) and I.S.B.D. for other non-book materials. These International Standards are describing the documents have been given precedence over the rules for choice of headings and that too the rules for I.S.B.D. (G) have been put at the top priority as Chap. I which could be applicable to all type of documents-books, booklets and non-book materials. The catalogue is supposed to describe the document first and then he will provide access points to the document consult.

The rules are based on conditions of authorship rather than type of works and as such there are no separate rules for dictionaries. Encyclopedias, Concordence, correspondence and others. There are certain stated principles for the rules for choice of entries.

There is tendeney towards growing number of cases for title as main entry. Works under editorial directions and 'collections with collective title' are new cases where title entries have been provided.

The confusing rule for 'collection without collective title' have been amended in A.A.C.R.I., for such works, the catalogue had to face difficulties with the rules number 5th B-which is sole arbiter for choice of heading and rules number 146 that is for "Bound with" notes would also be applicable. The detailed rules given under rule 146 proved to be contradictory if applied along with rule number 5th B. These two rules taken together proves to be contradictory against the established unit card principles.

The rules for differentiated and Undifferentiated multiple author have been provided along the same time as in the A.A.C.R. I. Among first catagory of authoriship the rules for translation, revision etc. and for so called joint authorship traditionally have been provided where in the find dominance in document of Bibliographical unit rather than document as literary unit. The availability of principal author recognised by way of typographical differences is the testimony to this fact. While in case of differentiated multiple authors there is dominence of

Literary Unit where in translations, revisions and artistic works are entered under the author of the original or the author responsible for the main portion of the book.

Corporate authorship is one such controversial area which prove to be a great obstacle in reaching an agreement in Anglo American Cataloguing Practices. The Principles, agreed upon at the ICCP (1961) could not be formulated into a single act of rules, which could not be acceptable in both the countries. The result was the two simultaneous editions for A.A.C.R.-1. Thanks to the Joint Steering Committee of the A.A.C.R. Second that an agreement has been reached over the rules for corporate bodies and thus in making the code as a true International code of cataloguing A.A.C.R.-2 does not have artificial distinction between society and Institution but these bodies are now covered under a single generic rules for all types of corporate bodies.

The recent developments like MARC project. Shared Cataloguing Programme, Cataloguing-In-Publication programme and other mechanised cataloguing programme have rendered it essential to bring out the code of Cataloguing having such areas in cataloguing: entries with distinct punctuation marks acceptable to mechine Immediately after the development of ISBD's, the some were implimented in the cataloguing of the Library of Congress, in "National Union Catalogue" in the BNB and in numerous other bibliographical services through out the world. A.A.C.R.-2 can. therefore, be deemed as a code having a standardization is not only Author and Title cataloguing but Descriptive Cataloguing also.

Besides rules for choice of headings, form of headings and descriptions, there are rules for analytical cataloguing and reference entries. The chief sources of information for different items in the catalogue entries had been stated and here again we find definite impact of Ranganathan and its "Canon of Ascertainability." The chief source of Information for the body of entry in A.A.C.R. I was too right which is now modified. Besides these there is a glossory of technical terms and there are standard abbreviations listed and extensive index of course to add to the value of the code.

Limitation of A.A.C.R.-II

On practice to the code two difficulties come in way: How to describe documents first and add access points after words and when the code provides to retain main and added entries systems. The author entries having the name of author at the top is to be the main entry. While added entries are replicas of the main entry. The distinction between main and added entries is artificial and academic only. The best course for the code would have been if it had provided for title as main entry and added entry headings including the heading for the author have been given as access points, There is author problems when to enter work under the title. In such cases title will be repeated if consistency is to be maintained. A face saving device of option has been adopted by the cataloguer in such cases. But it will effect consistency in the structure of catalogue entries.

LAYOUT OF CATALOGUE CODE

Catalogue code is a technical juncture of various systems, principles, terms, canons and rules framed in a line of thougbt covering various aspects of cataloguing procedures, maintaining consistency in nature, framing a structure and representing several aspects of author, title, subject at various levels and distinctions.

Dr. Ranganathan bas described the layout in 3 parts:

(1) Idea plane,

(2) Verbal plane,

(3) Structure plane.

Idea Plane

Idea plane is based on Principles of Unity of Ideas in a catalogue. Ideas are break up in:

(a) Sentences,

(b) Paragraphs,

(c) Chapters,

(d) Parts.

Verbal Plane

Verbal plane is based on discussion and exchange of conversation. It has some specific breakup:

(a) Syntactical Unity-each sentence should have syntactical unity,

(b) Accuracy in Homonym and Synonym-Fault of homonyms and Synonyms should be avoided,

(c) Proper tautalogy-Fault of tautology should be avoided,

(d) Proper terminology- Tecbnical terms should be used wherever warranted taking them from an accepted glossary of technical terms for the subject of study, and its absence, by defining them.

Structure Plane

The structure should be based on idea plane and verbal plane. It is divided in 8 parts:

(a) Structure, (Parts, Chapters, Sections, Rules)

(b) Area of catalogue code. (Author, title. subject, collaborator entry)

(c) Unity at all levels, (Rule level, Chapter level, Part level and Code level)

(d) Standard technical terminology, (Free from Hemonyms, Synonyms)

(e) Rules, (Rules, sub-rules, canons, principles)

(f) Transparency, (transparency of a code)

(g) Tautology, (No repetition)

(h) Notation, (helpful notation)

Basic Features. There have been several efforts in early history to construct several codes by several authorities. All propounded several rules of author, title and subject, but none formulated rules for structure and out line of code. There should be a proper planning and consideration of other requisites for the structure of a catalogue code:

(a) Proper planning,

(b) Open discussion,

(c) Broad mindedness,

(d) Universal recognition,

(e) Thoughtful foundation,

(f) Systematised knowledge,

(g) Timely review.

Structure

We may divide the structure of a standard code in following catagories.

1. Structure. Structure is based on Idea plane, verbal plane, and notational plane. Idea and verbal planes are the work of mind (thoughts) and verbal discussion and conversation. The Notational plane is a written work which is exchangeable. We accomodate letters and numbers. These may be pure or mixed notation.

CC—Ranganathan has used mixed notation-Roman capital and Indo-Arabic numerals. Roman Capitals are used for parts in single digits. Indo-Arabic numerals are used for sections and laws.

Part K (class Index Entries)—K

Chapter KA (Terminology of classification)—KA

Section (Basic Class) —1

Sub-Section (Class) —11

AACR—Mixed notations are used. There have been used Arabic numerals for parts, Chapters and Sections. Roman Capital for sub-sections and rules.

Part I (Entry headings)	—1
Chapter 2 (Headings for persons)	—2
Section	—42
Sub-section	—42 B

Priliminary

Every code has some priliminary characteristics. Priliminary consists

(a) Normative principles,

(b) Typing,

(c) Style of writing,

(d) Printing of entries,

(e) Construction,

(f) Punctuation,

(g) Capitalisation,

(h) Arrangement of entries.

Normative Principles. The CC has adopted the principle of consistency, relevence, permanency, osmosis, part, section and rule. Rule has permanent place in their sequence throughout. Ranganathan has suggested the application of canons and principles in place of rules.

Typing. Shorthand style, specific printing with specific letter-capital roman, small capital roman, ordinary letters and italics have been used in various codes. Capital roman for chapters, small capital roman for sections, ordinary letters for sub-sections, italic for references, are used.

Punctuations. Various cataloguing codes have used several symbols and signs like fullstop, Comma, Semicolon, Das, circular bracket, oblique and hyphon.

CC has used fullstop for completing the sentence comma for separating two consecutive blocks, semicolan for descriptive element, Das for consecutive numbers and circular individualising element.

Style of Writing. Capitalisation and Arrangement of entries. Fast colour ink, ordinary ink, ordinary ink pencil, library hand, letter, words, lines, capitalisation, underlining, etc are used in the layout of code. CC—has used fast colour ink, ordinary ink, library hand (ABCD-Z, abcd-x, 1234—0), lines (leading line, first verticle, second verticle, capitalisation according to grammer, Entry arrangement in alphabetic part, section. space. fullstop, comma, numerals in natural sequence, bracket, words in roman, italic, underlined, and word 'and', 'etc.' and semicolon.

AACR. It has followed more or less CC. Placing of rules are changeable and sequence is not determined all through.

ISI. The part on priliminaries shall be devoted, to normative principle, style of writing, typing or printing of entries, Construction, punctuation, Capltahsation, arrangement of entries, etc.

Terminology

The terminology should be precise and minimum in use. It should avoid homonyms, Synonyms as these are more or less found in natural language.

CCC has used technical terminology which makes the point clear and explain the things in short. In CC there is a separate chapter on terminology and defined in precise manner.

AACR. This code has followed ALA except few new terms. Code consists a separate chapter *i.e.* Appendix I. The language of terminology is ordinary and of laymens use.

No doubt CCC has adopted its over technical terminology, but it had used bombasting and superfluous words. CCC has not adopted a lay mans language. The plus point for CCC is that it has adopted the proper terms suitable and fit for a standard catalogue code.

ISI. The part on terminology shall contain definitions of technical terms and terms of Art used in the catalogue code.

Tautology

While layout a Catalogue code, it is always avoided to repeat the partial or full contant of any other rule. The rule should be full in itself and explanatory.

CCC—Has taken all precautions that rule are not repeated. Rules are full in sense and context, brief and systematically arranged.

But rules are partly shown and dependent on other rules. One has to compel to consult several other rules, if he consults one rule. It is time consuming. Rules are also lengthy and takes sometime to understand.

AACR—Rules are full in sense and no other rule is required to be consulted for the context of a particular rule. Rules are lengthy but small and understandable. Rules are sometimes confusive and not explanatory.

Determination of author and Collaborator:

Codes should have separate chapters on choice of author whether person or corporate. It should give guidance for determining the author and collaborator of a document.

CCC—There is a separate Chapter on choice of heading and rules on conflict of authorship. Ranganathan has discussed the problems in systematic way in CCC to avoid any confusion:

1. Person-vs-person,
2. Person-vs-Corporate body,
3. Government-vs-Institution,
4. Institution-vs-Institution,
5. Delegation-from-body-vs-Delegated to body,
6. Legal publications,
7. Author's name merged in title.

AACR—The code consists of chapter I which includes works with author ship with mixed character, related works from rule 1-16. Chapter II includes persons, choice and form of names from rule 40-58. So far corporate author is concerned this code consists of rule 17-33 with certain religious publications.

TOTAL RULES IN CCC AND AACR

	Total rules	Personal author	Corporate author
CCC	65	22	3
AACR	272	35	79

These rules have with them several sub-rules and sub-subrules.

ISI—The Section on the definition of author (s) and Collaborator (s) in this part, shall give guidance for the determination of the author (s) and the Collaborator (s) of a document.

INDIVIDUALISING ELEMENTS

Homonyms are the bad conductor of a Catalogue code. Code should avoid homonyms and form necessary rules to resolve homonyms.

CCC—has described homonyms in 3 senses. Sense 1-Rule FR 12, Sense 2-rule FR 22, Sense 3-rule FR 32. Homonyms are also described separately with every type of author and title. Rules for individualisation for homonymsare given in chapter BD under "Canon of individualisation" and adopted bracket as individualising element.

AACR—Code has not provided any specific rule for homonyms and its rendering.

ISI—The section of the part shall deal with individualising element to resolve homonyms.

Subject Entries

IS1—This part shall provide the structure of such a entry. It shall prescribe:

(i) The rules for determining the subject of a document either with the aid of its class number or otherwise.

(ii) The rule for rendering the name of a subject in the heading of a general subject entry for a document either with the aid of its class number or otherwise.

(iii) The individualising element to resolve homonyms in the main heading and sub-headings.

CCC—A separate part K has been alloted for Class Index entries. It is divided in to 12 chapters *i.e.* terminology, terminology of chain procedure, Choice of subject index heading, rendering of class index Heading, class index entry and examples of class index entries, classics, commission report, homonyms in class index entry, feature heading, and modification of dictionary catalogue.

AACR—It has no (separate) provision.

CCC has specific provision of class index, which is an important aspect of a classified catalogue code.

Cross Reference Index Entry

ISI. This part shall prescribe the structure of such an entry. It shall contain a chapter on each kind of cross reference index entry, laying down the rules for the choice and rendering of a referred from and referred to headings.

CCC—This code has described the rendering and choice of cross reference index entry in a separate part 'L' which includes chapters of structure and types, alternative name entry, varient-form of word 'entry, pseudonym-real name entry, editor-of series entry, and Generic name entry.

AACR—This code has provided some specific rules for reference. Under rule 120-126 in 17 pages, there are separate rules of references in case of name of persons, name of corporate body, special headings for legal publication, uniform title, collective title and references in lieu of added entries.

Both codes have made provision for cross reference entry. But AACR has not made provision for Editor of series entry and Generic name entry separately and with full explanations.

Simple Single Volumed Book

ISI. The chapter shall prescribe:

(i) The structure of a main entry.

(ii) Rules regarding the contants of each section of the main entry and their rendering.

CCC. Ranganathan has described the rendering of main entry in Part 'M' with its aspects source, sections, leading section, heading, title section, note, accession number, tracing section, cross reference entry.

Book index entries are also provided the place under main entry under chapter MK. Main entry in dictionary catalogue has been described in MZD.

AACR. Choice of main entry are described in the Chapter I, This chapter includes general rule, individual author, joint author, composit work, collection and serials.

Composit and Multivolumed Books

ISI. This part shall prescribe the structure for the different kinds of entries of ordinary composit books, artificial books, and multivolumed books. It shall contain the special rules for simple and single volumed books.

CCC—This code has separate provision for part N and chapters of ordinary composit books, artificial composit books, multi-volumed books.

AACR—This code has made provision for composit books in Chapter I, Rule 3- composit books. It has made separate rules for added entry for title.

CCC has specific rules and followed the ISI in real sense.

Perodicals and other Publications

ISI. This part shall deal with the nature of the complexities in periodical publications as viewed from the angle of cataloguing. It shall prescribe rules on the kinds of entries needed, the structure of of each kind of entries and the contents of each section of an entry for each kind of complexity.

CCC. This code has made provision for periodicals in chapter 'P'.

Chapters—Complexities

Simple periodical publications.

Irregularity in volume number.

Interrupted publication.

Change of title and sponsor.

Amalgamation.

Splitting up.

Supplement.

Combination of Complexity.

Dictionary Catalogue

Desiderata.

It has covered all possible aspects of periodical publications and rendering entries.

AACR- This code has made provision under Chapter I, Rule 5

A. Collective title.

B. Without Collective title.

C. Serials not issued by Corporate body.

D. Serials issued by Corporate body.

E. Serials issued by personal author or name of corporate author.

CCC. has adopted a organizational view in deciding the chapters and based on possible problems. While AACR has adopted a concept of type of periodicals along with their problems.

Other Chapters

ISI. A code may have following Chapters:

(i) Union Catalague.

(ii) National bibliography.

(iii) Abstracting and Indexing.

(iv) Other bibliographies and Cataloguing.

CCC. This code described in separate Chapters

Chapter Q—U.

Q. Union Catalogue

(Coverage, Modification in Catalogue rules, library number, cards for union Catalogue)

R. Union Catalogue for periodical publications.

S. National Bibliography.

T. Indexing periodical.

U. Abstracting periodicals.

AACR. This code has made no provision for Union Catalogue. It has made provision for Indexes.

Chapter I-Rule 27 Indexes.

Non-book Material

ISI. A code may have following Chapters regarding Conventional and non-Conventional documents

(i) Manuscripts,

(ii) Incunabula,

(iii) Picture,

(iv) Maps,

(v) Charts,

(vi) Films,

(vii) Gramophone records,

(viii) Audo-Visual meterial,

(ix) Automatic record.

CCC—This code has described non-book material in separate part V and Chapter V. A.

Chapter V—Incunabula and Non-book meterial.

VA-Kind of documents for consideration.

AACR. This code has described Non-book meterial in separate part III and Chapter 10-15.

Chapter 10—Manuscripts,

11—Maps, Atlas etc.,

I2—Motion pictures & film strips,

I3—Music,

I4—Phonorecords,

15—Pictures, designs.

AACR has specifically described various aspects of each type of Non-book material. While CCC has not gone in detailed studies.

❐

7

Subject Cataloguing

Subject cataloguing is an important area of subject. The speedy growth of authors, long titles of works and heavy production of reading material have led to the dominance of subject approach. Subject is the first preference of the library users on which he wants information as it discloses books exclusively devoted to the specific subject, book of a greater extension than the specific subject, books of a smaller extension than the specific subject but dealing with some aspect of it, books in collateral subject which contents some Information, though indirectly, on the specific subject. In a large library maximum number of users consult the catalogue by subject approach particularly when one requires a specific book.

Subject Structure

While we discuss the subiect catalogue few lines may highlight the subject structure. Universe of subjects are developed by different methods-from individual experience, by applying fundamental laws and normative principles, with the aid of imagination, through deductive laws and canons and through other cycle of experience, principles and laws.

Ranganathan in 1957 submitted a press copy of theory of classified catalogue before the vice chancellor of Madras University for printing. His one friend 'Prohit Swami" presented a memiograph copy of the preliminary 2nd edition of the Anglo American code for comments. This draft copy of AAC (Anglo American code) made a cooperative study possible with classified catalogue code. A library catalogue is essentially a tool and a subject catalogue is a pinpointed cutter for a user to reach to the proper document.

Dr. Ranganathan as clearly mentioned in his book "Theory of Library catalogue" that subject approach in a substance derived from self education and principles crystallized on the basis of four categories of Upanisnadic seers, study, understanding, practice and teaching.

Objectives

Subject catalogue have two main objectives To enable a person to find the book of which the subject is known a to show what a library has on a given subject. According to Dr. Ranganathan most important function of the catalogue is subject retrieval and the catalogue has to take it bipartile, classified form one part holding entries arranged classified, in a hierarchical order between subject and given information about library resources holding on various subjects. He attributed the tardiness in its emergence to the enability of a classification scheme which was capable of serving adequatly as a base for the classified file of the catalogue. The degree of efficiency of the classified file in literature searching is directly proposional to the ability of classification scheme on which it is based to individualise specific subject of any degree of intension and to arrange them in a helpful hierarchical order.

Cutter's Attempt

Cutter was the pioneer to have for the first time ettempted to set up rules governing the choice and rendering of subject entries. Dr. Ranganathan was the other land mark evolving a system of chain Indexing and POPSI. The other effort was the library of Congress-List of subject headings for respectively. These lists lacks some appropriate terms and forms new concept. Libraries have to made their old heading to make the consistency by preparing authority files.

A subject catalogue is one which shows documents on a specific subject, by a given library.

Subject catalogues have four categories:

1. Alphabetical direct catalogue,

2. Alphabetical Indirect catalogue.

3. Alphabetical classed catalogue.

4. Classified catalogue.

In alphapetico direct catalogue form of heading are taken from ordinary uses and opposed to indirect heading. In alphabetico indirect catalogue indirect headings are used and a alphabetical filing of these headings provides collocation of material relating to traditional fields of study. In Alphabetico classed catalogue terms are listed in the form of indirect heading and the terms used do not belong to natural language, style of writing.

In classified catalogue headings are arranged on the besis of notation used in the scheme of classification. Tbe catalogue using notation and symbols to arrange entries are called classified catalogue.

Subject Headings

Bhattacharya discusses Ranganathan's work in formulating a general theory which is extended to the work of transforming, forms of names of subject for the purpose of finding information on the subject concerned. The structure of a subject classification, organising, associative and semantic relationship have been examined. He mentioned that the form of subject heading whether it be an artificial verbal language or notational language is important. The principle as enunciated by Cutter, that subject headings are necessary for both organising and associative classification and the symbolic relationship between these types of classification.

Cutter did for subject heading while Dowey did for classification. Library of Congress show some bias and confusion of thought. Eric Coates produced a system of cross references which could be computerised and Austin, through PRECIS, solved the problem of incomplete cross references and that of choosing the most important heading word. U K. Classification Research Group has analysed the kinds of sementic relationship between terms in thesauri and has isolated 3 groups: equivalent hierarchy and affinitivej associative. The Library of Congress affirmed that, although Changes in its subject headings were planned to replace absolete terminology, modernise spelling elminate antiquated patterns broaden or alter standard sub-divisions, and accomodate AACR 2, the publication of Library of Congress subject headings would continue.

Chan identified L.C.'s recent use of split subject files as representing a departure from the long-standing LCSH principle of uniform heading.

Chain Indexing

A subject index which governs the name of subject and refers to their class number is, therefore a *Sine quanon* of a classified catalogue. Dr. Ranganathan is the originator of chain procedure which is also known as Chain Indexing. Chain procedure is a procedure for deriving Class Index Entry from a class number, in a more or less mechanical way. It is used to derive Class Index Entry in Classified Catalogue and specific subject entries, subject analytical and see also subject entries in dictionary catalogue. In other words chain procedure is a semi-machenical method to derive Class Index Entries (Subject word entries) from a chain drawn out a successive sub-division of a class number. The approach is more or less mechanical because it helps in avoiding taken of arbitrary decisions recording how to use, might approach the catalogue to the subject.

Its adoption by B.N.B.

Chain indexing system is one of the greatest contribution in the field of subject cataloguing. It was used by British National Bibliography for 2 decades. Over the last 20 years chain procedure has been considerable amended and improved. The 4th edition of classified catalogue Code (1958) contained a special terminology of chain procedure and tight it up with the special terminology of a synthetic classification. After applying chain procedure for BNB E. J. Coats has produced a more modified structure of headings in subject catalogue. He has analysed the chain procedure and explain Chain procedure indexing reflecting the modulated structure of classification scheme, tends to represent complex ideas by means of elementary combined terms, rather than by single complex terms: because of this, the coverage of subject relationship signalled by a classified catalogue supported by collocation of terms in a chain procedure index is probably greater than that produced by any alternative method of indexing.

Effectiveness in Classification Scheme

In 1950 B. C. Bickery numerated 5 requirements of an exhaustive catalogue. 1. Alpha-betical index must be consistantly derived from a systematic organization of a subject matter. While Dr. Ranganathan has deviced a technique. "Chain Procedure" for transforming the relation in a synthatic classification system in 1953. It is a mechanical process of the ehoice and rendering subject heading, a symbosis between classification and cataloguing. It is an original contribution to the development of Library Science.

Chain procedure does not apply with Decimal classification due to many defects in that classification scheme. In D.C. notation has no hierarchical relation between terms. It is insufficient to relay in the digit of D. C. class numbers to produce all necessary entry words. There are many omissions and errors in the classification schedule.

Chain procedure has some demerits in its credit. It does not provide detailed rules of direct application except few guide lines to apply the chain procedure. Cataloguer has no liberty to use his knowledge and experience to decide which Cross Reference Index Entry to prepare and correct. Moreover chain procedure can not be applied to a scheme of classification having no canon of Hospitality in array and chain. The same case is applied in the classification scheme does not provide class number co-extensive with the specific subject of the book. Universe of knowledge is a changing procedure and the classification scheme should also be changed accordingly. If it did not follow it may create a serious problem, Dr. Ranganathan has suggested broad guide line for selection of sought headings and the individualization of heading.

Chain procedure is class number based and conventional. It was experienced that it should be made possible to apply the chain procedure in corporating classified catalogue system in the dictionary catalogue system.

P.O.P.S.I.

Research team of G. Bhattacharyya and A. Neelameghan developed chain procedure known as P.O.P.S.I. It is a superimposed version of chain indexing—Postulate based Permuted Subject Indexing. It is a procedure for implement the policy "Grouping by *Juxta* position" by keeping the structure of each specific subject heading parallel horizontally presented chain serving as the basis.

It implies the analysis of a subject into its components according to a set of postulates and principles, arrangement of the components in a definite sequence and derivation of desired specific subject heading and of the referred from subject heading on the basis of the sequence components of the subject concerned. A. Thoms on evolved method deriving subject heading which was based on a system of subject analysis into six factors-Pagination, Material, Processes and problems, Place, Time and Form.

Neelamaghan in his paper, has suggested at length the semantic and synthatic aspect of POP system. A comparative study of subject heading structure according to POPSI has heen discussed, by Rajan and Guha.

PRECIS—Derek Austin has developed the new indexing system known PRECIS—PRE served Context Indexing System. It is computer oriented system and being used in the BNB since 1971. Austin has made sufficient provision of necessary subject reference index.

This system owes partialy to Ranganathan facet analysis worked out in chain indexing procedure for subject index.

E. J. Coats described chain procedure as an alternative tool arbitrary limited permutation of index components. He also discussed its economy together problem of unsolved heading and the need the exclude genius-species pairs from qualifying terms. Coats conveyed the adoptability of PRECIS for the contribution of subject heading for the British Technology Index. Chain procedure is not full applied to the fully class number of a micro subject. Neelamaghan recommended to treat the micro subject as multifocal one and devide it into convenient smaller compound subject going with the one and same basic subjects. He further explained that a main entry be prepared each of these compound subject and class index entries derived from each class number by applying chain procedure.

Adhoc Committee

1960 and Adhoc Commission was appointed in order to determine the heading of the entry. Special rules were formulated for deriving Class Index Entries from the last saught heading of the chain contributed by a class number. These suggestions were accordingly corporated in CCC in chap. K.J. 1963 Dr. Ranganathan declared few homonyms among class index headings and suggested the use of auxiliary words with semantic value to resolve the homonym. In 1965 it was needed for standardisation of the style and rendering of subject headings derived by chain procedure in a frozen bibliography and suggested a new style for the purpose.

The efforts are made for the use of chain procedure in derived subject heading for dictionary catalogue also as the chain procedure is based on classified to help the dictionary catalogue deciding subject headings. E. J. Coats demonstrated how to adopt it for the preparation of the multiple subject headings to meet the requirements of an alphabetico specific catalogue.

Constructed stylized abstracts, which allows input, searching and retrieval in 4 languages; Switching between existing monolingual index language, through the use of an intermediate switching language, or by the saurus reconciliation; PRECIS which, because of its formalised syntax, has the potential to accept input data in one language and produce printed indexes in author; Freetext searching, involving the translation of the entries data base to produce parallel data based in different languages. This last approach appears unreasonable, but in a fully multilingual system the content of the data base has, in any case, to be translated.

TYPES OF SUBJECT CATALOGUES

A subject catalogue is a one which shows documents on a specifie subject passed by a given library. It attempts to bring together entries on a specific subject. A subject can be expressed either through words chosen to describe the different subjects or through notation based on a scheme of classification. In the first case it is called a subject heading and in the second case it is named a class number.

Subject catalogues are of the following four types:

Alphabetico-direct catalogue

Alphabetico-indirect catalogue

Alphabetico-classed catalogue

Classified catalogue.

ALPHABETICO-DIRECT CATALOGUE

It uses direct form of headings (that is natural form of a phrase) taken from ordinary usage as opposed to indirect headings. For example, headings like EDUCATIONAL SOCIOLOGY; RURAL SOCIOLOGY; CHRISTIAN SOCIOLOGY; are direct headings. On the other hand, headings like SOCIOLOGY, EDUCATIONAL; SOCIOLOGY, RURAL; SOCIOLOGY, CHRISTIAN are indirect headings.

Alphabetico-Indirect Catalogue

It uses indirect headings like SOCIOLOGY, EDUCATION; SOCIOLOGY; RURAL; SOCIOLOGY, CHRISTIAN. The alphabetical filing of these headings provides collocation of materials relating to traditional fields of study. The printed list of subject headings follow such a pattern.

Alphabetico-Classed Catalogue

Let us examine the example given below:

EDUCATION

EDUCATION, ADULT

EDUCATION, POST-GRADUATE

EDUCATION, SECONDARY

EDUCATION, SECONDARY, MANAGEMENT

EDUCATION, UNIVERSITY

EDUCATION, UNIVERSITY, EXAMINATION

EDUCATION, UNIVERSITY, MANAGEMENT

EDUCATION, UNIVERSITY, TEACHING TECHNIQUE

In the above example, terms have been listed in the form of indirect headings. The terms used do not belong to natural language style of writing. Every heading belonging to EDUCATION has been brought together. Thereby limited collocation has been achieved. Within EDUCATION, there is alphabetical scattering. Headings beginning with EDUCATION, UNIVERSITY have been brought together. Amongst these, there is again alphabetical scattering. This type of catalogue is called alphabeticoclassed catalogue.

Classified Catalogue

Let us examine the following example:

S1 CHILD PSYCHOLOGY

S2 ADOLESCENT PSYCHOLOGY

S3 POST-ADOLESCENT PSYCHOLOGY

The above headings have been arranged on the basis of notation used in the scheme of classification. The notation of Colon classification, the scheme used here mechanizes a preferred order. Its notation is also brief as compared with the natural language. The catalogues which use notational symbols as explained above to arrange entries are called classified catalogues. The arrangement achieved is a systematic on providing maximum degree of collocation. In order to get the best out of this type of catalogue, an alphabetical index has to be provided. The user will have to consult the index first and the index will provide him with a class number and with the help of the class number he will be able to reach the entry or entries in the classified catalogue, which will guide him to a particular part of catalogue containing entry or entries of his interest. However, the quality of this type of catalogue depends greatly upon the qualities of the scheme of classification used.

Evolution

Pettee has done detailed study about the evolution of subject catalogues. She is of the view that the alphabetical subject catalogue is of very recent origin, probably beginning from the middle of the 19th century. According to her, the subject catalogue is derived from the classed catalogue. The catchword entries in the early author and catchword catalogues, alphabetical subject index as a supplement to the author list, have contributed to its development.

Purpose

The basic purpose of a subject catalogue is to provide a direct and prompt approach to finding a document or group of documents on a given subject. According to Cutter, purposes of the subject catalogue are to enable a person to find a book of which subject is known and to show what the library has on a given subject. There is a conflict between these two purposes.

The first one considers a book as an individual item and the second one regards a book as an item belonging to a group of items. Thus, the first purpose requires that subject cataloguing should be done to distinguish one item from another, the second one requires that subject cataloguing should attempt to integrate the individual book with other books like it. Library literature shows many other statements of purpose. The fact remains that we have not been able to achieve complete agreement regarding purpose of a subject catalogue. The same still remains a fundamental question.

Theory

There is certainly a need to develop an agreed body of theory or principles upon which to base practice or method to derive subject headings for the preparation of a subject catalogue. In fact, we also require a comprehensive manual for practical application based on body of principles. Although Sears list of subject headings and Library of Congress subject headings are useful manuals, yet these are not fully satisfactory. Of course, Ranganathan did make an attempt to develop principles, but there is an urgent need to develop a comprehensive manual of subject headings based on chain procedure for practical application.

Rules

The alphabetical subject catalogues in most libraries are based on Cutter's Rules for a dictionary catalog. Cutter has provided detailed rules for the preparation of a subject catalogue covering rules 161 to 188. Many codes have been formulated after Cutter, but for Ranganthan's CCC to some extent, all derive from and indicate the influence of Cutter's rules.

Frarey rightly questions the validity of basic rules and techniques, because "the rules rest almost' solely upon a tradition of assumed needs derived from experience, and the techniques, lists and manuals of practice do no more than translate the rules into ways and means, the validity of the entire apparatus rests ultimately upon the reality of the needs assumed and the legitimacy of the purposes and functions which have been sensed in general ways but not defined with precision."

Problems in Determining a Subject Heading

Many times it becomes difficult to determine the subject of a document. Sometimes multifarious relationships of subject headings can be bewildering. The major problems in determining the subject are given below:

The subjects, very often, do not exist in separate compartments by themselves, they overlap in their extension and intension.

Subjects shift their scope and coverage, and change their nomenclature.

Subjects may have no specific name, because it is not always possible to find a single term or phrase to represent a specific subject.

Subject may have more than one name.

The document may deal with no precise subject or it may cover more than one subject.

How specific should a cataloguer be in determining the subject in relation to a given document?

Comments. The degree of specificity depends on the number of books available in the library and the types of readers to be served. However, the degree of specificity cannot be stated precisely.

Methods of Deriving Subject Headings

The following are the two major methods of deriving subject headings: (i) use of a printed list of subject headings; (ii) chain procedure.

Standard Lists of Subject Headings 710 Evolution

For many years printed dictionary book catalogues of libraries like those of the Boston Athenaeum and the Peabody Institute of Baltimore were used for the preparation of subject headings. These catalogues were more suitable for large libraries than small ones.

After the publication of Cutter's Rules for a printed dictionary catalogue in 1876, there began a demand for a standard list of subject headings based on rules provided by Cutter in his code. Thus an ALA Committee on Index to Subject Headings was formed in 1892. This committee succeeded in bringing out ALA List of subject headings for use in dictionary catalogs in 1895.

This list was brought out to serve the requirements of small or medium-sized public libraries. It reflected the conformity to the principles described by Cutter in his code. The list was mainly based on practice of five great catalogues of public libraries. It was revised and published in second and third editions. The list was received with enthusiastic response initially. Later, it became increasingly out of date and as a result this began to be given up by most libraries. The emergence of to important lists like Sears list and LC list led to the abandonment of ALA list by many libraries. Now this list is out of date.

Sears List of Subject Headings

It was first published in 1923, consisting of a collection of subject headings used in representative small libraries and later its scope was expanded to provide headings suitable for small as well as medium-sized libraries. It serves the requirements of general libraries. On the basis of experience and practices of several libraries, it has been revised from time to time. The latest edition being the tenth, having been published in 1972..

Aim

The list aims to provide one form of subject headings, under which all documents possessed by a library on a given subject can be listed. Besides, it lists headings after x, xx, which can be used to prepare see and see also subject references. Headings enumerated after see also are used to select appropriate subject heading(s) to be given for a document being catalogued.

Entries

Under the heading Catalogues, Classified, the following entry is given in the list:

Catalogues, Classified

See also Classification-Books

x Catalogues, Systematic; Classed catalogues; Classified catalogues

xx Classification-Books; Library catalogues.

Explanation. (i) Heading after See also is used to choose an appropriate heading. The list provides an entry similar to the above under Classification-Books.

(ii) If Catalogues, Classified is chosen as a subject heading, then a subject entry with a following heading will be provided:

CATALOGUES, CLASSIFIED

(iii) Headings after x will lead to the following see references:

CATALOGUES, SYSTEMATIC

see CATALOGUES, CLASSIFIED

CLASSIFIED CATALOGUES

see CATALOGUES, CLASSIFIED

CLASSED CATALOGUES

see CATALOGUES, CLASSIFIED

(iv) Headings after xx will lead to the following see also references, provided the referred from headings for these have also been used as subject headings in the catalogue:

CLASSIFICATION-BOOKS

see also CATALOGUES, CLASSIFIED

LIBRARY CATALOGUES

see also CATALOGUES, CLASSIFIED

Note: A library in India will have to adopt British spellings instead of American spellings.

Specific Entry

The principle of specific entry is recommended by the list. In order to obtain specific entry, the user of the list is required to prepare entry under the "most specific term, *i.e.* subject heading, which accurately and precisely represents the content of the book."

However in practice the list very often provides broader headings, so as to meet the requirements of small libraries, thus sacrificing the principle of specific entry.

Common Usage

The word or words used represents common usage in America. Thus, current American spellings and terms have been used. In fact, popular or common names are preferred over scientific or technical names.

Uniformity

If there are several synonyms, then one uniform term must be selected out of these and it must be applied consistently for the same topic.

Consistency

The Sears list is based on experience and practices of several libraries. Therefore, a cataloguer by using, it can achieve an element of consistency in the practice of subject headings.

Relation with LC List

As far as possible, the headings, terminology and subdivisions in Sears list follow the practice of Library of Congress subject headings. Therefore, it becomes easy for a library to change over to Library of Congress list, when the library becomes large enough.

Revision

It does not make provision for revision between editions except new headings or changes in old headings are incorporated for H. W. Wilson Co. publications.

Sub-divisions of Subjects

Under JESUS CHRIST, SHAKESPEARE, UNITED STATES, CHICAGO, OHIO, ENGLISH LANGUAGE, ENGLISH LITERATURE detailed sub-divisions have been provided, similar sub-divisions can be used for other headings of the same type.

Directions have been provided as to how subject headings involving subdivisions of subjects can be obtained.

Examples: PHYSICISTS—DIRECTORIES

LIBRARY SCIENCE—BIBLIOGRAPHY

PHYSICS—PERIODICALS

PHYSICS—HISTORY

LIBRARY SCIENCE—PHILOSOPHY

PHYSICS—STUDY AND TEACHING

Geographic Names in Subject Headings

The list provides guidelines, for subject sub-divided by place. For subjects like art and music the adjective forms as given below are to be used:

ART, INDIAN

MUSIC, INDIAN

Detailed rules have been provided for biography, language and literature.

Examples: HINDUS-BIOGRAPHY

NEW DELHI-BIOGRAPHY

LIBRARIANS-BIOGRAPHY

HINDI LANGUAGE—GRAMMAR

HINDI DRAMA—TECHNIQUE

HINDI LITERATURE—HISTORY AND CRITICISM

SANSKRIT DRAMA-COLLECTIONS

Plural Form

Headings usually have been provided in plural form, with a few exceptions. The singular form is used in order to distinguish between subject and form headings.

Subject headings:

ESSAY

SHORT STORY

DRAMA

Form headings for collections:

ESSAYS

SHORT STORIES

DRAMA-COLLECTIONS

Direct Headings

Basically the headings provided in the list are direct headings but in certain cases inverted headings are used, so as to collocate them. That is the basic approach of classification to collocate material is applied.

Examples: CATALOGUES, BOOK

CATALOGUES, CARD

CATALOGUES, BOOKSELLERS

CATALOGUES, CLASSIFIED

Comments on Sears List

Sometimes the list equates non-synonymous subjects.

Examples: RELIGIOUS HISTORY

see CHURCH HISTORY

The possible reason for the above approach would be to reduce the number of specific subject headings. However, an Indian librarian would find choice of CHURCH HISTORY as a heading to be wrong one. Because it may have hardly any book dealing with CHURCH HISTORY and it may have many books on REUGIOUS HISTORY.

There are many inconsistencies in the form of subject headings used. LIBRARIES, SPECIAL but MUSIC LIBRARIES; EDUCATION, HIGHER but PROFESSIONAL EDUCATION.

There are inconsistencies in the choice of headings. Under EDUCATION, there is a reference to EDUCATION OF WOMEN but none to EDUCATION OF PRISONERS, though both the later headings have been enumerated as subject headings in the list.

There are certain headings, which are vague, without a scope note having been provided. In such cases, scope notes are essential.

The terminology used by the list is American. A library in India or Pakistan or Great Britain would have to face some problem due to the variation in American and British spellings. However, it should not be considered a major drawback.

Subject headings of importance and special interest to American libraries have been provided in great detail. Thus, an Indian library would find the list inadequate for subjects of special interest to it.

The references do not seem to have been based on any set of principles.

LC Subject Headings

The Library of Congress began printing its subject headings in parts in 1909. However, a complete list covering all areas of knowledge was issued in 1911. The list is in its seventh edition published in 1966. The list includes terms which can be used as subject headings for a library catalogue. The list records the practices of the Library of Congress. Each subject heading included in it was chosen for the dictionary catalogues of the library.

Principles

Cutter's precepts are followed in many respects. The list includes terms, which can be used as subject headings and as well those from which references should be prepared. Terms have been given in various forms including single nouns, adjective form of nouns, complete phrases, compound nouns to express relation, paired terms, etc.

Revision

Supplements are issued every month, listing new and revised headings. Approximately 9,000 new subject headings are established every year.

Usage

The headings from this list appear in the tracing on printed cards issued by the Library of Congress and H.W. Wilson Company. Hence this list is followed extensively by those libraries which use the above card services.

As the list includes more terms and provides comprehensive subject coverage it is therefore considered more suitable for larger libraries than Sears list of subject headings.

Sears List of Subject Headings and LC Subject Headings

Sears is based on LC, but it is smaller than LC because of the elimination of many specific headings. It makes use of more combined subject headings forms and provides for fewer sub-divisions.

Both have similar headings, references, and terminology, thus making it possible for a library to change from Sears to LC, in case it becomes sufficiently large. However, Sears contains fewer specific headings and sub-divisions. In many cases, specific headings found in LC are rejected by Sears and put under broader headings. For example, PLANE GEOMETRY.

Both have similar limitations, but they have set a high standard. Great care is required to apply them properly.

Special Lists of Subject Headings

After the development of general lists of subject headings, a large number of special lists to cater to special requirements or special collections have been developed. In general, these are based on the LC pattern. These have greater specificity in subject headings and provide for detailed sub-divisions.

Comments

Although, the lists are based on logical and pragmatic considerations, still, they cannot be accepted completely by all libraries. Each library should chalk out a policy of its own, taking into consideration the size of collection, demands made upon the catalogue, and needs of the users. The lists can provide most of the terms required. To meet the special requirements, the cataloguer should not hesitate to adopt a new heading or term. However, this requires judgment, experience, and knowledge of the field. Otherwise too much of autonomy is likely to lead to chaos.

In standard lists of subject headings, general practices have been developed on the basis of experience. But there is a need for a code of practice which should be acceptable to cataloguers. Perhaps, it is the result of a lack of agreement that such a manual has not appeared so far.

Chain Procedure

S.R. Ranganathan is the originator of chain procedure which is also known as chain indexing. It was first mentioned in his *Theory of library catalogue.* It is a "Procedure for deriving Class Index Entry from a class number, in a more or less mechanical way". In other words, chain procedure is a semi-mechanical method to derive class index entries (subject word entries) from a chain drawn out of successive sub-divisions of a class number. The approach is more or less mechanical because it helps in avoiding taking of arbitrary decisions regarding how a user might approach the catalogue through the Subject. This method may be used to provide subject indexes to classified catalogues and classification schemes. This can also be used to prepare subject headings for a dictionary catalogue.

Usage

From 1951 onwards, it was adopted by British National Bibliography successfully. But since 1971, it has been abandoned. This must be because of many difficulties arising from the application of chain procedure to Dewey decimal classification which is less suitable for the purpose. However, a large number of Indian libraries following Ranganathan's Classified catalogue code are using chain procedure successfully to derive subject headings.

Relation with Scheme of Classification

For the full efficiency of this technique, the scheme of classification to be used for the purpose should possess the following qualities: *(i)* satisfaction of the canons for growing universe; *(ii)* class numbers to be provided should be coextensive with the specific subjects of the books being classified; and *(iii)* notation of the scheme must indicate subordination at each step of division (follow hierarchical pattern).

Chain procedure was originally intended for use with Colon classification. However, it may be applied to any scheme of classification, whose notation follows hierarchical pattern. This method of deriving subject word entries demands great care in its application especially when used with schemes, where steps of division are not always clear.

Procedure of Finding Links

Let us consider a class number from which subject headings are to be derived. The first digit in the class number provides the first link, the first two digits provide the second link, and so on. The last link is made out of the whole class number.

Links are of various types (CCC, chapter KB) as given below:

False link-"a link is a false link, if it ends with a

1. Connecting symbol; or

2. Digit representing a phase relation; or

3. Digit representing an Intra-facet relation; or

4. Digit representing an intra-array phase relation; or

5. Time-isolate representing time itself in the time facet of the class, and not representing any other fundamental category space, energy, matter, or personality-in their respective facets in the class number."

Unsought link-"Link which

1. Ends with a part of the isolate focus in a facet of a class number; and

2. Represents a subject on which reading material is not likely to be produced or sought or which is not likely to be looked up by any reader seeking materials on the specific subject forming the last link of the full class number."

Sought link—"Link which is neither false, nor fused nor unsought, and link ending with an after-time anteriorising common isolate digit." In practice, each library will have to take its decision keeping in view the documents to be organized, types of users, and nature of service to be provided.

Missing Link—"A link in a chain-with-gap, corresponding to the missing isolate in the chain."

The class number taken from Colon classification from which subject headings are to be derived may be represented in the form of chain as following:

Class number 0111,2J64, 6=Macbeth

0 = Literature (Sought link)

↓

01 = Indo-European literature (Unsought link)

↓

011 = Teutonic literature (Unsought link)

↓

0111 = English literature (Sought link)
↓
0111, = (False link)
↓
0111,2 = English drama (Sought link)
↓
0111,2J64 = Shakespeare (Sought link)
↓
0111,2J64, = (False link)
↓
0111,2J64,6 = Macbeth (Sought link)

Note: J64 in the above class number has been got with the help of a chronological device. According to Ranganathan. "The part of a class number, got by chronological device, should be treated as a whole, as if it were a single digit" Thus both the intermediate link have not been provided in the above chain.

A class number taken from Dewey decimal classification may be represented in the form of a chain as given below:

Class number 336.240942 = Income tax in England
300 = Social science (Sought link)
↓
330 = Economics (Sought link)
↓
336 = Public Finance (Sought link)
↓
336. = (False link)
↓
336.2 = Taxation (Sought link)
↓
336.24 = Income tax (Sought link)
↓
336.240 = (False link)
↓
336.240942 = Income tax in England (Sought link)

Derviation of Class Index Entries

A class index entry is a subject entry consisting of the leading section, directing words and a class number representing the terms in the leading section. The leading section consists of term represented by the last digit of each of the sought links of the chain representing the class number of each main entry and each cross reference entry. Each sought heading contributes one class index entry. Thus the number of class index entries depends upon the number of sought headings. In case, the heading is not an individualizing one, then sub-headings necessary to secure individualization are derived with the aid of canon of context, from the last digit of one or more of the upper sought links. Each heading or sub-heading should be a single noun in nominative case except when a qualifying adjective is necessary. We should prefer to use proper names or single words in popular usage. The terms should be taken from the scheme of classification used. However, if the scheme provides for American spellings and the library follows British spellings, then the former must be replaced by the latter. The detailed rules for choice and rendering of class index headings are given in chapters KD and KE, which should be followed.

Thus out of class number 0111,2J64,6, we are able to obtain the following class index entries:

MACBETH, SHAKESPEARE (William) (1564).

For documents in this Class and
its Sub-divisions see the Classified
Part of the catalogue under the Class
Number O111,2J64,6

SHAKESPEARE (William) (1564), DRAMA.

For... O111,2J64

DRAMA, ENGLISH.

For... O111,2

ENGLISH, LITERATURE.

For... O111

LITERATURE.

For... O

SOCIAL SCIENCE.

For documents in this Class and
its Sub-divisions see the Classified
Part of the catalogue under the Class
Number 300

ECONOMICS.

For....

330

PUBLIC FINANCE. For....

336

TAXATION.

For....

336.2

INCOME TAX.

For....

336.24

INDIA. INCOME TAX.

For....

336.240954

The above examples show, how chain procedure can be used to derive class index entries in a classified catalogue from class numbers obtained with Colon classification and Dewey decimal classification. It may be added that class index entries can also be derived for a dictionary catalogue.

Merits

Chain procedure is nearly mechanical and is applicable to those schemes of classification for classified catalogue as well as a dictionary catalogue, whose notation indicates subordination at each step of division.

Ranganathan has prescribed a set of rules for the application of chain procedure. His approach is such that many of the problems faced in the formulation of subject headings are solved automatically.

This procedure has been found to be more economical than other methods of deriving subject headings because it does not index all permutations. Take the example of a class number L2:3, the following subject headings are possible:

MEDICINE

DIGESTIVE SYSTEM, MEDICINE

PHYSIOLOGY, DIGESTIVE SYSTEM

MEDICINE, DIGESTIVE SYSTEM

DIGESTIVE SYSTEM, PHYSIOLOGY

According to rules give in CCC, we will choose first three Subject headings, rejecting others. A person looking under DIGESTIVE SYSTEM will be directed to the classified part, where he will be able to locate entries relating to the physiology of the digestive system. As a result, there will be no need to give last entry.

The subject headings contain characteristics in a reverse order as compared with scheme of classification. As a result, the elements which are scattered by a scheme of classification are found together in the subject headings.

Let us consider the following class numbers:

D1:4

D65:4

D66:4

ND:4

Here the documents on design get scattered depending upon the context.

Consider the following subject headings based on above-mentioned class number:

DESIGN, CIVIL ENGINEERING

DESIGN, ELECTRICAL ENGINEERING

DESIGN, ELECTRONICS

DESIGN, SCULPTURE

The headings beginning with DESIGN are found together. Thus a special purpose is achieved by the subject headings.

The drawing of the chain, choice, and rendering of subject headings can help in locating faults in the scheme of classification used regarding the hierarchical pattern, terminology, etc. Thus, chain procedure can prove to be an excellent check on the schedules of a scheme of classification.

If chain procedure is used along with a classified catalogue, then a class number once indexed will not require any further class index entries for that class number irrespective of the number of documents classified under that class number. Of course, if the terminology of a subject changes, then entries may have to be replaced. Occasionally, provision for synonyms, key words not already provided for, may have to be taken care of.

In case, a cataloguer applies chain procedure to a classified catalogue, then a reader approaching the catalogue from a broader or narrower subject will be directed to the classified part within easy range of the specific subject of his actual interest.

Demerits. It is not possible for a code to provide detailed rules of direct application, only broad guidelines can be given to apply the chain procedure. For instance, the rules for chain procedure and other ruies in CCC provide guidelines for preparing cross-reference index entries but the cataloguer will have to use his knowledge and experience to decide which such entries to pre pare. Often, it would be difficult to take a decision.

If the scheme of classification violates the canons of hospitality in array and chain, then that will cause a defect in the subject headings (*i.e.* headings of class index entries) derived on the basis of chain procedure. Out of a class number D66, the following class index entries can be derived for a classified catalogue:

ENGINEERING. MECHANICAL ENGINEERING

For.... D For... D6

ELECTRICAL ENGINEERING

For... D66

From the above we find that D6 stands for mechanical engineering and D66 represents electrical engineering. Both subjects are coordinate ones at the idea plane but at the notational plane, these have been put at the subordinate level. Thus canon of hospitality in array is violated. A reader looking for mechanical engineering will be able to locate an entry under it in the alphabetical part. This entry will direct the user to consult the classified part under the class number D6 and its sub-divisions. As D66 is a sub-division of D6, a reader is likely to look under D66 for books on mechanical engineering. On the other hand, D66 represents a subject different from mechanical engineering. This will certainly mislead the reader.

In case the scheme of classification does not provide class numbers coextensive with the specific subject of the book, then either further steps of division have to be provided by the cataloguer, or he must choose broader subject headings.

A change in the universe of knowledge may force a change in the scheme of classification, thereby affecting the already used subject headings in the catalogue. This can create a serious problem.

For selection of sought headings and individualization of headings, Ranganathan has suggested broad guidelines. In order to put the guidelines into practice, a cataloguer is expected to use his flair. At times it may not work.

In the case of compound subject headings derived from a class number with the help of chain procedure, sometimes it is found that order of terms thus obtained does not conform to the order which most enquirers might look for. This is because of the fixed citation order of concepts in a faceted or enumerative scheme of classification.

Solution. According to Mineur "The failures of chain indexing arise mainly from an inherited overemphasis on generic relationships, encouraged by careless use of the term 'chain'." He suggests the use of symbols to represent relations between terms, so as "to emphasize syntagmatic relations and prevent ambiguity." Further, "These relationships can be used to manipulate the index terms into likely additional index approaches, employing the logical concepts of Symmetry and Transitivity which derive from a structure inherent between relations, a sort of 'metarelations'." Thus there is need to carry out research along the lines suggested above.

Latest Developments. The version of chain procedure described above is class-number based, which is a conventional one. Researches have led to the fact that chain procedure has immense possibilities, different versions depending upon the variation of several factors, such as the set of postulates about the structures of names of subject policy of subject indexing, and the set of rules for deriving subject headings.

Thus, we now have postulate-based chain procedure, logical unit-based chain procedure and computerized chain procedure besides, of course, class-number based chain procedure. These versions of chain procedure have been explained in detail by Bhattacharya.

G. Bhattacharya and A. Neelameghan14 have showed that the features of the classified catalogue system could be incorporated to a great extent in the dictionary catalogue system with out affecting its advantages, by developing POPSI (Postulate based Permuted Subject Indexing): It is a procedure for imple menting the policy "Grouping by Juxtaposition" by keeping the structure of each specific subject heading parallel to the horizontally presented chain serving as the basis. Attempt is made to bring the members of the same group in juxtaposition, supplemented by the provision of all possible points of approach. Economy is achieved by providing only necessary and sufficient number of terms in the specific subject headings. From 1971, British National Bibliography has been following PRECIS (Preserved Context-Indexing System) to derive subject headings, which is another version of chain procedure somewhat similar to POPSI. Both differ mainly because the first does not recognize the concept of a basic subject, while other does.

Colon classification can be used successfully for postulate-based subject indexing. Here rules formulated to implement the policy of subject cataloguing by policy "grouping by references" is applied. These rules are analogous to those provided in CCC.

Logical unit-based subject indexing (LUSI) is a system which lies in between post-coordinate indexing at one extreme and POPSI at the other, aiming at the advantages of both systems the necessary basic chain is broken into a few logical units according to a set of rules. Subject heading is derived from each unit. Such subject headings are used as an "as if" specific subject heading for the document concerned.

The DRTC experiment on application of computer for information retrieval has found the chain procedure fully amenable to computerization. POPSI has also been found to be quite compatible with the computerized information.

Conclusion

The chain procedure is extremely versatile to the extent that almost all the systematic methods of representing a subject in a subject heading can be either derived or considered its corollary.

New versions of chain procedure are being experimented upon but these have led to techniques which are difficult to understand and apply. However, today we have a better understanding of subject cataloguing. The work in this area is going on and much remains to be achieved.

❐

8

Study of AACR and CCC

AACR

Rules for Choice of entry (problem of determination of responsibility for authorship) and construction of heading (problem of name involves, firstly, choice of a particular name and a particular form of that name; secondly, it covers conformation in which name should be presented as a catalogue heading) have been separated except when form headings are involved. Conformation is "based on considerations of morphology, language and custom that determine the entry element of the name, considerations of the possible dependence of the name on another name, and considerations of the relationship of the name to other headings in the catalog". The rules are based on statement of principles adopted by the International Conference on Cataloguing Principles held in 1961.

CCC

Rules are given at three levels. The levels are terminology, conflict of authorship (determination of responsibility for authorship, that is rules for choice), and rendering of the name. The rules are based on normative principles, which have been developed by the author himself.

1 CHOICE OF HEADING FOR THE MAIN ENTRY

AAGR	*CCC*
1	*2*
The following general principles underlie the rules for entry:	MDI The heading is to consist of the earliest of the following

1	*2*
	which the document admits and the rules for conflict of authorship prescribe as the author:
1. Entry should be under author or principal author when one can be determined.	1. The name of a personal author;
2. Entry should be under editor when there is no author or principal author and when the editor is primarily responsible for the existence of the work.	2. The names of joint personal authors;
3. Entry should be under a compiler named on the title page in the case of collections of works by various authors.	3. The name of a corporate author;
4. Entry should be under title in the case of other works whose authorship is diffuse, indeterminate or unknown.	4. Names of a joint personal anthor and of a joint corporate author;
	5. The names of joint corporate authors;
	6. A pseudonym or two or more pseudonyms;
	7. The name of a collaborator.
	8. The names of joint collaborators; and
	9. The title of the Document.
AACR considers author, "the person or corporate body chiefly responsible for the	CCC regards authors of work in two senses as below: Sense 1, Person creating the

1	2
creation of the intellectual or artistic content of a work". Thus principal author is the one, "to whom principal responsibility is attributed, *e.g.* by wording or typography"	work, that is, the thought and the expression constituting it. Sense 2, Corporate body owning responsibility for a work that is, for the thought and the expression constituting it.

Comments. The rules in AACR basically conform to the general principles. There are some rules in AACR which form exception to these principles. It is suggested that the principles should have been better named as general rules rather than principles. In CCC the rules are definite and there are no exceptions.

Both the codes are agreed about the definition of an author. However, AACR has put forward the concept of principal author, "to whom principal responsibility" can be 'attributed and its rules are based on this idea. CCC bases its rules on the canon of ascertainability, which directs that the information provided on the title page and its overflow pages of the document to be catalogued should be used for choosing the heading. As AACR specifies that choice of heading should be based on the concept of principal authorship, therefore, the canon of ascertainability will get violated quite often.

Unlike CCC, AACR considers editors, revisers, translators, etc. as authors. These should be regarded as collaborators rather than authors.

CHOICE AND RENDERINC OF PERSONAL NAMES

The rules regarding choice and rendering of personal names have been dealt in chapter study of personal names.

MARRIED WOMEN

AACR

46B3b Married women. Names of married women that include both the maiden surname and the husband's surname are entered under the husband's surname unless the woman's language is Czech, Hungarian, Italian, or Spanish. In these cases entry is under the first surname, regardless of its derivation.

Stowe, Harriet Beecher

Wang Ma, Hsi-ch'un

but

Landova-Stychova, Luisa

46G3 Include the term of address of a married woman when she is identified only by her husband's name.

Ward, Mrs. Humphry

Comments: CCC has not provided any rules to deal with cases of married women as mentioned above. Therefore, it is suggested that in the next edition, provision should be made to deal with such cases.

PSEUDONYMOUS WORKS

Definition AACR defines pseudonym as "a name assumed by an author to conceal or obscure his identity".

Choice

3 C Joint pseudonyms.

3Cl If collaborating authors consistently use a joint pseudonym instead of their individual names, enter under the pseudonym and refer to it from their real names.

> **Title Page.** The detective short story, by Ellery Queen (Ellery Queen is the joint pseudonym of Frederic Dannay and Manfred B. Lee)
>
> Main entry will be under Queen.

3C2 If for any reason the pseudonym cannot be used as a heading, enter the work under its title, unless 3A above should be applied. Rule 3A prescribes entry of a work of shared authorship under the person or corporate body, if any, to whom Principal responsibility is attributed (*e.g.* by wording or typography).

Title page: Philip; the story of a boy violinist, by T.W.O. (T.W.O is a pseudonym of M.C. Hungerford and V.C. Young) Main entry will be under title.

Rendering

40 Basic rule

Enter a person under the name by which he is commonly identified, whether it is his real name, assumed name, nickname title of nobility, or other appellation.

42A If all the works of an author appear only under one pseudonym, enter him under the pseudonym.

42B If the works of an author appear under several pseudonyms or under his real name and one or more pseudonyms, enter him under the name by which he is primarily identified in modern editions of his works and in reference sources.

However, an alternative to rule 42B as a footnote has been provided, which reads: If the works of an author appear under several pseudonyms or under his real name and one or more pseudonyms, enter each work under the name he used for it.

51A If a person is always identified in his works or in reference sources by an appellation or pseudonym consisting of a word, phrase, or expression that is obviously not intended to be taken as a *bona fide* name, enter him under the appellation or pseudonym in direct order unless it has the structure of a name consisting of a forename, or forenames, and a surname. Enter such a name under the pseudo-surname and refer from the name in direct order.

CCC

Definition. According to CCC, pseudonymous author is "an author assuming a false or fictitious name or any other specification different from the real name" (pp. 127-128).

Choice

A pseudonym or two or more pseudonyms are chosen as the heading, provided the document in hand admits them and rules for conflict of authorship in chapter G prescribe the same as the author(s) (Rule MDI).

Rendering

Pseudonyms with structure like that of a name of person are to be rendered, according to the rules of chapter JA, which deals with rendering of names (Rule MD2). An individualizing element (part J) and descriptive element (Rule MD4) can be added when required.

If the title page gives only a pseudonym in the place of the author's name, the pseudonym is to be used as the heading and it is to be followed by the descriptive element "pseud" (Rule MD41).

Example: TWAIN (Mark), Pseudo

If the title page gives the real name of the author also in a subordinate manner, it is to be added in circular brackets after the descriptive element "Pseud". The real name of the author is to be preceded by the symbol 'ie." The bracket is to be preceded by a comma. The words in the real name are to be written in their natural sequence (Rule MD 421).

Example: TWAIN (Mark), Pseud, (*ie* Samuel Langhorne Clemens).

MD422 deals with the title page giving the real name of the author, adding the pseudonym in a subordinated manner.

MD423 deals with the case when real name can be found from outside.

MD424 and MD425 deal with pseudonym representing join authors.

MD43 If there are two or more pseudonyms occurring in the place of the authors' names, they are to be connected by the conjunction "and."

Example: JKFRS and SASe, Pseud, [ie James Keir].

Comments: (1) Both the codes have provided special rules to deal with pseudonymous works.

(2) AACR regards pseudonym as a "name assumed by an author" but CCC considers an assumed name as well as "any other specification different from the real name" within the scope of a pseudonym. Thus if the title page reads "by ABC," then according to CCC this will be regarded a pseudonymous work. However AACR regards such a work not a pseudonymous one.

(3) AACR mixes together the rules for choice and rendering of heading. CCC has also not succeeded fully in separating the rules for choice from those of rendering.

(4) The basic approach of the two codes differs. AACR makes an attempt to bring the various works of a given author together This is done by choosing a single form of heading for all the works of the same author. However, alternative Rule 42B is an exception which allows to "enter each work under the name he used for it." CCC follows the canon of ascertainability. The entry is prepared under the form of the name given on the title page, thereby using the information provided on the title page. However, "if the real name of the author can be found out from outside the work, it is to te added." Here the assumption is that a user of a catalogue is more likely to look under that form of a name, the one found on the title page of the document itself. This does scatter the works of a given author.

A person interested in the works of an author will have to consult the catalogue under as many headings as the number of different forms of the name used by him. This will be found very inconvenient by the students of literature.

(5) Very often AACR suggests consultation of reference sources, various works of the author, etc. to identify the names which can be a time-consuming process. On the other hand, CCC bases the preparation of the entries on the information usually found on the title page, whereby the work of cataloguer becomes easier.

(6) Rule 51 of AACR is a little confusing because it mixes together rules of entry for an appellation and a pseudonym.

(7) Rules in CCC have suggested the addition of the word "pseud" to represent pseudonym, which is superfluous and likely to cause confusion to the reader.

(8) Rules of AACR are a little difficult to apply and rules of CCC are simple to understand and apply in practice. To a user, who is interested in reading a given document, whose author and title as given on the page is known to him, then he would find the approach of CCC highly suitable. But if a reader is interested in knowing about all the works by a given author, he would find AACR more useful which is certainly the case of a student of literature.

CHANGE OF NAME

AACR

6D If the title of a serial changes, if the corporate body under which it is entered changes, or undergoes a change of name, or if the person under whom it is entered ceases to be its author, make a separate entry for the issues appearing after the change.

If the change in title is either of very short duration or of a very minor character, however, it is simply noted on the existing entry.

41....If, however, a person changes his name, if he acquires or becomes identified by a title of nobility, or if the title by which he is identified is changed, enter him under the latest name or form of name or title unless there is reason to believe that an earlier one will persist as the one by which he will be better known.

68 If the name of a corporate body has changed (including change from one language to another), establish a new heading under the new name for cataloging publications appearing under this name.

Footnote to rule 68 reads:

If the change is so slight that the distinction between the names might be easily confused in citations or escape notice by users of the catalogue, it may be preferable to enter all the publications under the later form of name with a reference from the former.

100-102 These rules deal with provision for uniform titles. Uniform titles provide the means for bringing together all catalogue entries for a given work (including compilations and collections that require uniform titles) when its editions, translations etc. have appeared under various titles and for properly indentifying a work when its title is obscured by the wording on the title page.

52 CCC

JD5 Change in the name of an institution is looked after by the canon of ascertainability and the rules on cross reference index entry.

Comments. AACR provide a number of rules to deal with change of name. This is because it does not follow a set practice. In CCC,there is no need to have special rules because general direction is to follow the canon of ascertainability and provide cross reference index entry(ies) to take care of alternative approaches. Above Rule JD5 is a redundant one, instead there should be a general rule applicable to all kinds of changes of names.

CORPORATE AUTHORSHIP

Corporate Body

Definition: A corporate body may be defined as:

"Sense 1 A number of persons taken collectively—usually as united, or organised, or coming together informally, in a common cause or for common action such as governmental business or commercial or industrial or service or political or any other business, or for deliberation, or for collective expression of opinion or statement.

"Sense 2 A number of corporate bodies in sense 1, taken collectively—usually as united, or organised, or coming together informally, in a common cause or for common action such as government business, or commercial or industrial or service or political or any other business, or for deliberation, or for collective expression or opinion or statement".

According to AACR corporate body is "An organization or group of persons that is identified by a name and that acts or may act as an entity."

For example, Government of India, American Library Association, Mount Wilson Observatory, All-India Radio, Birla Mandir, Indian Congress, etc.

Corporate bodies occur in large numbers and great variety. This has important implications for the use and preparation of library catalogues. The number of corporate bodies is ever increasing because the number of co-operative ventures is increasing. Not only is their number increasing but their functions are ever widening.

Corporate Author

Definition: According to CCC, a corporate body becomes the author, provided, "the responsibility for the thought and expression constituting the work resting solely on it or any organ of it, and not on the private capacity of any person or persons forming part of or holding office in or in any other way connected with that body".

According to AACR, a corporate becomes the author, if it is "chiefly responsible for the creation of the intellectual or artistic content of a work."

Sharp has rightly pointed out, "... corporate authorship, which, by general consent, is the most difficult and controversial aspect of the whole field of practical cataloguing, not only for teachers to put across and for students to assimilate, but equally so for practising and even experienced cataloguers, and infinitely more so for subsequent catalogue users." In fact the complexity of present catalogues is directly, related to the problem of corporate entries.

Growth of the Concept of Corporate Authorship

The concept of corporate 'authorship was employed in early catalogues. However, the concept was not used in a well defined form. The early catalogues did not actually consider corporate bodies as the authors of their publications but corporate bodies were thought important and it was supposed that generally the readers will remember the name of the body or the place of location better than the title itself.

Panizzi recognized the concept of corporate authorship but he did not have precise and clear conception of the significance as well as the concept of principle of corporate authorship as we understand it today. But perhaps he was the first to establish the principle of entry under corporate bodies as bodies. It seems that C. C. Jewett gave the first definition of corporate bodies as authors of their publications. The credit goes to Cutter who for the first time in 1876, in his Rules for a printed dictionary catalogue? provided a definite description of the principle of the recognizing corporate bodies as the author of their works.

It may be mentioned that the USA, in particular, Great Britain, and certain European countries had recognized the principle for a long time. On the other hand German, Austrian, Swiss, and Dutch librarians, along with some support from Scandinavians and other countries, refused to accept this principle until very recently. They strongly believe that only persons could be recognized as authors, and treated corporate body publications as anonymous works.

Rendering of Heading for Corporate Bodies Basic Rule

631 AACR

60 Basic rule. Enter a corporate body directly under its name except when the rules that follow provide for entering it under a higher body of which it is a part, under the name of the government of which it is an agency, or under the name of the place in which it is located.

632 CCE

CCC does not provide basic rule for corporate bodies as a whole because it gives general rule, specific to a particular type of corporate body.

64 FORM OF THE NAME

AACR: 61 When the name of a corporate body found in reference sources varies from that used by the body on the publications of which it is author, publisher, or sponsor, the latter form is preferred.

62 Applies if the form used in the body's own publications varies.

63 If the body has acquired a conventional name, then the provisions of this rule will take precedence.

64 This applies, if the name appears in different languages.

65 Is concerned with individualization.

66 Prescribes the omissions to be done from names.

67 Prescribes modifications of names to be carried out.

Comments: CCC does not have to provide special rules for form of the name corresponding to Rule 61 to 63 of AACR because CCC follows the canon of ascertainability and cross" reference index entries are provided to take care of alternative names. CCC provides rules for individualization, omissions from names, and modifications of names along with rules for particular type of corporate body.

Legal Publications

AACR: Rule 20 to 32 deal with choice of entry for certain legal publications.

CCC: Rule GC4l and GC42, along with Rule GB6 cover choice of entry for legal publications.

Comments. AACR has provided special rules for certain fegal publications "because the framers of the code consider that "such types involve special problems in authorship responsibility or require special headings that could not be dealt with satisfactorily in the general rules." On the other hand, CCC has not provided special headings for these publications, as a result, three rules suffice to solve the problems of choice of entry.

66 GEOGRAPHICAL NAMES

AACR: Rule 72 to 74 cover special rules for geographical names.

CCC: Chapter JB deals with geographical names.

Comments. The rules in AACR are biased in favour of the English-speaking world. Rules in CCC are based on the concept of "favoured language of the library." Thus CCC prefers the name of a geographical entity in the favoured language of the library.

67 CONFLICT OF AUTHORSHIP

Conflict of authorship is a major problem faced by cataloguers. In such cases it becomes difficult to decide as to who should be the author because it may not be easy to determine primary responsibility. Variety of cases of conflict is so large that no code can possibly provide rules to cover all such cases. However, codes can provide general principles to deal with these.

671 ISSUES INVOLVED

Some of the major issues involved are enumerated below:

Person versus person

Person versus corporate body

Government versus institution.

Ecolesiastical polity (relating to church organizations)

Institution versus institution

Delegation from body versus delegated to body

Legal publications

Author's name merged in title.

672 SOLUTION

Conflict of authorship can best be resolved at the level of definition. For this purpose, the definition of the term "author" and terms denoting different kinds of author along with appropriate interpretative definitions of each such term as a sequel should be given. The interpretative definitions will often serve as illustrative enumerative form.

CCC follows the above prescription. AACR has not been able to give a completely satisfactory solution because it has not followed the above solution.

6721 PERSON VERSUS PERSON

AACR: Rule 7 to 16 are concerned with person versus person cases of conflict.

GCC: Chapter GB covers person versus person cases. *Comments:* Both the codes base their rules on the question of responsibility.

I6722 PERSON VERSUS CORPORATE BODY

AAGR: 17 Al Enter under the corporate body. . .a work that is by its nature necessarily the expression of the corporate thought or activity of the body. Such works include official records and reports, and statements, studies, and other communications dealing with the policies, operations, or management of the body made by officers or other employees of the body.

17A2 Enter under the corporate body a work, other than a formal history, describing the body, its functions, procedures, facilities, resources, etc., or an inventory, catalog, directory of personnel, list of members, etc.

Note: Rule 17 applies to works issued by or bearing the authority of a corporate body, but with authorship or editorship specifically and prominently attributed to one or more persons, either by name or by official title.

CCC: GC31 The work in the document is of corporate authorship, if it is of a deliberative, legislative, directive, judicial, administrative or routine character limited by the purpose or function or outlook of the corporate body. The mere fact that a document is published, financed, aided, approved, sponsqred, or authorized by a corporate body is not sufficient reason to deem the work in it to be of corporate authorship, and not of personal authorship.

Rule GC2 If the title page does not mention the name(s) of person(s) in the author-statement, but mentions or indicates somewhere in itself or in the overflow of title page the name of a corporate body(ies) other than a body belonging to the publishing trade mentioned in the imprint, and if there is also internal evidence of corporate authorship, the work in the document is of corporate authorship; provided that, even in the case of the name(s) of the corporate body(ies) mentioned in the Imprint being only that of a body belonging to the publishing trade, if it is a work by the corporate body itself-such as its catalogue, administration report, history-the work in the document is of corporate authorship.

AACR: 17 A-1 Single reports, however, that are made by officers or other employees and that embody the results of scholarly investigation or scientific research are excluded unless written by more than three persons, none of whom is represented as the principal author. All reports and studies prepared by consultants engaged for the particular purpose are excluded.

17B If the work would not be entered under corporate body under the provisions of 17A or if there is doubt as to whether it would, enter it under the heading under which it would be entered if no corporate body were involved.

CCC: GC32 The work in the document is of personal authorship, if its primary function is the extension of the boundary of a field of knowledge or its intensification, and the responsibility for the thought and expression of it rests on the person and not on the office held by him in the corporate body, in spite of his being a paid or an honorary employee or a member of the corporate body. The mere mention of the personal name of an official of the corporate body in the place in which author's name is usually mentioned in a book, is not sufficient reason to deem the work in it to be of personal authorship and not to be of corporate authorship.

GCI If the 'title page mentions the name(s) of person(s) only in the author statement and does not mention or indicate the name of any corporate body(ies) other than the one(s) belonging to the publishing trade mentioned in the imprint, the work in the document is of personal authorship.

AACR: 17Cl a Enter an official communication (*e.g.* a message to a legislative or governing body, a proclamation, an executive order that does not come within the provisions of 20A) issued by a chief of state, a head of a government, or a head of an international inter-governmental body under the corporate heading for the office which he holds. In case of doubt as to the official character of a communication, however, enter it according to the provisions of 17C2.

17C2 Treat any other speech or writing by chief of state, heads of governments, etc., other than, official communications as a work of personal authorship.

CCC: Note under Rule JC4:

Head of the government should be treated as organ of government as corporate author only in the case of official publications such as messages, proclamations, despatches, ordinances, and so on, emanating from the head of the government. This kind of heading is not applicable to works written by a king, a president, etc. in his private capacity.

The note given in CCC Rule JC4 finds a place under rules for rendering of government publications; instead, it should have been given in chapter GC.

Comments: Both the codes have tried to provide guidance for the determination of the author in type of cases, which are to be found usually. AACR gives a solution based on the consideration of "expression of the corporate thought or activity of the body." CCC takes into consideration the responsibility for "thought and expression" constituting the work as well as the canon of ascertainability.

68 GOVERNMENT

680 DEFINITION

AACR: Footnote 15 The word "government" is used here to mean the totality of corporate bodies, executive, legislative, and judicial, exercising the powers of a given jurisdiction.

CCC: FC22 Sense 1 Coporate body with full or limited sovereign power over a territory. It has generally functions of execution, legislation, justice, and administration. Other functions, such as defence, taxation, regulation of commerce, public transport, communication, etc., will vary with the degree of limitation in the sovereign power.

Sense 2 Local authority in charge of regulation, promotion, and/or provision of specified local public services in an area, under power delegated by the government within the territory of which its own area lies, and with a defined extent of autonomy.

Sense 3 Organ of government in sense 1 or 2 defined above.

Comments: AACR has not provided a specific definition of a government in its glossary but describes the scope of the term as used in the code.

681 CHOICE OF HEADING

AA CR: 17 deals with cases of person versus corporate body. This is equally applicable to works of government as a corporate author. In fact, Rule 17C is a specific rule, applicable to chiefs of states, heads of governments, etc. Rule 17 has been briefly discussed. 18 covers cases of corporate body versus its subordinate unit. 78 covers cases of corporate body versus corporate body dealing with cases of corporate bodies created and controlled by the government. This rule prescribes that "agencies through which the basic legislative, judicial, and executive functions of government are exercised should be entered as sub-headings under the heading for the government; other bodies created and controlled by the government should be entered, if possible, under their own names." The code has defined the activities, institutions, which can not be regarded as basic to.govermental function and examples have also been given. Rule 86 prescribes choice of heading for delegations to international and inter-governmental bodies. It prescribes that "Enter a delegation, commission, etc. representing the government of a country in an international or inter-governmental body, conference, undertaking, etc. as a sub-heading under the country represented and in the language of that country..."

CCC: This code decides the choice of heading with the help of rules on "conflict of authorship" given in part G.

Comments: Conflict vith regard to person versus corporate body is resolved with Rule GC31 and GC32. Rule 17 of AACR resolves the conflict on the similar lines.

Rule 18 and 78 of AACR help in resolving conflict between government versus institution. Rule GO2 and GO3 of CCC take care of this conflict. CCC also provides synopsis of cataloguing convention, which lists the headings to be chosen in such cases.

Conflict with regard to delegation to a conference is solved in AACR by means of Rule 86. CCC has got Rule GD71. Both codes give a similar solution.

682 RENDERING OF HEADING WHOLE GOVGRNMENT

AACR: 75 Use the conventional name of a country, province, state, county, municipality, or other political jurisdiction as the heading for its government, unless the official name of the government is in more common use.

Note: Above rule has to be used along with the aid of Rules 72-74. These rules are for rendering of geographical names. For instance,

Rule 72 directs the cataloguer to prefer English form of the geographic name if there is one in general use.

CCC: JCI If the corporate body is a government as a whole its name is to be the name of its territory.

Comments: Rule ofCCC is easier to apply and Rule 75 of AACR requires the cataloguer to make a search to determine conventional and official names and their usage.

AACR directs the preference for English form of geographic name. In this regard CCC follows the principle of favoured language of the library, which is a direction, which can give general guidance, suitable for all types of libraries everywhere.

AACR: Rule 77 prescribes elements required to distinguish governments with same name.

Comments: Both Rule 73 and 77 prescribe the elements to be added to individualize name of place. It is suggested that provisions of Rule 77 should have been given under Rule 73. CCC has not provided a similar rule but examples under rule JCI indicate how name of a territory can be individualized.

683 ORGANS OF A GOVERNMENT

AACR: Rule 78B If the body is not of the type listed in 78A, or if there is doubt that it is one, enter it as a sub-heading under the heading for the government and in accordance with the provisions of Rule 79-86. Omit the name of the country, state, etc., or an adjective derived from its name when either occurs at the beginning or the end of the body's name, unless objectionable distortion would result. Under the rule are given examples to illustrate application of Rule 79 to 86. Rule 79 deals with subordinate agencies and units of the government.

CCC: JC21 If the corporate body is an organ of a government, a multiple corporate heading is to be used.

JC22 The first heading in the rendering of the name of an organ of a government is to be the name of the government as a whole.

JC3 The rendering of the name of a constitutional organ of a government, used as second heading, is to be the name of the organ as it is current in the language of the library and otherwise in the language of the territory concerned.

6831 EXECUTIVE ORGANS

AACR: 76 deals with administrative districts of cities, towns, etc., which are identified by a number.

80 applies to chiefs of state etc., heads of government, governors, and governing bodies of dependent or occupied territories and other officials of the countries and other states that have existed in post-medieval times.

Examples: Gt. Brit. Sovereign, 1952-(Elizabeth II)
Gt. Brit. Prime Minister.

84 Armed forces

85 Embassies, legations, etc.

86 is concerned with delegations to international and inter governmental bodies, which has been discussed.

Note: Besides the above rules, examples under Rule 78 and 79 illustrate examples for executive organs.

CCC: JC4 The rendering of the name of the head of a government, used as second heading, is to be provided with the name of the occupant of that office as an individualizing element.

Example: INDIA, PRESIDENT (S. Radhakrishnan).

Note: Examples under JC31 illustrate the rendering of executive organs as sub-heading under the name of the government.

JC6 The entry element in the name of an administrative department of a government is to be the word or the word group denoting its sphere of work. The sphere of work if possible be reduced to a noun form in the nominative case. The other words in the name of the administrative department are to be deemed to form secondary element.

Examples:

INDIA, FINANCE (Ministry of-).

In AACR, above example would be rendered as:

India. Ministry of Finance

JC65 Provides for elements required to remove homonyms in the names of administrative departments.

Comments: Why should a special Rule 76 have been given for administrative districts, identified by a number? It should have been put along with Rule 79 to 86.

AACR makes a distinction between the provision for chief of the state and head of government. In the first case, the years as well as the name of the person are added and in the second case, they are omitted. The distinction seems to be illogical. CCC does not provide special rules corresponding to armed forces, embassies, legations, etc.

Provision of entry element in JC6 under the sphere of work is a better treatment.

6832 LEGISLATIVE ORGANS

AACR: 8lA and 8lB Deal with legislative bodies. Rule 8lC prescribes individualizing element for successive legislatures numbered consecutively.

82 Prescribes rules for constitutional conventions.

CCC: No special rules are provided.

Comments: Examples under rule JC32 illustrate the rendering of legislative organs as sub-heading under the name of the government.

6833 JUDICIAL ORGANS

AACR: 83 describes rules for courts.

CCC: JC5 Prescribes the elements of individualization for two or more courts of law of the same government having similar names.

Comments: Examples under Rule JC33 illustrate the rendering of the judicial organs as sub-heading under the name of the government.

6834 TEMPORARY ORGANS

CCC makes special provision for temporary organs in Rule IC7 and its sub-divisions. In case of temporary organ, its year of formation is to be added as an individualizing element. In case of ad hoc commissions, committees, etc., the name of the chair man is to be added further.

Example:

INDIA, INDIAN FINANCE COMMISSION (1951)

(Chairman: K.C. Neogy).

AACR does not make such a provision. It would be useful, if AACR gives a special treatment to temporary organs.

684 CONCLUSION

Both the codes prescribe that the publications of government as corporate author should be entered under their name. In AACR, it is a conventional or official name. In CCC, it is the name of the territory.

The publications of which their organs or agencies are the author are rendered under the name of organs or agencies as the sub-heading(s) under the name of the government. But both codes have enumerated cases in which exceptions will take place, where the entry will have to be made directly under the name of the organs or agencies.

In case the headings happen to be homonymous, then AACR individualizes it by putting an individualizing term in parentheses, but sometimes it is added after a comma.

691 CONFERENCES, CONGRESSES, MEETINGS, ETC.

6910 DEFINITION

AACR has not provided a definition of terms like conference, congress, meeting in an explicit manner. However, in the introductory note the code has indicated that rules for conferences, congresses, meetings, etc. "apply to meetings of persons, either as individuals or as representatives of various bodies, for the purpose of studying, discussing, or acting on a particular topic or on various topics of common interest." The legislative or governing congress, council, or convention of an organization, consisting of representatives of its membership, is treated under the provisions of Rule 69-70. A meeting of the general membership of an organization that is simply called 'conference [convention, etc.] of the [organization]' is considered to be an activity of the body as a whole and without corporate character of its own."

CCC: FC24 Conference—Sense 1 Ad hoc assembly for deliberation or formulation and expression of opinion or sentiments.

1 Not convened by

11 A government and made up solely of its own personnel or as a constituent assembly to form a sovereign state,

12 An institution and made up solely of its members or as a foundation assembly to form an institution, or

13 More than one government jointly and confined solely to their own personnel, or

14 More than one institution jointly and confined solely to their members;

2 Convened and conducted by

21 A number of persons and/or corporate bodies, spontaneously, to consider matters of common interest, or

22 A body with no function or existence beyond the conference convened and held by it, or

23 A body with only the convening and holding of confetences at intervals, as its primary function.

For example, the Indian Mathematical Conference of 1957 is a conference in sense 1. The Reception Committee of the Indian Mathematical Conference of 1957 is a conference in sense 2.

241 Organ conference—Any category of assembly excluded from the definition of a conference in Rule FC24. It is an organ of the corporate body(ies) convening it.

Comments: AACR has not given definitions of terms like conference, congress, meeting, etc. But the scope of these is implied in the introductory note. Similarly definitions of their organs have not been given. CCC uses the term conference to cover meetings, congresses, etc. It has also provided a clear definition of organ conference. In AACR, legislative or governing congress, council, or convention of an organization, consisting of representatives of its membership, is treated under the provisions of Rules 69-70 which deal with subordinate and related bodies. In CCC also such types of corporate authorship have not been treated under rules for conference publications.

In AACR, Rule 87 indicates, in case a meeting lacks a name then rules meant for conferences, congresses, meetings, etc. are not applicable to it. The code has explained when a meeting is considered to have a name or not.

6911 CONFLICT OF AUTHORSHIP

PERSON VERSUS CONFERENCE

AACR: 17C2c Enter a collection containing both official communications and other works of such persons as a work of personal authorship, if by one person; as a collection, if by several persons and monographic in character; or as a serial, if by several persons and serial in character.

CCC: GC5 A conference is deemed author only of its agenda, minutes, resolutions, report of proceedings, and similar collectively created thought. But a collection of learned papers or memoranda presented by person(s) or corporate body(ies) at the conference is deemed to have the respective person(s) or body(ies) as author(s).

Comments: CCC makes a sharp distinction between a mere collection of papers and report of proceedings. It goes strictly by the question of responsibility for thought and expression constituting the work. However, the readers would most likely rtot make such a distinction. They would rather look under the name of the conference than the editor or compiler.

DELEGATION TO A CONFERENCE

AACR: 86 Enter a delegation, commission, etc., representing the government of a country in an international or inter-governmental body, conference, undertaking, etc., as a sub-heading under the country represented and in the language of that country. If the name of the delegation is uncertain, the sub-heading is formed in the language of the country represented by using the terms found in the work being cataloged in the form normally used, *i.e.* Delegation [Mission, etc.] to—. If it is uncertain that the body represents the government of the country, enter directly under its name.

CCC: GD71 The delegated-from-body should be taken to be the parent body of a delegation to a conference or to a body such as the United Nations or a Peace Conference in respect of any work embodying any thought and expression created by the delegation.

Comments: Both codes direct that delegated-from-body should be considered as the parent body of the delegation to a conference.

6912 RENDERING

AACR: 87 Enter a conference, congress, or other meeting under its name, followed in many instances by one or more of the following elements: number, place, date. If a heading is required for a projected conference that was never held (*e.g.* for its pre-conference publications), establish the heading as if it had been held but add at the end of the heading:(Projected, not held). If a meeting lacks a name, its publications are treated according to the applicable general rule for entry (2A, 3 or 6A). For unnamed diplomatic conferences see 63B.

88A If the formal presentations of the name vary and one form includes the name or abbreviation of the name of a sponsoring body, prefer this form.

88B If a conference has both specific name and a more general name as one of a series of conferences, enter it under the specific name.

88c Omit words in the name of a conference that denote its number, frequency, or year of convocation.

CCC: JEl·The name to be used in rendering the name of a conference is to be the one in the shortest form found in the title page; or on half-title page; or any other part of the document.

JE11, If the name of the conference occurs in two or more languages, the name in the language occurring earliest in the scale of languages of the library is to be used for rendering.

JEI2, 13, 14 prescribe the elements in the name of the conference to be omitted, while rendering it.

JE15 In rendering the name of a conference beginning with a numeral figure, the numeral is to be spelt out in the language of the rest of the words in the name of the conference.

JE16 In rendering the name of a conference, in whose name trivial variants occur in different documents, the uniformized name is to be used. (Uniform name is the one uniformized by popular or cataloguing usage.)

JE3 The name of the place of a diplomatic conference is to be prefixed to the name of the conference not held periodically, so as to form a word group, if it is not already in the name of the conference; and the year(s) of the conference is (are) to be added as individualizing element.

JE4 The name of a conference without specific name and not held periodically is to be made of the class of persons meeting together as conference, such as citizens, Indian residents, ladies, merchants, and musicians.

Comments: Rules 87 to 91 are meant for meetings, which have a name. Qualifies when a conference has a name or does not have one. Strangely enough, there are two exceptions. A conference without name, but having sequential numbers or dates, combined with these terms in a formal presentation on their publication, is treated like a meeting with a name. Similar treatment is given to a conference which lacks a name but possesses a conventional name. However, it would be difficult to determine a conventional name. AACR suggests choice of a longer name including the name of a spon-soring body. On the other hand, CCC favours a shortest name.

CCC has not made provision for a projected conference that was not held, which is an omission. It violates the canon of ascertainability in its Rule JEl because a cataloguer is expected to search for the shortest name from any part of the document. The treatment of a diplomatic conference is an exception as the name of a place has to be prefixed to it, which is difficult to understand. Its treatment of a conference without specific name is easier to apply than that of AACR.

69121 INDIVIDUALIZATION

AACR: Rule 89, 90, 91 in general, suggest the use of place, date to individualize the name of a conference.

CCC: JE2 The name(s) of the place(s) of a conference and its year are to be added as individualizing elements to the name of a conference which is not held periodically.

JE41 and 42 prescribe name of place and year or month or date as individualizing elements for conferences without specific names.

Comments: The rules in both the codes are similar, however Rules JE41 and JE42 are superfluous because these repeat the directions already available under Rule JE2.

69122 PERIODICAL CONFERENCE

AACR: 89 If a conference is one of a series of numbered conferences of the same name, follow its name by the abbre viation of the ordinal number in English.

CCC: Rule JE2 A periodical conference is to be catalogued in accordance with rules for periodical publications.

Comments: The solution suggested by CCC is much better, because it will lead to economy in number of entries to be prepared and also have better control by the periodical section.

69123 ORGAN CONFERENCE

Both codes AACR (Rules 69 and 70), CCC (Rule FR 57) give a similar treatment except for joint parent bodies.

692 INSTITUTION

6920 INTRODUCTION

In AACR, broadly speaking, the corporate bodies as the authors of their publications can be divided into the following categories:

Governments, government bodies, and officials; conferences, Congresses, meetings, etc.; others.

In CCC, corporate bodies have been divided into governments, conferences, and institutions.

The three categories of AACR and CCC correspond to each other. Thus CCC uses the term "governments" to include governments, government bodies, and officials. Similarly the term "conferences" covers conferences, congresses, meetings etc.

Therefore, we may assume that AACR rules coming under the category of "others" will correspond to the CCC rules for institutions.

Thus in this chapter, the rules for AACR and CCC have been discussed on the basis of the same assumption. However, it may be mentioned that the term institution in the present context will include associations, business firms, churches, institutions, societies, etc.

6921 DEFINITION

AACR: No definition has been given.

CCC: FC23 Sense 1 Independent or autonomous corporate body other than a government. It may be created by a government, or constituted under a statute, or formed voluntarily either formally or informally. It has or it is intended to have continued existence and functions beyond that of merely convening a conference.

Sense 2 Organ of an institution in sense 1 defined above.

Comments: In the second edition of ALA cataloging rules for author and title entries, 3 the code had recognized societies and institutions as corporate authors and provided separate rules for these. However, in this edition the code has not used these terms. Thus we do not find definition of the term "institution." CCC has given a clear definition.

6922 CONFLICTING CASES

AACR: 17 deals with cases of corporate body versus personal author. 18 deals with corporate body versus subordinate units.

CCC: Chapter OC is concerned with cases of conflict between person versus corporate body.

OD2 For a work bearing on the discharge of primary functions-administration report, report of deliberation, direction, and any kindred work embodying thought created and expressed by an organ of government of first remove, second remove, etc.—the government or its appropriate organ(s), as the case may be, should be taken as its author.

GD3 Any autonomous or even non-autonomous organization engaged in the work of research, production, commerce, and supply of commodities and services to the public may have to be taken to be the institutional author for a work for whose thought and expression it is responsible. It is so even if the institution is owned and managed by the government.

GD8 contains synopsis of cataloguing conventions, which can be very helpful in deciding certain cases of institution as the authors of their publications.

Comments: AACR has provided general rules. CCC has provided general as well as special rilles for conflicting cases has taken advantages of conventions to help in taking a decision. Strangely enough, in OD82, 83 and 84 Ranganathan decides the problem of parent body versus organs on the basis of whether or not the organ has a distinctive name? He has not defined, what is a distinctive name. Even otherwise it would be difficult to recognize a distinctive name.

6923 RENDERING

AACR: 69 Enter a subordinate body as a sub-heading under a higher body if its name belongs to one or more of the following types:

Type 1 A name that includes the entire name of the higher body. Omit this portion of the name in the sub-heading.

Type 2 A name that contains a term that by definition implies that the body is a component part of something else, *e.g.*, "department," "division," "section," "branch.'

Type 3 A name that contains a word ordinarily implying administrative subordination, *e.g.*, "committee."

Type 4 A name of a university, school or college that simply indicates a particular field of study.

Type 5 A name that is entirely descriptive of the body's functions and that has a character that is common to the names of both subordinate bodies and independent bodies, *e.g.*, many "institutes," "centers," "laboratories," etc. of universities.

Type 6 Any name that is so general that the name of a higher bod is required for its identification.

69A directs whether to enter under direct or indirect sub-heading. Rule 69B is about form in the language of the name to be used. Rule 69C is concerned with additions to names.

70A Enter a subordinate body directly under its own name if its name does not belong to one of the types described in 69.

71 takes care of related bodies.

78A Enter a corporate body created and controlled by a government directly under its name, if it is one of the following types:

Type 1 Organizations engaged in commercial, cultural, or scientific activities or the promotion of such activities.

Type 2 Institutions (typically with their own physical plant). Type 3 Installations and parks.

Type 4 Bodies created by intergovernmental agreement. Type 5 Authorities and trusts for the operation of utilities and industries.

Type 6 Banks, corporations, manufacturing plants, farms, and similar specific enterprises.

Type 7 Established churches.

The exceptions are given below:

(1) bodies that are designated as ministries, or a foreign equivalent, or by terms that by definition denote that the body is a component part of something else (*e.g.* "department," "division," "section," "branch," and foreign equivalents).

(2) libraries, archives, and other government bodies that normally function primarily as service units of a particular agency of government if their names contain the name of the agency as the sole identifying element or require the addition of the agency's name for their identification.

Rules 92-96 deal with religious bodies and officials. Religious bodies are generally entered under their name.

97 Enter a radio or television station under its call letters followed by the words Radio [television] station (within parentheses) and the place which the station is identified....

CCC: JD1 The name to be used in rendering the name of an institution is to be the one in the shortest form found in the title page; or half-title page; or any other part of the document.

JD11 If the name of the institution occurs in two or more languages, the name in the language occurring earliest in the scale of languages of the library is to be used for rendering.

JE16 In rendering the name of an institution, in whose name trivial variants occur in different documents, the uniformized name is to be used.

69231 OMISSIONS

AACR: Rule 66 prescribes elements which should be omitted from the name of a corporate body.

CCC: JDI2, 13, 14 prescribe the elements to be omitted in name of an institution, while rendering it.

69232 MODIFICATIONS

AACR: Rule 67 lists modifications of names to be carried out in the names of corporate bodies.

CCC: JD15 in rendering the name of an institution beginning with a numeral figure, the numeral is to be spelt out in the language of the rest of the works in the name of the institution.

69233 INDIVIDUALSATION

AACR: Rule 65 prescribes the elements to be added to corporate bodies having the same name or names so closely similar that they are likely to be confused.

CCC: JD2 and JD21 prescribe elements required to individualize the bare name of an institution.

69234 ORGANS

Both codes, AACR (Rules 69 and 70) and CCC (rules on the analogy of government-JC2 to JC8) provide a similar treatment.

6924 CONCLUSION

In ALA cataloging' rules for author and title entries (2nd ed. 1949), a distinction between a society and institution was made. In general, societies were entered under their names and institutions under the names of place, where located. In AACR the distinction between the two has been rightly abolished and both are entered under their own names. Thus, the treatment in both codes is similar.

❐

9

Resource Sharing

CENTRALISED CATALOGUING

Centralised cataloguing is one such which has recently witnessed considerably developed. The centralised cataloguing being limited to that method of cataloguing which is commonly adopted in large system of libraries, where by all the cataloguing classifying and possibly other operations are carried out at a central point in the system, usually the central library.

There is a great shortage of well trained cataloguing man power in the country. But the libraries are growing in number as a result of a current renaissance. The economical method of meeting the situation will be to adopt the centralised cataloguing. This can not be done for the country as a whole. There should be a diversified organization for it. In each of the constituent States, there should be a State Central Cataloguing Body for the books in the language of the state. There should be a Union Central Cataloguing Body to take charge of the books in English, Sanskrit, and in any other Indian languages in which books are published in different parts of the country.

Cataloguing activity limited to library system, which have number of branches or departments. There is no commercial basis involved in production and distribution. The entire cataloguing process is carried out at the central and head-quarter library, just as the book for all the branches are purchased and distributed. Centralised cataloguing is defined as cataloguing of document by some central organisation.

Centralised cataloguing provides a varying degree of cataloguing services to its clientele from a central point. This form of cataloguing can take place within an library system of within a number of library systems. Some times centralised cataloguing may be done by another agency.

Centralised cataloguing has many objectives to:

1. avoid duplication of works,
2. reduce cost of cataloguing,
3. raise the level of quality of cataloguing,
4. enable member libraries to provide better services to users,
5. achieve uniformitty in classification and cataloguing and
6. put cataloguer to more effective use.

Centralised cataloguing was first brought in the United States in 1901 from than the Library of congress prints the catalogue cards of each book.

These cards are available for sale, Many countries have also introduced national centralised cataloguing entries among which may be mentioned the Library of Congress (U.S.A.), the Central Book Chamber (U.S.S.R.), The State Lanin Library (U.S.S.R.), Dansk Bibliogralisk Kontor (Denmark) The Swedish State Library Committee (Norvey), Rumanian Ministry of Culture (Canada). There are other commerical ventures take up centralised cataloguing printed cards, like H.W. Wilson printed catalogue card service, the Deuthche Bucherei publication in Germany, British National Bibliography also followed printed catalogue card since 1950. It has begun to supply catalogue card within 48 hours of order. Sharp has suggested 3 stages of the procedure of centralised cataloguing-initial processes, after processes and future development.

Non-fiction books are covered in centralised calaloguing as soon as non-fiction books are accessioned. These are passed to the cataloguer, who divide them into two groups. Book not previously catalogued, 2-books previously catalogued The books of first group are catalogued and classified, their entries are made on catalogue slips or cards after final checking the verification stamp is made behind the title page and written the class number. Shelf register card are stamped in a corner and the date of "First Cataloguing" and copies are sent to various libraries.

Books covered under grouped two to the cataloguer extract from the Union Shelf Register the appropriate shelf register cards and check them to ensure that there is no variation in edition, date etc. If however any variations is found books are re-catalogued. The serving stage of procedure is very important. The Union Shelf Register cards are now collected for author indexing and immediate filing by subject. A catalogue slip is written by cataloguer to include them in the list of Recent Additions. Its reproduced copies are sent to libraries. Suplementary List of Additions is published at intervals. The entries in the list will become affective & informative to the libraries.

Third stage of procedure is future development. A full set of catalogue cards and a District Shelf Register card shall be sent out with each book. Catalogue slips are marked to show number of copies to be purchased. The cards are re-produced. The book number are allotted centrally in order to have exact the same call number.

FORMS OF CENTRALISATION

The first form is card or sheaf service. It means the central organisation produced the actual physical entries (unit entries) which individual library can buy. They are distributed to individual libraries who file them in their catalogues after adding the appropriate headings to the basic unit. B.N.R card/sheaf service, printed catalogue cards are distributed. Library of Congress also give such services, they distribute proof sheets which can be re-produced.

Second form is MARC Machine Readable Catalogue service. It is an production of cataloguing data in machine readable form *e.g.* magnetic tap). In fact the central organization/agencies catalogues the document and records the data on magnetic taps and supply them to the libraries. These taps can be computerised and printed catalogue can be produced. Library of Congress started this operation in 1969. Its main aim was to minimize and eventually eliminate a problem of card being out of stock and the storage and inventory of card production. The system reproduces card automatically through the use of computer driver, photo composition machine and option set printing machine. MARC has been modified to the automation position. MARC service is receiving full response all over the world, Magnetic taps are replacing card catalogue. NASI-National Aeronoutics and Space Administration is following the system.

The third form is information service. It is a production of a bibliography or from which libraries than construct their own catalogue either the cutting out tbe entries and pasting them on cards or using the information provided as a guide in their own cataloguing or possibly by using the bibliography as a substitute for a catalogue. BNB Services were of this kind before the starting of card service in 1956. Such bibliographies are also useful for blok selection and acquisition, identification and location. Indian Nationa1 Bibliography has the same nature. BNB and Library of Congress are giving these services jointly.

The fourth form is Cataloguing-in-Source. It is an important form of centralisalion. Under this service cataloguing of books is done by a central organisation, in association with the publishers, before publication the catalogue entries, then printed in book form. This venture is possible with the collaboration of book trade. Library of Congress started this work in June 1958. It published 1203 Publication of 157 publisbers on a cost of dollar 25 per publication. The eatry generally appear the version of title page in the form of fecsimile of LC card catalogue entries. Thus prepared were called CIS entries. This venture could not be continued because of its high cost. Library of Congress was also not so much interested as it could heavily stain on cataloguers owing to a close schedule.

The fifth form of centralisation is cataloguing-in-Publication (CIP). This venture was began in July 1971 of the Library of congress. It was a galley proof system. Entries are prepared from galley proofs and data returns to pulisher. Informations recorded subtitle, imprint and callation are omitted but a complete record of other' description is entered in M.A.R.C. C.I.P. cataloguing is under taken from folded sheats or pre-publication bounded copies is varified C.I P. is a modern method. It attracts the publishers and encourage them to send galley proof of their yet unpublished book. This is a venture of optimistic nature but it is a success depends on the association of publishers and tenchical capacity of Library of Congress.

The sixth form of centralisation is Pre-Natal Cataloguing (P.N.C.) Dr. Ranganathan introduced Pre-natal technical work which includes prenatal cataloguing and classification. Ranganathan recommended that prenatal technical work sbould be undertaken by the Natiional Central Library of the country and each book before its release before the publisher. The National Central Library prepared a master stencil of the catalogue card for each book before its release and provide the call number and catalogue entries for each book The class number can be printed in the back of the title page. The catalogue card can be printed even when the book release. This is called prenatal cataloguing.

All three founds C.I.S., C.I.P. & P.N,C. have the same object to prepare catalogue cards before the release of the book. C.I.S. fails to serve this purpose. C.I.P. proved more sucessful. Pre-Natal Cataloguing is under consideration of many more countries.

Pre-requisites for centralised cataloguing are as necessary as the planning factor for a building. The success of centralised cataloguing is solely depend on five requisites.

1. Uniformity of cataloguing and classification in sufficient number of libraries: Uniformity is a important factor. It is very necessary to have a prior aggreements as to the scheme of classification, the cataloguing code to be used. and where physical entries are to be provided. There must also be a prior aggreements in regard to the physical from of cataloguing. Centralised agencies

make necessary provisions specially when computers are used. But It will become impracticable if too many libraries belief their requirements to be unique.

2. The existence or establishment of some machinery by which new documents can be seen by the central agencies. One should think prior to start to venture of centralised cataloguing, of such methods which are quick and speedy. Show as to make the entries available as soon as librarians receives to documents. Any selectress, or delay may result a failure of the scheme. Usually the central organization is based on the copyright library. Where publishers are forced to send atleast one copy of every book published.

3. Duplication of stocks in libraries. In special libraries stock often consists of high proportion. It will be easy to centralised cataloguing if the stock of all libraries is identical. It is assumed that libraries are duplicating cataloguing but it is in few cases, particularly the books published in the country for the local language. B.N.B. limited its service to British material. This cost of a set pack to B.N.B. as most of the libraries taken a large proportion of a foreign material could not cooperate B.N.B. services, while in a modern age all libraries are taken foreign and special material. Hence a cataloguing centralised can only be entered with the cooperation of other centralised agencies. Such cooperation referred to as Shared Cataloguing is now being initiated.

4. Financial backing to establish the service when centralised cataloguing services are prompt and covers the maximum area and seek cooperation from all libraries, and central agencies. There may not be any financial problem. BNB established the services with the satisfactory finance.

5. An economic method for printing the bibliography or catalogue cards and taps. Economy should be maintained by central organisation as much as possible. The scope of cooperation and service will be more effective. Sophisticated machine should be installed. Waste of labour and material should be minimized.

Centralised Cataloguing and B.N.B.

British National Bibliography is an organization supported and controlled by Council of Library Association, British Museum, Publishers' Association, and Booksellers' Association. The documents are seen as they arrive at the copy right office B.N.B. issued its. first bibliography in 1950. The card system began in 1956 and the British Catalogue of Music for entries recorded in which cards are not available, started in 1957. B.N.B. appears weekly (classified with an author/title index). The index cumulates monthly and subject index entries are added. It is further cumulate four monthly, anually and further cumulation every five year.

B.N.B. includes all British books except maps. Music scores are covered by British Catalogue of Music. Music books are covered by both B.N.B. and B.C.M. The most important coverage of museum is government publications, research reports and publications of organisations. It is a comprehensive trade bibliography.

D.C. is used for classification and A.A.C.R. for cataloguing. B.N.B. has used a modified version of D. C. and based on 14th edition. The extensions of schedule is necessary for specific headings, being verbally expressed after the symbol. Such verbal extensions. have allowed Indexing of Key Concepts by chain procedure regardless of the limitations of the classification scheme. More recently 17th edition D.C. numbers are given. In addition of B.N.B. numbers. They have also made a plan to adopt the 18th edition of D.C. supplemented by detailed indexing. Cards service of B.N.B. is used by increasing numbers of library as it is cheaper and has raised standards of cataloguing in this country. Computer assisted techniques are being rapidly adopted and these are likely to facilitated improvements in indexing and in the speed of the cumulation. National Cash Register Company has evolved a new techniques known as Photo Chromic Micro Image (PCMI). By this techniques data can be transferred at a reduction of 150 : 1, from microfilm to a transparency approximately 4" x 6" in size. The micro-film is produced by C.O.M. (Computer Output Micro-filming) by which data from magnetic tap is transferred at high speed on to microfilm. These two processes accommodated six transparencies a bibliography of all books in English published in one year throughout the world. B.N.B. is also testing for introducing subject index data. Very soon a file of transparencies as inch or so thick will contain more information in a more accessible form than a whole shelf of bibliographies.

Centralised Cataloguing and Library of Congress

In 1840 Edward Edwards has suggested for the adoption of centralised cataloguing in Britain. But it was a slow process and it took a century to take up this process. In U.S.A. Library of Congress has been serving and supplying printed cards since 1901. L.C. is originator of card service. Each item catalogued by the Library is given a serial number and these numbers are noted in "Cumulative Book Index" through which the cards are ordered. Library of Congress is regularly printing its catalogue in the "National Union Catalogue" Cards can also be ordered through National Union Catalogue, L.C. catalogue is a National Bibliography. L.C. also supply cards of foreign books. Its coverage is limited and cataloguing details are restricted according to the limited cataloguing practices. L.C. follow author/title headings and based on 1908 code with few modifications from ALA code. In addition to Library of Congress rules for Descriptive Cataloguings, subject headings are taken from the Library of Congress list.

There is a growing need for International Standardization. It is effected with the development of Shared Cataloguing and MARC. Efforts are being made to adopt AACR by Library of Congress. Though there are differences between British & American rules over rule 98 concerning the entry of corporate bodies under place.

COOPERATIVE CATALOGUING

Cooperative cataloguing refers to "a situation where a number of independent libraries share the work of producing a catalogue for their mutual benefit." It is done in two or more libraries for the benefit of each participant and results may or may not be made available to other libraries.

Forms of Cooperative Cataloguing

(1) The Library of Congress is running a cooperative programme in which other libraries are expected to contribute catalogue card copies for printing. The Library of Congress edits each copy so as to correlate it with other entries provided on Library of Congress cards. These edited copies are printed and distributed to subscribers.

(2) Under the Higher Education Act (passed by Congress in 1965), since 1965 the Library of Congress (LC) has established a global network of national and regional offices for international cooperation. Each office is now responsible for the selection, acquisition and despatch of materials published locally. In addition, these offices supply bibliographical data which serves as a basis for cataloguing by the Library of Congress. In many cases, LC accepts cataloguing undertaken for the national bibliographies in the countries concerned, adding only the supplementary information required for the special requirements of LC. In Britain, the office is located with the bookseller Stevens and Brown, and the bibliographical information is supplied by BNB in MARC tapes. The above concept of cataloguing may be called shared cataloguing.

(3) Creation of a 'union catalogue on the basis of data supplied by individual libraries is a good example of cooperative cataloguing.

Union Catalogue

The term union catalogue needs some explanation. Larson defines it as "a catalogue listing in one sequence the holdings or part of the holdings of two or more libraries." It is an important tool for a librarian.

Types

We may recognize local, regional, and national union catalogues. Further division may be done on the basis of the kinds of material included, *e.g.*, books, periodicals, films, etc.

Functions

(i) To serve as a tool for the location of a given document; *(ii)* to help in inter-library loan; *(iii)* to serve as a tool for selection

of documents; *(iv)* to help to achieve coordination in acquisition as well as in the selection programme of a group of libraries (it can help to avoid unnecessary duplication of materials like periodicals etc.); *(v)* to serve as a useful source for obtaining bibliographical information; and *(vi)* to reveal the total document resources of libraries in a given geographical region, thereby indicating the strengths and weaknesses of the holdings in that area.

Compilation

First consideration to compile a union catalogue is to prepare a statement of the purpose. This should be followed by the decision regarding: *(i)* libraries to be included; *(ii)* materials (form, period, subject, language, region) to be covered; *(iii)* types of entries and description of each entry; *(iv)* arrangement; *(v)* physical form; and *(vi)* method of compilation and revision.

It is only when decisions regarding the above have been taken that the actual work of compiling information should be started.

Libraries

It is necessary to decide whether the union catalogue is going to be local, regional, or national in scope. The local union catalogue, though limited in scope, has the great advantage of being able to show at a glance total holdings of local libraries within reach. This is also easier to maintain and up-date.

A national or regional union catalogue is likely to cover a large region having many libraries. Experience shows that these are unwieldy and difficult to maintain. Comprehensive national union catalogues of books showing their location in a country are difficult to prepare and not necessary. Either there should be a series of regional catalogues, or a national union catalogue showing location of materials in a highly selective set of libraries.

Materials

Form of material, period, subjects, and languages to be covered will have to be decided.

Usually, union catalogues of periodicals are preferable because of: *(i)* low cost of compilation; *(ii)* easier to maintain and up-date; *(iii)* less bulky; and *(iv)* saving in case of periodicals because these may have to be acquired as a set.

Types of Entries

Rules for headings and description must be decided by the compiler. The cooperating libraries should adopt these fully.

(1) For a union catalogue of books, two entries consisting of author entry and title entry are prepared. Author entry is the main entry, and title entry is an added entry. Title entry is a brief entry which refers to the main entry for maximum information. After each main entry is added the holdings section, indicating the name of libraries having the document.

(2) For a union catalogue of periodicals, main entry is provided under the class number and, in addition, there should be class index entries and sponsoring body entry. The reference to main entries should be through serial numbers.

Description

(1) It is necessary that only minimum details required for the identification of a book should be included in the main entry. Author, title, edition, and date of publication are considered sufficient. The holdings section should show completely the volumes available and also indicate when the complete file is not there, along with symbols representing the concerned libraries. Title entry should contain the title and a serial number referring to the main entry.

(2) The main entry should include class number; information about change of title (if any), volumes published, cumulative indexes, complexity section and holdings section (library number for each library along with the holdings of each). Class index entries should be prepared for the class number preceding the digit denoting "Periodical publication." These entries should consist of subject in the leadir.g section followed by the class number.

Arrangement

Union catalogue for books should be arranged in a single file alphabetically. In filing, if forenames are disregarded, then it provides greater speed in filing and searching.

A union catalogue for periodical publications should have two files, namely, classified file and alphabetical file. Main entries will go to the classifieid file, and class index entries to the other file.

As some of the union catalogues are being compiled with the help of a computer, it is becoming increasingly possible to provide multiple approaches.

Physical Form

Sheaf form (4" X 6") is preferable to card form. If printed, it becomes a valuable tool. However, it becomes almost impossible to print a national union catalogue unless the libraries are included on selective basis.

Method of Compilation and Revision

If a large library circulates its catalogue of holdings amongst other co-operating libraries, then each may be able to indicate items available with them and also add further titles if not listed therein. This is certainly a time-consuming method.

A second possibility is that instead of one copy, a number of copies of the basic catalogue are circulated and a final catalogue would be a unified one.

A third possibility is that each library may make a catalogue of its holdings and these catalogues may be cumulated.

A fourth possibility is that one or more persons may go from one library to another to collect information.

It is to be noted that photography has been made use of successfully in the compilation of union catalogues. Here, catalogues of cooperating libraries are photographed and catalogue entries made from the film by some suitable method of reproduction. It is to be kept in mind that problems of compilation depend a great deal upon the uniformity of cataloguing practices.

The development of computer-based union catalogues has been achieved successfully even in developing countries. This is neither expensive nor difficult.

There must also be an adequate provision for continuous revision. Somebody or some agency must be regularly notified about the additions and withdrawals. A file of those should be maintained, so that at the time of bringing the new edition, the work would become easier.

Some examples of union catalogues of periodicals:

Ranganathan, S.R., etc., comp.

Union catalogue of learned periodical publications in South Asia, *v. 1: physical and biological sciences,* Indian Library Association, 1953.

Union list of learned American serials in Indian libraries, Delhi, Indian Council for Library Development, 1966.

Regional union catalogue of scientific serials: Kerala; Delhi, Union Catalogue Division, National Science Library, Indian National Scientific Documentation Centre, 1969. (A series of such union catalogues are being compiled by INSDOC. The above one represents just a sample.)

The National Union Catalogue: a cumulative author list (The author catalogs of the Library of Congress-National Union Catalogue series vary in title, form, and coverage. These are complemented by the subject catalogue of the Library of III Congress).

Union list of serials in libraries of the United States and Canada, 3rd ed., edited by Edna Brown Titus, New York, Wilson, 1965, 5 v.

CENTRALIZED VERSUS COOPERATIVE CATALOGUING

According to Sinkankas: "Although centralized units aim to provide a complete job at one place and distribute the results to others, cooperative cataloguing aims to complete a job by sharing the work involved, and then trading the results from one unit to another. Thus the site and organization of the effort are the distinguishing points. Centralization gathers the work in one site and organizes the work force as a unit; cooperation divide's the job among several sites and seeks not to control but, to coordinate the scattered work force." Sharp thinks that "The cataloguing of a large library system is often centralized, but it is not cooperative, except in a very insular sense. One simple form of cooperative cataloguing may be said to exist when a number of libraries take a share in cost or work of providing and maintaining a centralized cataloguing bureau, and reap the benefits accruing from it, by being freed from the necessity of having to provide entries for such books as are catalogued by the central bureau."

Some regard cooperative cataloguing as a part of centralised cataloguing, provided centralized cataloguing is coordinated by a central agency and the product is distributed from a single site. But in practice, the lines of demarcation break down. However, we can make a functional distinction. Centralized cataloguing reduces cataloguing effort by providing centralized services, and cooperative cataloguing makes it possible to put existing library resources to better use.

There also seems to be general agreement that centralized cataloguing is to be preferred to cooperative cataloguing for reasons of increased uniformity, more prompt availability of cards, and economy of operation.

Conclusion

In ultimate terms, the success of the various ventures mentioned in this chapter would depend on the degree of agreement on principles and techniques for carrying out these programmes, availability of financial support, willingness on the part of libraries to participate in these or subscribe to their products.

Centralized cataloguing is most relevant to countries like India, where bad, indifferent, and terrible cataloguing is the order of the day. This is surprising, considering the fact that this country has given birth to one of the most advanced catalogue codes in the world. With a gulf separating theory from practice, the techniques of cataloguing applied in actual practice in Indian libraries are inexcusable. The multiplicity of languages adds to the woes of a cataloguer because of inadequate staffing of cataloguing departments in Indian libraries. The availability of chain procedure as a tool which should be an advantage in the normal circumstances turns out to be a liability because of the mechanical translation of class number into headings of class index entries. The preparation of classindex entries is less of a strain to libraries following catalogue codes other than CCC because of the availability of accessory aids like Sears list of subject headings and Library of Congress list of subject headings.

Centralized cataloguing could also lead to improvement of the other services in Indian libraries, because some of the staff engaged in cataloguing can be released for performing other services in the library. The most important advantage in introducing this service would be the possibility of training a whole generation of librarians in India in the art of true cataloguing. The reference services can also be streamlined in most libraries because of the advantage in possessing a catalogue in the proper sense of the term. Scholars are bound to be grateful because for them the process of preparing bibliographies can be less strenuous. It should have been the responsibility of the Central Reference Library, which brings out the Indian National Bibliography. Who is, however, going to bell the cat?

LIMITED CATALOGUING

Owing to increase in the amount of literature being published and its complexity, the costs of cataloguing have been increasing steadily. They have become so high that ways are being constantly thought of to achieve economy. Limited cataloguing is one such approach to reduce costs, which refers "to any reductions in the amount of cataloguing." These reductions can take place in terms of number of entries and amount of information in each entry.

Types

Limited cataloguing can take two forms, namely, selective cataloguing and simplified cataloguing.

Selective Cataloguing. This is concerned with reduction in the number of entries for a document. At times, it may be decided to have no entry for certain documents. Selective cataloguing is an extremely useful idea which leads to saving in time and space. However, it is not always easy to apply.

Ways to Selective Cataloguing

(1) In case subject and title entries are the same, title entry can be avoided. Even otherwise, title entry is often prepared in case of those documents where a user is likely to remember the title.

(2) Joint author, joint editor, joint translator, joint illustrator entries are often omitted.

(3) If an index which contains analytical entries is available then there is no need to prepare these for those books which have already been analyzed in the index. Theoretically, it is a good piece of advice, but in actual practice it is found that users do not appreciate it.

(4) If a given library is acquiring all the British books, then their entries can be avoided altogether, provided the British National Bibliography (BNB), which contains the entries, can be provided to users to serve the purpose. Here we have assumed that BNB will list the publications as soon as published, which may not be true atleast in case of the Indian National Bibliography (INB), with its delayed publication programme. Users will find it inconvenient to consult the BNB or INB in a number of places because of lack of cumulative volumes for recent publications.

(5) The normal accepted practice is that, if a book deals with three or more sub-divisions of a subject, an entry is prepared under the general heading and references are made to satisfy other approaches.

(6) Chain procedure as compared to printed lists of subject headings is considered economical with regard to number of subject headings to be prepared. Therefore, application of chain procedure can lead to reduction in the number of entries.

(7) The printed lists of subject headings like Sears list of subject headings and Library of Congress subject headings suggest a large number of references which might have to be prepared for a dictionary catalogue, but one can be selective.

(8) The extent of selective cataloguing to be practised in a library would depend upon the set of circumstances existing in a particular library. The types of users to be served and number of staff available for cataloguing are two of the most important factors.

Simplified Cataloguing

This is concerned with reduction in the descriptive cataloguing as well as simplification of heading. It is essential that a cataloguer must limit the provision of description to items which are essential for the identification of particular editions of a given document being catalogued. In this connection, a cataloguer should always ask himself whether all the details he is including are really necessary. The answer to this is related to the significance of each item in an entry and requirements of the users being served.

The two catalogue codes, AACR and CCC, represent two extremes. Application of AACR demands inclusion of details regarding imprint, collation, notes, etc. But CCC prescribes omission of items like imprint and collation and there is less emphasis on notes. CCC thus favours simplified cataloguing. The difference in approach between the two codes is not a matter of accident but is determined by different philosophical and historical approaches. CCC considers the catalogue as a key with minimal information opening the floodgates to the document of interest to the reader. The catalogue is expected to provide so much information as is necessary for the purpose of identifying the document. Author, title, notes (in a few cases) are considered sufficient to constitute the data bank for identification purposes. AACR is motivated by a different philosophical approach. The catalogue is considered a storehouse of information containing maximum information about the document including the publisher, place of publication, size, pages, notes, etc.

In historical terms, the less concern of CCC with descriptive cataloguing can be explained by the fact that CCC took birth in the Madras University library at a time when the catalogues were mainly intended for undergraduates. The bibliographical information which is such a special feature of AACR is of much interest to research scholars because of their special requirements. The development of the two codes is historically determined to some extent.

FACTORS

Kind of Library. In special libraries, enquiries are often detailed ones, requiring detailed cataloguing. This would leave less scope for limited cataloguing. On the other hand, limited cataloguing can be practiced to a greater extent in a public library.

Types of Services. If a given library provides reference service of a very intensive variety, then the reference staff would insist for the provision of more information and entries in the catalogue to enable him to get the information that he may require.

Accessibility. It is accepted that in a close-access library more entries and more information in entries is necessary than in an open access library, because in a close-access library the cataolgue will be the only source which will help users in the retrieval of documents.

Types of Materials. All materials do not require the same amount of information to be given in the catalogue. For example, in case of fiction, no specific subject entry is usually prepared in dictionary catalogue practice. As regards children's books, only broad and simplified subject, headings need be given. Similarly, pamphlets belong to a category of material which often has temporary value. Therefore, such material would require limited cataloguing. Some libraries prefer to shelve such material under broad subjects and do not prepare any entry for them.

Indexes, Bibliographies etc. If an index which contains analytical entries is available then there is no need to prepare analytical entries for books which have already been analyzed in the index. Theoretically, it is a good piece of advice but in actual practice it is found that users do not appreciate the omission. The same is true about published bibliographies, catalogues, etc.

Physical form of Catalogue. In case a catalogue is printed, then limited cataloguing can be adopted to reduce the cost. If the catalogue is handwritten or typed, then the number of entries may have to be reduced and descriptive cataloguing may also have to be decreased. But if the entries are reproduced by a mechanical process, then there may be less need to practice limited cataloguing.

The above factors will help a cataloguer to decide the type and extent of limited cataloguing to be practiced in a given library. The factors to be considered will certainly differ from library to library. Each cataloguer will have to take a decision for himself as to the type and extent of limited cataloguing to be applied in his library. However, once a decision has been taken, one should stick to it consistently unless the decision is revised because of change in the situation.

Conclusion

Limited cataloguing provides great scope for economy in cataloguing. This can enable cataloguers to reduce the cost of cataloguing and also increase their output. However, the application of limited cataloguing should be considered rather carefully. It should not be practiced at the cost of service to users or for the sake of short-term gains.

Limited cataloguing has great practical utility for libraries constantly confronted with the headache of reducing mounting arrears. This is a worry equally shared by large libraries, like the

British Museum and the Library of Congress on the one hand, and local public libraries on the other. Limited cataloguing is desirable for all such categories of materials as are rarely used or are of interest to a limited number of readers. There are as yet no norms established to measure the utility of documents over a period of time. Commonsense, however, demands that economy in cataloguing is necessary for documents rarely consulted, being of interest to a limited clientele, in unfamiliar language, or concerning subjects or areas of less direct interest to the readership of a library. These are value judgements that are difficult to apply, and with change in environment what was of marginal interest yesterday may come to occupy the centre of the stage tomorrow. We are thus standing on slippery ground that in the best of times needs to be avoided. Having said all this, it needs to be stressed that the preposition is not entirely invalid because where logic fails, instinct can provide the answer. In other words, the flair of the librarian should be such as to be able to tell where to apply limited cataloguing and how to draw parameters delimiting boundary lines.

MECHANIZED CATALOGUING

Mechanization applied in one operation previously performed by a human is than done by a machine but which itself operated by a human *i.e.*, instead of copying information by hand a typewriter is used. Following this a punched typewriter may be used which can be programmed or instructed by a human before the operation is started theoritically. It can be set up, switched on and left to operate itself.

Mechanized Cataloguing is easily the process of reproducing catalogue entries in quantity by some methods of duplication, whether this be done by photographic, mechanical or chemical means; in a wider sense also including the administrative and routine methods attendent upon the introduction of such duplication. Where a library system established a cataloguing department mechanized cataloguing a frequently instituted, particularly where tbe department must provide entries for incorporations into many individual catalogues.

Under mechanical processes much of the impersonal and routine work is done with mechanical aids. Copying is done photographically. The development and use of post cordinate indexing during the 1950's created an impression which was only apparent, that subject indexing could be converted into routine clerical process and deducting the tagging documents with term labels. Almost at the same time the tremendous possibilities of the computers of bibliographical data handling work just showing up. Mechanization is a distributed relative. There may be a mechanization aspect to it : simple and complex. Cataloguing should not be considered in isolation from other libraries technical processes, but as one use of common record of stock data, to be used for both catalogue and other purposes.

Literature Explosion. The speedy growth in amount and diversity of literature will in abilitability bring us more major switching elements devided between specilised information centers, abstracting periodicals, central depositaries and technica libraries. The increase flow of documents abstract and kee-word list devided between convensional periodicals, journals of specific natures, reports and manuscripts. With the growth of the system obstructions to easy flow will become more and more disabling.

There is an ever-growing quantity today of important library materials which cover an increasingly complex range of subject, language and authorship. Unless proper documentation is made, vital information may be overlooked, causing duplication of costly research. On the other hand, busy and highly paid research workers do not have time to scane large numbers of documents only to have to reject most of them as irrelevant. Many professional and clerical workers would have to be employed to do this job, and still they might not be able to work fast and accurately enough to keep up with demand. We reach the point when it becomes impossible to use humans in the traditional technical processing of documents, especially since these people require longer and more expensive education in both subject awareness and in library science.

Therefore, there is need to investigate the potential of mechanisation in information retrieval of all sorts part of such an investigation involves a systematic and detailed analysis of what is required from an information service and how these requirements are met. It may so happen that an investigation will result in a decision not to mechanise, but to streamline human processes. The important thing is to decide on a system which is most efficient, speedy and economic in the prevailing circumstances.

Basic Factors

(l) The important basic factors in mechanization are many. With the exception of the American 'flexo-writer' automatic duplicating typewriter all methods of duplication relay upon the production of correct of 'Master' entry upon a printing plate. Lithographic plate, sprit of set stencil, silk screen stencil etc. which is used to produce all the entries required. In relation to cataloguing, therefore the choice of duplicating method will depend to some extent on the qualities required of the 'Master'. Ideally the masters should enable errors to be corrected easily, be easily adjustable for the insertion of different headings or delition of parts of the entry, and should be an expensive in relation to the number of copies produced from it.

(2) It should also be able to be stored easily if required for future use,

(3) Speed,

(4) efficiency,

(5) accuracy,

(6) simplicity,

(7) cleanliness in operations,

(8) ability to produce,

(9) economical.

Computerised Cataloguing. Neubaver describes the system for the EDP (Electronic data processing) cataloguing of monographs in England. He presents the projects for retrospective cataloguing, especially since at present there are no large projects of this type in West Gecmany. He presents the developments at the British Library, London and South Eastern Regional system, and the university libraries of New Castle and Southampton. He discusses the methods for tile acquisition and transfer of bibliographic data and compared with conditions prevailing in West Germany. Bryant comments arising from a study visit. The following are among the topics covered: the use of microfilm, especially for catalogues and indexes; the use and future of UOC, the potential for key-word catalogues within academic libraries; the development and future of MARC-based services both nationally and regionally. He also describes developments and studies as a number of S.E. Autralian Universities and colleges, and microfilm and reprography in Australia.

Malinconico considers the trends in automation of duties aucilliary to cataloguing which avoid the inclusion of the entries cataloguing process. In a fully automated system a rigidly controlled structure is essential to ensure the true function of the catalogue.

Ceadel points out the adaptation of computer programmes for catalogues for use in another library. He concludes that the system is suitable for adoption with some adaptation. Out lines the consequences of the implementation of automated system for: *(1)* filing and catalogue production using KWIT (Key word in title); *(2)* cumulative catalogue using COME-several libraries have a copy of the Quetelet library catalogue on microfiche; *(3)* successful on-line retrieval with STAIRS; shared cataloguing system and their implication; the application of the AACR and CIP; standard bibliographic description; and catalogues in book-form and computer-output-microform.

Davis and Anderson deal with the cataloguing procedure of the library a combination of LC and NLM (National Library of Medicine) practice, so quick retrieval of LC and NLM catalogue copy is important. They point out that ATLINE provides information both before publication, for CIP materials and soon after publication. Author describes the practice followed previous to using CATUNE (installed in September 1973). In April 1975 the NLM published the On-line services manual which increased expertise, with the result that both service cost and time were out. They discusses the following factors affecting search costs and the hits ratio: *(1)* form of search statement; *(2)* type of material; *(3)* imprint data; *(4)* costs of terminal connect time. Nurminen points out that Joemuu University Library started an off-line cataloguing system in autumn 1975, but no output was ever produced. The British library package was due to be initiated in early 1977; this system will have many advantages over manual cataloguing, which will be abandoned Baxter points out that the library's card catalogue was closed in late 1975 and a computer produced catalogue was adopted. In 1977 the serial collection was incorporated into the data base.

The system is based on a master-file which generates 3 catalogue files; author/title; subject/classified. Data preparation consists of initiating new master life records and amending master file records when catalogue alterations are required.

Miller gives a very brief review of the advantages of the computerised cataloguing of music, emphasising that the most successful systems are those run rationally or cooperatively. He mentions the long term plans of the British Broadcasting Cooperations to construct a data-bank to hold details of all materials in all BBC libraries.

Royan describes the Scottish libraries, Cooperative Automation project. He discusses the structure and introduction of the scheme and outlines the economics of 'stagging' (*i.e.* the holding of information on a medium appropriate to its current usefulness. He also justifies the use of film rather than fiche and considers the possibility of large scale retrespective conversion using computer Input-Microfilm (CIM). Bajema discusses negotiating for innovative service. He concludes that successful negotiations depend on honesty with vendons, library staff understanding prices and technology, deadlines being established and kept and the existance of mutual understanding and flexibility between the two sides.

Duerden covers the development of the Marconi Automated Microfiche Terminal System, which has a capability for storing 56 million pages of information, including diagrams, on a high reduction microfiche and retriving and displaying anyone of term in a few seconds under computer control. Experiences in several application areas is reffered to, along with cost avaluations against other systems and magnifications.

Harada states that cataloguing of monographs in the David Lubin Memorial Library (Library and Documentation System Division, Food and Agriculture Organization, Rome) has been computer aided since 1976, using the AGRIS-ISIS package. He outlines the events and re-organisation leading to computerisation and developments in 1976. It is planned to have on-line terminals for input and up date operations and retrospective retrieval and to use external data bases as well as those produced by FAO.

Piney describes a system developed for the acquisition of bibliographic data which comprises part of a project to machinise 'library cataloguing and related operations of the scientific information system at CERN, Geneva.

Wilson describes the Aldermaston Mechanised cataloguing and ordering system (AMCOS). He states the factors involved in setting up the new mainfile, AWRE Reports. file, and concludes that the future is unpredictable and that library policy will continue to produce pragmatically step-by-step. Emmtrt describes METCAT automated library cataloguing system for North Brisbane College of Advanced Education. He discusses difficulties, particularly in over loading the University's computer and future plait). Waston described that in 1976 Foodscray Institute of Technology (FIT) Library implemented a MARC based COM cataloguing system and during last year there was continuing interest in this development from other librarians.

Nose describes the Mechanisation on the National Diet library. Describes the National Diet Library's Kanji Information Management system which is capable or representing 4,059 Chinese characters as well as the cyrillic and a total range at some 6,000 characters and symbols. Input is either by paper tape or cassette magnetic tape. He Outlines some of tbe problems this system raises for potential users of the NDL's tapes.

The Bath University Programme for Catalogue Research has announced two projects: (1) A study of contents and sources of catalogue Data for Local use (CASCADE); and (2) Prevision of subject Access to Library Catalogues through Key Word Indexes (SALCKIND).

Balling discusses the FAUST project, a cooperative automated acquisitions, cataloguing and circulation system of three Danish Library organizations.

National Dielt library (NDL) has automated its processing svstem for printed card orders and is producing by computerized method the Japanese National Bibliography. Christensen describes the cbanges in daily work resulting from the implementation of electronic data processing at Denmark's Bibliotekscentralen.

The British National Bibliography (BNB) announced that its service would be contracted to the Birmingham Libraries Cooperative Mechanization project.

Yeoh presents the use of the OCLC system in a hospital library. He preferred the installation of an OCLC computer terminal in a hospital library which can develop cataloguing system, the staff, the hardware and the future potentiality.

Spyens Duran contends that automated cataloguing has eliminated the need for many professional-level cataloguing positions, and staff cutting has been a by product of the shift to automation; Berman tooks the opposite view, that automation has created a need for more and not less well qualified cataloguers to improve mass production cataloguing and create a local catalogue that will make a library collection accessible to its users.

Cowan and Chaput states that the 11 decentralised units of the University of Quebec lacked documentary resources of adequate quantity and quality. The data base BADADUO was introduced for integration and resource-sharing. The use of BADADUO has facilitated use of external data bases, provided an automated system of management and will eventually control loans, reservations and interlibrary loans and communications.

COMPUTERISED COOPERATIVE CATALOGUING

Corbett presents report on the 2 days workshop at Sterling University. Jan. 75 run onbehalf of the Aslib Computer Applications Group and the Scottish Libraries Cooperative Automation Project (SCOLCAP) which brought together experts/suppliers in mechanised cataloguing services and systems and staff from major Scottish libraries. As a result of the workshop a 2nd SCOLCAP conference was called on 11 March to discuss the report and recommendations of the SCOLCAP Working Party. A Steering Committee has been formed to direct and manage a draft, provisionally costed 2½ year project programme the objective of achieving cooperative cataloguing in the 6 libraries of the working party by 1977. Cain discusses the Scottish Libraries co-operative Automation Project (SCOLCAP). In 1975 SCOLCAP was formalised by a 2nd meeting of the original conference. A rent was received from the British Library R & D Department of investigate the alternatives for an on line network for bibliographic processing in Scotland, to implement the chosen alternative expenimentally with 6 participating libraries, and to integrate the Scottish network with any national network established by the British Library. In the present iluid situation, the matter of whether to adopt an offline system during initial phase of SCOLCAP remains undecided.

Jane and Reeds points out that the Washington Library Network is developing a computer-assisted bibliographic system to speed and expand library oprations throughout the state. Features include MARC format with all content designators, subject and name authority files, sorting by LC rules and stringent quality control. They describes the present batchmode cataloguing support sub-system, its history, operation, impacts, problems and costs, They indicates developments towards on-line integrated acquisitions and cataloguing support.

There is a need to develop a bibliographic data base providing a foundation for total service, including acquisitions, circulation and serials control-a-goal witch does not conflict with national plans for the BIBDATA system.

Beckman discusses automated cataloguing system and network practiced in Canada. He describes system in British Columbia, Alberta Saskatchnwan, Manitoba, the Atlantic provinces, Ontario and Quebec. Reasons for the increasing activity in automated cataloguing may be summarised as: *(1)* the desire to make internal operations more cost effective; and *(2)* the possibility of increased user services through detailed case studies of OCLC, UNICAT/TELECAT, the University of Guelph Library System and others. It will fulfil two stated objectives-librarians mustremain flexible and always open to new ideas, so that technology and the information which it organises does not pass them by.

☐